E-COMMERCE

E-COMMERCE

Lindsay Percival-Straunik

THE ECONOMIST IN ASSOCIATION WITH
PROFILE BOOKS LTD

Published by Profile Books Ltd
58A Hatton Garden, London EC1N 8LX

First South Asian Edition 2002

The greatest care has been taken in compiling this book.
However, no responsibility can be accepted by the publishers or compilers
for the accuracy of the information presented.

Where opinion is expressed it is that of the author and does not necessarily coincide
with the editorial views of The Economist Newspaper.

Typeset in EcoType by MacGuru
info@macguru.org.uk

Printed and bound in India by
Replika Press Pvt. Ltd., 100% EOU, Delhi 110 040

A CIP catalogue record for this book is available
from the British Library

ISBN 1 86197 283 0

For Alex and Marusa

Contents

Preface

I BEGAN WRITING this book amid the hullabaloo about e-commerce; how it would change the economy, devastate high-street shopping and make millionaires out of many. The scene today could not be more different, but the landscape is much clearer. The rubble is gone and the dust is beginning to settle. We can now say with some certainty what the real rather than the imagined potential of e-commerce will be. But we should keep an open mind. Andy Grove was right when he likened himself to Columbus in the New World. The journey has only just begun.

This has been a challenging book to write. Keeping abreast of developments in the rapidly changing world of e-commerce is no easy task, but it has given me ample food for thought. Some of the companies written about will disappear and many things will change, but the essential lessons of the book will remain valuable. I have made every effort to keep the information as fresh as possible up to the time of going to print.

In writing this book I have drawn heavily on the resources of *The Economist*. I am especially grateful to Sam Ahmad, Chris Anderson, Matthew Bishop, Frances Cairncross, Emma Duncan, Simon Long, John Peet, Ludwig Siegele and Matthew Symonds, who wrote the surveys and articles listed on the following page.

I am also grateful to staff at Jupiter Media Metrix, Forrester Research, Analysys, Boston Consulting Group, Arthur Andersen, Baring Communications Equity Emerging Europe and the *E-Commerce Times*, who were all particularly helpful with my research.

I would like to thank Tim Hindle for providing me with opportunities and encouragement over the years and for first suggesting I write this book; Stephen Brough, who helped bring the germs of my ideas to fruition; Penny Williams, who helped give the book its final shape; and Jonathan Harley, who did all the page make up.

On a more personal note, I thank my husband Alex for his love, support, advice and diligent proofreading, and my daughter Marusa for her enthusiasm and spirit of adventure. Lastly, I thank my mum, who always enjoyed a good book. I hope I made the grade.

LINDSAY PERCIVAL-STRAUNIK
May 2001

Material previously published in *The Economist*

Chapter 2
The chapter reproduces most of a survey by Frances Cairncross on e-management, published November 11th 2000. The ideas in this chapter will be expanded in a book called *The Company of the Future* by Frances Cairncross, to be published by Harvard Business School Press in January 2002.

Chapter 3
The sections "The Dell way" and "The Cisco way" come from a survey by Matthew Symonds on "Business and the Internet", published June 26th 1999.

The section "Banking and financial services" is based on an extract from a survey by Simon Long called "The Virtual Threat", published May 20th 2000.

The section on "Books" is based on material from a survey by John Peet on "E-commerce", published February 26th 2000.

The section just before the conclusion is based on an article "Uncertain prize", published October 21st 2000.

Chapter 4
The section on "Mass customisation" on page 83 is drawn from an article called "All yours", published April 1st 2000.

The section on "Delivering the goods" that starts on page 84 and ends on page 85 is drawn from a survey by John Peet on "E-commerce", published February 26th 2000.

Chapter 5
The section identified that starts on page 100 and ends on page 102 comes from "The container case", published October 19th 2000.

Chapter 6
The section identified that starts on page 108 and ends on page 112 comes from "Living in freefall", published November 16th 2000.

The section on consultants starting on page 122 comes from "Consultant, heal thyself", published December 7th 2000.

Chapter 7

The section "Churning at the top" that starts on page 129 comes from an article with the same title, published March 17th 2001.

The list of ten qualities e-managers need starting on page 137 comes from Frances Cairncross's survey on e-management (see Chapter 2 on previous page).

Chapter 8

The section on "Regulation" starting on page 141 comes from "The consensus machine", published June 10th 2000

The section "Domain strain" that starts on page 146 comes from an article with the same title, published March 10th 2001.

Some of the material in the section on "Security" starting on page 156 comes from "Denial of service", published February 5th 2000, and other *Economist* articles.

The section on "Taxation" starting on page 160 is based on extracts from a survey by Matthew Bishop, published January 29th 2000.

E-BUSINESS KNOWLEDGE IS GENERALLY INVERSELY PROPORTIONAL TO BOTH
AGE AND RANK IN THE ORGANISATION.

Jack Welch, chief executive, General Electric

THERE WILL BE NOTHING IN THE 10-YEAR WINDOW EXCEPT E-COMPANIES.
THAT DOES NOT MEAN THAT BRICK-AND-MORTAR WILL GO AWAY, BUT
CLICK-AND-MORTAR WILL BECOME THE ONLY MEANS OF SURVIVAL.

John Chambers, chief executive, Cisco Systems

BETTER TO DO FIVE THINGS AT 100% THAN 10 THINGS AT 80%. AND WHILE
WE HAVE TO MOVE VERY, VERY FAST, I THINK YOU ARE NOT WELL SERVED
BY MOVING INCREDIBLY RAPIDLY AND NOT DOING THINGS THAT WELL.

Meg Whitman, chief executive, eBay

IT IS LIKE A NEW CONTINENT – THE DEEPER WE GO, THE MORE WE KNOW
ABOUT IT, BUT THE DIFFERENCE BETWEEN THE INTERNET AND, SAY, AFRICA
IS THAT THE INTERNET IS CHANGING UNDER OUR FEET – ONE MONTH IT
LOOKS LIKE A GARDEN AND THE NEXT MONTH IT LOOKS LIKE A
WASTELAND.

Jiri Hlavenka, Czech Internet entrepreneur

THIS IS JUST A CATALOGUE RETAIL BUSINESS WITH LOWER BARRIERS TO
ENTRY. MARGINS, IF THEY EVER MATERIALISE, WILL ALWAYS BE CRUMMY.

Michael Murphy, American high-tech investor

THE GAP BETWEEN WHAT WE CAN IMAGINE AND WHAT WE CAN ACHIEVE
HAS NEVER BEEN SMALLER.

Gary Hamel, management guru

WHAT'S MY ROI ON E-COMMERCE? ARE YOU CRAZY? THIS IS COLUMBUS IN
THE NEW WORLD. WHAT WAS HIS ROI?"

Andy Grove, co-founder, Intel

1 Introduction

MUCH HAS BEEN written about e-commerce. Many claims have been made about the impact it will have. Paper and some real fortunes have been created on the back of a dotcom boom that in so many cases has turned to bust. This book aims to provide an understanding of one of the most important business topics today. By cutting through the jargon and the hype it will provide a clear picture of the potential of e-commerce and how it can be harnessed. It will highlight some of the successes and failures of the pioneers and examine the factors that are expected to shape the industry in years to come.

What is e-commerce?

Electronic commerce, or e-commerce, is the buying and selling of goods and services on the Internet, especially the World Wide Web. Clearly, the influence of the web is much wider than this when taken in its commercial context. For example, many people may use it as a source of information to compare prices or look at the latest products on offer before making a purchase online or at a traditional store.

E-business is sometimes used as another term for the same process. More often, though, it is used to define a broader process of how the Internet is changing the way companies do business, of the way they relate to their customers and suppliers, and of the way they think about such functions as marketing and logistics. For the purposes of this book e-commerce is taken to mean doing business electronically.

Other terms that are often used when talking about e-commerce are B2B and B2C, shorthand for business-to-business, where companies do business with each other, and business-to-consumer, where companies do business with consumers using the Internet. These are considered to be the main forms of e-commerce. The creation of online auctions has spawned two other terms, C2B, consumer-to-business, and C2C, consumer-to-consumer (see Figure 1.1). The biggest volume of trade on the Internet is business-to-business. Technology companies, such as Cisco and Oracle, have been among the first to transfer their purchasing and indeed most of their sales to the web and independent B2B exchanges have mushroomed.

Online retailing is often referred to as e-tailing. The best-known example of an e-tailer is probably Amazon, whose name itself has become synonymous with e-commerce. Bricks-and-mortar refers to companies with traditional outlets. Bricks-and-clicks refers to companies that use a mixture of offline and online channels.

A short history of e-commerce

The first thing that should be said about electronic commerce is that it is nothing new. It is not just the latest IT buzzword as some would believe. If you take a Darwinian view of technology, then doing business electronically has certainly been an evolutionary process. Or as Paul Saffo, a futurologist, puts it: "Progress isn't built on the spires of successful technologies; rather it's built on the rubble of failed technologies that went before."

In fact the origins of e-commerce date back some 30 years and lie in Electronic Data Interchange (EDI), a standard way of exchanging data between companies. Created by the trucking industry in the early 1970s, EDI became a major force in industries such as food manufacturing and car making, where suppliers replenish in high volumes. At its simplest, it is a way to automate purchasing. Retailers often use it because it allows stores to link their suppliers directly into their stock databases. The "paperwork", including the order and the bill of sale, also takes place in this secure, safe and verifiable electronic environment.

Much as it has changed some industries, EDI has some serious shortcomings. It can still save time and money, but it usually requires an expensive private or dedicated network connection between two established trading partners. It is not interactive, meaning there is no opportunity for discussion or negotiation. It also resists change. According to Forrester Research, a high-tech consultancy, "EDI is so deep in the bowels of old systems that changes cost an arm and a leg." These disadvantages mean that EDI has been typically confined to and used by large firms.

Of the 2m American companies with ten or more employees, only 100,000 choose to deploy today's EDI, according to Forrester. This leaves another 1.9m small and medium-sized companies that have not been reached by EDI. Smaller companies highlight everything that EDI cannot do, yet they typify the new economy and the new, fluid, "virtual" world of business.

After 30 years EDI is out of synch with the business environment. Speed is the order of the day. Companies need safe, reliable access to a large, fluid pool of partners and suppliers so they can find customers and deliver the goods quickly. The arrival of the Internet promises a solution. Now EDI is being integrated into some Internet technologies. Security is the biggest concern and is holding back developments.

The Internet is everything EDI is not. It is cheap and easy to run. It is ubiquitous – anyone can use it. It can work both inside and outside the company in intranet or extranet form. And it is global.

The e-commerce matrix 1.1

	Business	Consumer
Business	B2B GM/Ford EDI networks	B2C Amazon Dell
Consumer	C2B Priceline Accompany	C2C EBay QXL

Source: The Economist.

Before the Internet, e-commerce was largely a hidden business-to-business affair. The dotcom gold rush brought it into the public limelight for the first time. Back in the heady days of summer 1999, everyone in Europe was scurrying to start a dotcom, invest their money in a dotcom or become the boss of a dotcom. If 1999 was the year of the dotcom start-up, some say 2000 was the year of its demise. As the year drew to a close the list of dead or dying dotcoms grew longer by the day. According to Webmergers, a company that tracks mergers and acquisitions, more than 100 e-commerce firms shut up shop mostly because they could not find a way to make any money. Internet-based e-commerce, said the sceptics, was finished before it had started.

So has e-commerce been a passing fad after all? On the contrary, this book will argue that the unruly child is beginning to grow up. There is information to be processed. There are trends to be examined and understood. And industry experts can now base their predictions on something more than just a hunch.

Like the scramble for Africa, for the first generation of e-commerce firms it was land grab: getting on to the Internet and getting there fast to gain first-mover advantage. Doing it took guts and money – heaps of it. Or as Thomas Wurster and Philip Evans put it in their article "Getting Real about Virtual Commerce" in the *Harvard Business Review* in late 1999: "It took speed, a willingness to experiment, and a lot of cyber savvy." Companies that were good at it like Dell Computer and Cisco understood the technology and ran with it. Old-economy firms were left at the starting post, dazed and confused.

Now the dust is beginning to settle. Companies once chided for sitting back on the sidelines are realising that second-mover advantage is not so bad after all. Having witnessed the rise and fall of the upstarts they know the real race is yet to be run. This time the giants of traditional industry will be ready too.

2 A changing world*

WORLDWIDE SPENDING ON Internet services was $7.8 billion in 1998, up from $4.6 billion the year before. By 2003 the market is predicted to reach $78 billion, according to International Data Corporation. The Internet is changing the way businesses do business. It affects many areas of a company from managing the supply chain to fostering customer loyalty. But companies need more than good technology to make the most of the Internet. They need flexible and self-confident management too.

How to manage e-management

In the mid-1990s, the managers of established, old-economy companies concentrated on running their business well: making cars, perhaps, or selling life insurance. They had to contend with constant change, of course, but normally of a fairly predictable kind: costs had to be cut, new products launched, mergers and acquisitions dealt with. Now life has become much more difficult. Change has not only become more rapid, but also more complex and more ubiquitous. Established companies are no longer quite sure who their competitors are, or where their core skills lie, or whether they ought to abandon the particular business that once served them so well. Behind this new uncertainty lies the Internet (which in this survey is used as shorthand to include the whole cluster of technologies that depend upon and enhance it). Since 1995, this has begun to transform managers' lives.

Why is it causing so much trouble? After all, the Internet as now used by many companies performs familiar functions, although more cheaply and flexibly. The e-mail is not really so different from the memo; the electronic invoice looks much like an on-screen version of its paper predecessor; the intranets that companies install to connect different departments resemble the enterprise resource planning (ERP) systems that many companies bought in the 1990s; even the networks that link companies with their suppliers had their electronic predecessors.

But new technologies often begin by mimicking what has gone before, and change the world later. Think how long it took companies to realise

*This chapter reproduces most of a survey on e-management, written by Frances Cairncross, that first appeared in *The Economist* (see acknowledgements page xi).

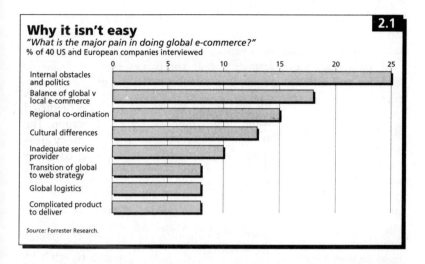

Why it isn't easy

2.1

"What is the major pain in doing global e-commerce?"
% of 40 US and European companies interviewed

	0	5	10	15	20	25
Internal obstacles and politics						
Balance of global v local e-commerce						
Regional co-ordination						
Cultural differences						
Inadequate service provider						
Transition of global to web strategy						
Global logistics						
Complicated product to deliver						

Source: Forrester Research.

that with electricity they did not need to cluster their machinery around the power source, as in the days of steam. They could take the power to the process, which could even be laid out along a production line and set in motion. In that sense, many of today's Internet applications are still those of the steam age. Until they make the next leap, their full potential will remain unrealised.

Yet even what the Internet has already achieved is puzzle enough for many managers. Why should it cause more bewilderment than, say, the arrival of the mainframe or the PC before it?

The answer lies in the Internet's chameleon qualities. It is not simply a new distribution channel, or a new way to communicate. It is many other things: a marketplace, an information system, a tool for manufacturing goods and services. It makes a difference to a whole range of things that managers do every day, from locating a new supplier to co-ordinating a project to collecting and managing customer data. Each of these, in turn, affects corporate life in many different ways. The changes that the Internet brings are simply more pervasive and varied than anything that has gone before. Even electricity did not promise so many new ways of doing things. (See Figure 2.1.)

At the root of the changes is a dramatic fall in the cost of handling and transmitting information. Almost every business process involves information in some form: an instruction, a plan, an advertisement, a blueprint, a set of accounts. All this information can be handled and shared far more cheaply than before. That has its drawbacks, of course: a fall in production costs is all too likely to lead to an increase in supply, and plenty of managers now feel that they are drowning in information. But it also brings immense advantages.

In particular, the investments that companies need to make in hardware and software are small in relation to the pay-off. Gary Reiner, chief information officer of GE, one of the pioneers of the Internet, describes how the company set out to build its own electronic-auction site. "It was less expensive than we thought," he says. "We built the software for $15,000 internally." Charles Alexander, who heads GE Capital in Europe, makes the point even more forcefully. "What we have rapidly begun to understand is that the incremental investment required is extraordinarily small compared with our overall investment. A $300m investment for a company making $4 billion–5 billion is weeks of cashflow to get a payback which is months away, not years. We thought, if we are completely web-enabled in two years, that's good. Then we realised we could do it in weeks – and the productivity gain is almost instant."

Of course it is not really that easy. Companies have to do a lot more than buy terminals and write software. Erik Brynjolfsson, a professor at the Massachusetts Institute of Technology's Sloan School of Management, argues that software and hardware account for only about a tenth of true corporate investment in information technology. A far larger investment goes into new business processes, new products and the training of employees. Such spending does not show up as investment on corporate accounts. Instead, it generally appears as expenses, such as payments to consultants, and is treated that way by the taxman (unlike investment in old-economy physical goods, which can be capitalised and depreciated). Nor does it appear on national accounts. Yet American companies, Mr Brynjolfsson calculates, have created a total of $1.5 trillion of "organisational capital" in the past decade.

A survey of 416 companies conducted by Mr Brynjolfsson, together with Lorin Hitt of the Wharton School at the University of Pennsylvania and Shinkyu Yang of the Stern School at New York University, identified such organisational capital by picking out companies in similar industries where employees tended to have a great deal of authority over the way they worked; where they were paid for performance; where they were well educated; where the emphasis was on teams; and where most information flowed freely across the company. Financial markets valued organisational capital highly, to judge by market capitalisation, but they were keenest on those firms with both high investment in information technology and a high degree of organisational change.

How's your organisational capital?

The reason for this correlation, Mr Brynjolfsson believes, is that in order to get the best out of their information technology, companies need to make a host of changes in a co-ordinated fashion. They cannot simply mimic others: if they do, the results may be disappointing or even disruptive. Organisational capital is far harder to reproduce than the more visible, marketable sort.

So the success of a company's Internet strategy depends on the way the company is run. It is not just a matter of designing a shrewd strategy – although that obviously helps. In addition, a company needs strength in depth. It needs intelligent, empowered employees, a culture of openness and a willingness to experiment, good internal communications and a well-designed pay structure. It also needs absolute commitment from the top. The sheer scale of change is impossible without determined leadership. A company whose chief executive never deals with his own e-mail will not get far.

Many managers began to think seriously about the Internet only once the millennium-bug scare was over. Most large American companies started to develop their Internet strategies in 1999; the benefits began to show up only in their 2001 accounts. A survey conducted in 2000 by the National Association of Manufacturers found that more than two-thirds of American manufacturers did not use the Internet for business-to-business commerce. If that is true for the United States, it is true in spades for the rest of the world. "Whenever I visit software companies," says Andrew McAfee, a professor at Harvard Business School, "I get them to complete the sentence, 'The business-to-business revolution is x% complete.' The biggest number I have heard is 5%. Many say 1%."

Some of the remaining 99% will be accomplished only as the network effects of the Internet feed through. For example, only half of Dell Computer's customers are "online-enabled", as Joe Marengi, one of the company's senior executives, puts it: able to use Dell's web pages to configure their orders. And only 15% of customers place the order electronically. The remaining 35% design the order online and then submit it in some way that requires Dell to take a second step to feed it into the system, such as e-mailing or faxing it. As more companies can submit electronic orders, both they and Dell will cut costs and speed the process. Many more processes involving transactions among companies bring the same double benefits, and ripple outwards as more firms share some particular capability.

The companies that have gone furthest claim to save astonishing amounts. GE plans to cut 15% from its cost base of $100 billion in both 2001 and 2002. That is five times the typical annual growth in productivity, even for this fast-moving firm, of 3–4%. In addition, the company hopes to reduce the prices of the materials it buys by making most of its purchases in electronic auctions. That should save a further $2 billion over the same period.

Other companies are discovering the same sort of magic. In the summer of 1999 Larry Ellison, boss of Oracle, announced that the company would cut $1 billion from its global corporate expenses of $7 billion. Now it expects to have cut a second billion by October 2001, and has its eye on a third. "I've been in business for more than 30 years, and I think this is by far the biggest productivity advancement I've seen in my life," says Jeff Henley, Oracle's chief financial officer.

Such figures will have a dramatic impact on the overall productivity of the economy. In America, productivity growth appears to have accelerated sharply in the past few years – although Mr Brynjolfsson would argue that the acceleration would look milder if the costly investment in organisational change could be properly measured. Even if the pioneers of the Internet are exaggerating, a long period of big productivity gains seems to lie ahead.

These gains come from several different directions. Some of them are achieved simply by transferring part of the work from the company to its customers. If you are having trouble recruiting enough staff for your help desk, and you want to spare your customers having to listen to an entire CD's worth of gruesome music on hold, then well-designed online information may actually benefit everybody. If your customers can submit electronic orders, it saves you the trouble of doing the job yourself, and also greatly diminishes time-wasting wrangles over mistakes. You just e-mail the querulous customer the original order.

Other cost savings come from being able to feed better information to suppliers all the way up the chain, and thus reduce stocks. Paul Bell, who runs Dell Computer's operations in Europe, the Middle East and Africa, describes inventory as "the physical embodiment of bad information". His company now measures its inventory in hours rather than days. Still more savings come from being able to buy from a wider market, allowing competition to drive down prices.

These changes allow measurable savings. But there are other, more far-reaching benefits. As companies install software applications to take over many of the tasks that employees now do – such as "running errands" to keep information moving – they alter the balance between the internal and external demands on a company, an issue described in a book called *Harmony: Business, Technology & Life After Paperwork* by Arno Penzias, former boss of Bell Labs. "Though to my knowledge no computer has yet managed to replicate the performance of a single office worker," he says, "the right combination of computing and communications can frequently replace whole departments."

The "errands" jobs are not only wasteful; they turn the attention of organisations inwards towards the smooth operation of internal processes, rather than outwards to the customer. Now, though, Internet-based software applications are shifting the balance, shrinking the amount of human time and effort that needs to be spent on internal co-ordination. Companies will no longer need layers of white-collar workers to manage the steps between what the customer wants and what he gets.

All sorts of things can be done differently. Manufacturers can talk directly to their customers, or to their suppliers' suppliers. Customers can click a mouse and start a production process rolling, far along the supply chain. Training sessions can be carried on a laptop. Sales staff can do presentations to customers a continent away. Companies will often find it difficult to tell whether such measures save money or whether they simply provide a better service, but overall they will increase the proportion of time that goes on keeping customers happy rather than keeping the business running.

Once a company sets off down the Internet track, what does it find? First, a change in familiar boundaries, starting with those of the firm itself. Collaborating with others becomes easier and less expensive, as does linking different operations within and between firms and buying in everything from management skills and innovation to the human-resources department. The boundaries for employees are redrawn too: those between home and work, as people work from home and shop from work, and those between the individual and the company, now that employees' knowledge and skills may be worth almost as much as the company they work for. Geographical boundaries start shifting as well: within companies, different regional divisions need to collaborate and share customers more than they did, businesses can source more products globally, and new ideas and competition can spring up anywhere on the planet.

Life in the fishbowl
Second, the Internet brings management out into the open. "You put a piece of glass into your organisation and expose all your internal strife,"

says Pete Martinez, who runs the worldwide consulting arm of IBM's global services. Managerial privacy dwindles. "I have to assume that every bit of information about me is broadcast back to our employees and customers. It's the fishbowl effect," says Eric Schmidt, boss of Novell, a troubled software company. If you have failed to reply to an e-mail, you can no longer hide behind "my secretary lost the message". Pricing is also more transparent, as more deals can be put to the test of an occasional auction. Companies need to allow customers and suppliers "inside the machine", in the phrase of Peter Martin, editorial director of Internet activities at ft.com. Thus customers can track the progress of their orders, and suppliers are growing used to scooping information straight out of their customers' databases. Moreover, employees can see what they might earn in similar jobs in other companies.

Third, the Internet increases the importance of standards. Indeed, the glue that holds it together is essentially a set of software standards. Their user-friendly simplicity allows people to use the Internet in many different roles – as customers, suppliers, employees, job-seekers – without needing to be retrained. Electronic commerce needs standards in order to make it easy to transfer information between companies with different systems: hence the importance of XML, a programming language (see page 23). Companies also need rules about what can be bought online: the aggregation of many departments' orders for staplers will save money only if all departments are willing to buy from the same standard shopping list. And aiming for a standard technology, and standard look and feel for customers, is a way to reduce maintenance costs and to measure more easily how customers behave. However, standardisation is a force for centralisation in companies. Once the human-resources department decides it needs a single global website to keep employees up-to-date, head office will want to decide what should appear on it.

This survey begins inside the company to see how the Internet affects the way managers communicate with staff, and staff with each other. It then examines links with suppliers and customers. Lastly, it considers how the shape of the company itself may change, and offers some guidelines for good e-management.

Talking to each other
Corporate culture instilled online
At its most basic, the Internet is a wonderful way to communicate. Hit that "send" button and off goes the e-mail, trailing attachments, to

everybody in the firm and beyond. No wonder companies find it a perfect way to talk to their staff. No wonder it is so useful – but also so dangerous – when staff want to talk to each other.

Over and over again, the Internet's uses turn out to dovetail beautifully with current trends. As companies become more fragmented and their workers more geographically dispersed, managers need a way to rally the troops. In particular, they need a way to build a corporate culture: that intangible something that binds employees together and teaches them to understand instinctively the defining qualities of the business and the appropriate way to respond to any issue that confronts them. The Internet provides the means to do this.

In a stable, slow-growing and well-established company, a common culture may be easy to maintain. You take each year's new recruits off to boot camp for a fortnight and teach them the company history. But few companies today can afford to be stable or slow-growing. Instability and speed make culture-creation harder.

In Silicon Valley, people count as old stagers if they have been with the same employer for much over a year. But rapid turnover is not the only difficulty. In many companies, the salesforce or the maintenance folk rarely come into the office. A quarter of IBM's workforce, for instance, is now mobile – they spend at least 80% of their time off-site, usually working from home or on the road. Key people may be based in key markets abroad, a day's air travel away from the main office. Mobility goes right to the top: Douglas Daft, chief executive of Coca-Cola, travels 80% of the time. He boasts: "The headquarters office is where I am."

Add in mergers and takeovers, which create a need to proselytise a new bunch of employees and coax them to abandon one corporate creed for another. As companies outsource more and more activities, too, they look for ways to teach their subcontractors to share their values. And the faster things change, the more important it becomes to explain to employees what is happening, and why.

How to do it? "In a rapidly changing and geographically distributed organisation," observes Michael Morris, a social psychologist at Stanford's Graduate School of Business, "you don't have the option of the drink after work." But you do have the Internet. More than any previous technology, it allows companies to ensure that every employee has access to the corporate news, views and vision.

Some companies use it to teach their employees (as well as suppliers and customers) their ethical code. Boeing, for instance, offers an online "ethics challenge" where employees can test their moral instincts on such delicate issues as "acceptance of business courtesies" and "the minister drops a hint". Such applications are a way to spread a common approach throughout an organisation.

But the Internet is also a way for bosses to tell staff where they want the business to go. For example, at Ford, which claims to have the world's largest intranet, 170,000 staff around the world are e-mailed a weekly "Let's chat" note from Jac Nasser, the chief executive. A purpose-built newsroom maintains a website upgraded several times a day, and available to Ford's employees around the world (in English only), as well as to those of its new acquisitions, such as Volvo.

Not only does the Internet allow managers to talk to their staff; it lets them track whether the staff are at least pretending to listen. William Nuti, president of Europe, the Middle East and Africa for Cisco Systems, a high-tech giant, produces a monthly video to send to his staff, explaining where the business is going. What happens if the staff don't choose to watch? Well, the Internet allows you to track who opens an e-mail and when. "I know everyone who clicks on it, and those who throw it away, and I make phone calls to people, saying it's important you watch this." Not surprisingly, Mr Nuti's viewing figures are high.

But all this communication from on high can sometimes cause problems. SAP, a German business-software giant, is another company with an elaborate communications system. It allows material to be broadcast on the car radios of workers on the road, for example. The company found that middle managers objected to the chairman e-mailing all employees. Their authority had rested partly on their role as a source of information, and without it they felt exposed. As so often with Internet-driven changes, the implications of what appeared to be a simple, time-saving innovation turned out to be more complex and politically sensitive.

That sensitivity becomes more acute as communications become increasingly bottom-up as well as top-down. At Siemens, a large German company, Chittur Ramakrishnan, the chief information officer, has noticed a "very significant number of e-mails to top management. The idea of going through a secretary to get an appointment has changed. People can send e-mails to anyone and expect a response. It is very democratising."

Listen to us

Leaving aside pep talks, companies find all sorts of mundane tasks can be done online with greater efficiency and less expense. As a result, "B2E"

– business-to-employee – applications are flourishing. Tim Mead, chief marketing officer for Cambridge Technology Partners, a consultancy, thinks they may be the biggest growth area for Internet applications over the next couple of years. They include many tasks involving staff matters; the creation of an internal job market; and training. These are discussed in detail in the next section. It is one of the strengths of the Internet over previous, proprietary systems that it can be used to provide services to everyone in a company.

Once material of direct interest to workers (say, their holiday entitlement) is available online, they grow used to logging on. Many companies reckon this is a quick way to help their people come to terms with changing business methods. That is why Ford and some other companies, such as American Airlines, are giving their employees computers to use at home. Two-thirds of Ford's employees are hourly workers, who will not be able to use them to do company work from home. But that is not the point. Ford is hoping to get all its people used to thinking online, and to have a direct way to reach them all with a consistent global message.

Consistency becomes important as companies evolve their internal communications. Initially, every department tends to set up its own website, perhaps protected from the rest of the company by a password, and often designed to boost the department's self-esteem. To end such anarchy, or simply to pull all internal information together, a growing number of companies now have a "corporate portal": a centralised home page with links to various services, items of information and titbits to entice the staff to keep looking in. Click, and there is a map of each floor of the office; click again, and there are photographs and personal details about who sits where. Elsewhere on the page there may be links to the online services of the human-resources department, or the day's news clippings, or a page allowing workers to fill in expenses claims, order office supplies or find telephone numbers.

To persuade employees to look at the home page as often as possible, companies think up various inducements. Cisco Systems, keen to attract the attention of its option-owning employees, plonks its share price centre-screen. Other companies post a list of employees with a birthday that week. Scient, an Internet consulting firm in San Francisco, has an area called "Do you want to scream at anyone?", for employees to complain about colleagues who send excessive e-mails. The site shows the daily winner in categories such as "Take a chill pill".

The good thing about such pages is that they are accessible not only to employees in head office, but also to people in distant subsidiaries, on the road or at home (though this can cause culture clashes: Scient's British staff are bemused by its "stream of e-consciousness" site). Increasingly, employees can personalise their page, so that if they are working in the marketing department they do not receive a deluge of news clippings on camshaft design. Companies with lots of old "legacy" computer systems can use the home page as the entrance to a network designed to pull all the old systems together.

In time, these in-house portals may become important sources of revenue for many companies. Some already sell their own products to their employees online. Ford has a scheme to allow the friends or family of an employee to buy a company vehicle at a discount. The employee enters his social-security number, name and address on a website and receives a personal identification number which he can e-mail to his friend. That allows the friend to pick up the vehicle from a dealer. Rival car companies have similar schemes offline that involve lengthy form-filling.

Next, there is the prospect of turning the corporate workforce into a marketplace. It is an advertiser's dream: a stable group of people with regular pay and a known employer. Why not, for instance, offer a link from the page that informs an employee of her holiday entitlements to a travel company with which the company already does corporate business, and which will offer discounts on leisure travel? Why not charge local restaurants for the occasional advertisement?

Indeed, this is already starting to happen. For instance, Exult, a consultancy to which BP subcontracts much of its human-resources work, is discussing just such a proposition with companies offering financial services. But how will businesses feel about encouraging their staff to hunt for a home loan when they should be finishing a presentation? Alan Little, Exult's head of global client relationships, replies robustly that, if employees can work from home at the weekend on their company laptop, then surely they should be allowed to book their holidays from the office on a weekday. They should be judged by results.

Handle with care
Dangers on the web

The Internet is a dangerous thing. Allow it into offices, and plenty of disagreeable things may try to follow it. Like pornography, for instance. One large British company was aghast to discover not long ago that it had 18,000 pages of porn on its server. Companies as diverse as Dow and

Orange have sacked employees for looking at naughty pictures. The risks are serious – and not just to the employee's moral welfare. In the course of researching this survey, the author of this chapter stayed with a friend who was distraught to have found one of his business partners downloading porn. "If a secretary comes in and catches him, she could sue us for sexual harassment," he wailed. "And we have joint and several liability."

Happily, new screening technology from SurfControl, a company based in Scotts Valley, California, now claims to be able to discern from skin tones whether a picture is naughty or not. This will be a relief to companies and their information-technology managers, who usually know exactly who is watching what, and grumble about the computer memory clogged with the unspeakable.

But ogling is not the only dangerous activity the Internet encourages in the office. E-mail can also do plenty of damage. One obvious problem is the amount of time it gobbles up. Many companies try to limit that by blocking outgoing e-mails for several hours in the morning and afternoon. Michael Schrage, an academic at MIT's Media Lab and author of a book called *Serious Play: How the World's Best Companies Simulate to Innovate*, wonders whether companies should give employees an e-mail budget, or at least discover which 20% of the staff send 80% of the e-mails. In some American companies, sending an e-mail with a smutty joke can get you fired.

More dangerous than dirt, though, is anger. In a speech early in 2000, Michael Eisner, chairman of Walt Disney, argued that e-mail had served to increase the intensity of emotion within his company and become the principal cause of workplace warfare. "With e-mail," he noted, "our impulse is not to file and save, but to click and send. Our errors are often compounded by adding other recipients to the 'cc' list and, even worse, the 'bcc' list. I have come to believe that, if anything will bring about the downfall of a company or maybe a country, it is blind copies of e-mails that should never have been sent."

The blind copy, says Mr Schrage, is a "software stiletto": a way for someone to report a correspondence to someone else without the knowledge of the other writer. It offers the perfect way to shop a colleague. "If business ethics mean anything to a firm," he says, "it should surely disable the blind-copy field." Corporate life might be less spicy, but fewer careers would be wilfully destroyed.

The inside story

Better ways to manage your staff

When companies are learning to eliminate paperwork and speed up processes online, they often begin in their own backyard. They notice that many of the jobs that keep their human-resources people busy can be better done electronically. They discover ways to handle employee expense claims online. They create an internal electronic job market. And they put training online to keep dispersed and busy employees in touch with constant innovation.

Most of this is relatively easy to do because it is, on the whole, unthreatening. It may cut out some HR jobs, but it does not alter the main business. On the other hand, it helps to teach companies and their employees about applying the Internet. Techniques honed in the HR department can be readily transferred to the customer-services department, and filling in expenses claims online is a lesson in electronic procurement.

HR departments used to spend much of their time answering questions from employees. The move towards "cafeteria" benefits – a choice of various permutations of pension, health plan, holidays and pay – brings lots of calls from workers asking: "What happens if I ..." Such questions are often more easily answered by a computer than a human being. This has encouraged companies to put their employees' details on a website, protected by a password, and allow their staff to update their personal information or, in refined versions, to experiment with different combinations. The results can be dramatic. Even when staff could use the HR website only to update their records, Ford found that calls to the central help desk fell by 80%.

Once they realise how much of HR can be shifted online, some companies start to think about passing the chores on to someone else. BP, an acquisitive oil company that is digesting Amoco, Arco and Burmah Castrol, agreed in December 1999 to outsource much of its HR work to Exult, a start-up that has recently negotiated a second deal with Unisys, a computer giant. Exult is building a network that will give BP's staff in more than 40 countries information on all sorts of HR issues. It will alert a manager when staff turnover in his unit passes a certain level, for instance, or allow him to see how various permutations of pay for his staff will affect his budget. It will tell a worker how much holiday entitlement he has left, and whether he could roll some over to next year. Or it will allow an expatriate employee to look at terms and conditions for his next foreign posting.

One effect of handing over this project to Exult has been to draw BP's attention to the hundreds of different pay scales, holiday policies and benefit arrangements that have sprung up throughout the business. Deciding whether and where to introduce coherence is a job for BP's own management, not for Exult. But Exult's Mr Little argues that, although 20% of local variations may be justified, 80% are not. Reducing unnecessary diversity brings all sorts of benefits: pay scales become easier to explain and faster to alter. Once again, the impact of the Internet is to encourage simplicity and centralisation.

Expenses claims, too, can switch to self-service. Oracle's Mr Henley has got rid of a quarter of the people in his accounts-payable department who were doing nothing but filling in data from expenses forms. To get employees to submit their expenses claims electronically, the company simply e-mailed everyone to inform them that claims on paper would no longer be paid. There are few better incentives for even the most Luddite employee to learn to use a new technology.

Cisco Systems went through a similar process. Sue Bostrom, in charge of Internet business solutions for the company, says it was costing $50 a time to process a claim. That figure has come down to between $2 and $7. When she returns from a trip, she simply pulls up the record of her company's American Express account, fills in what each payment was for, clicks and submits. She gets paid much more quickly. But there is also, she points out, a further benefit. Cisco has an application called Metro that compares an employee's spending with the corporate average. If employees typically spend $250 on a night in a New Jersey hotel, but this one chooses to spend $350, the system will automatically flag it up and ask him to fill in an explanation. A couple of auditors review all flagged claims; if they disagree with an employee's explanation, they e-mail him and his manager. That not only educates employees about what they are expected to spend, but also makes it easy for managers to check out-of-line claims.

Picking winners

Most companies' top priority is to find the best people for a job, and then to keep their knowledge and skills bang up-to-date. Hence the enormous importance attached to recruitment and training.

Once you have details of employees' work experience on a database, you have a more efficient internal talent market and a faster way to recruit a team to work on a particular project. A manager, using a special password, can examine a potential recruit's work experience, past assignments and willingness to move home, together with the latest job review. Armed with such information, a manager can search the database for a particular set of skills, a job that would once have needed help from the HR department. The result should be a better internal job market.

There are, of course, some snags. Employees may not much like the idea that managers in other departments can sneak a look at their latest job review without their consent. If a company puts up employees' photographs, it may find itself dealing with a discrimination case if a black face is screened out of a suitable job online (the technology will reveal whose records were considered). Most important, though, a database will probably not be able to answer the recruiter's biggest question: is this person any good? At SAP, for instance, Thomas Neumann, director of human resources, admits that his vast database of 22,000 people in 50 countries works "better for skills than for competencies". But the managers that use it still claim it saves them time. It may be a coarse sieve, but for the harassed manager it may well be better than waiting for a telephone call from the HR department.

Recruiting from outside also becomes faster if a curriculum vitae can be sent in electronically: 71% of the Fortune 500 companies now accept applications on their corporate websites, according to a survey by recruitsoft.com. That allows them to be circulated around departments the same way. Faced with a mammoth skills shortage, some companies have found cunning ways to use the Internet as a lure. Siemens, which now gets 60% of its job applications online, was struggling to find clever young engineers as the number graduating from Germany's crack universities was declining rapidly. So, with the help of psychologists, the company designed an online game that would test for the skills it most needed, such as an ability to work in a team. The company ran the game on its website for six weeks, expecting perhaps 2,000 people to play. In fact, says Peter Pribilla, a member of Siemens's corporate executive committee, 10,000 did, many of whom were young engineers. The company interviewed those with the highest scores. Perhaps partly as a result, three independent surveys of engineering graduates in the past year have rated Siemens the best company in Germany to work for.

Once good people are on board, the next challenge is to train them and to keep their knowledge up-to-date. Training is the main way in which companies invest in their people, and good training is clearly one of the main ways in which companies can create value for shareholders. But it is not easy when your staff are constantly on the road. And that is by no means the only problem that corporate training programmes face.

Most people end up dozing through much of any training course, because either it tells them what they already know, or it tries to convey something so complicated that an hour's class is not long enough.

For years, companies have dabbled with using computers instead of teachers. The results have generally been dire. Online training programmes are often little better. But some companies now think that they have begun to crack the problems of teaching their staff electronically. At SAP, for example, Rainer Zinow, head of knowledge management, says that his web training programme is the most expensive one he designs, needing between 100 and 200 hours of production time to produce a single hour of material. The important thing, he says, is to realise that "my classroom is a room in a medium-sized hotel in Connecticut", with a dial-up connection and a consultant who will pay attention for at most an hour between 6pm and 7pm. So to work well, an online training programme has to be broken into small bits, be able to grade skill levels carefully, and be designed to cope with irregular sessions.

Any training programme needs to test how well employees do before and after. At Dell Computer, John Coné, the company's head of learning, measures "initial ramp time": how long it takes a newly hired salesman to achieve his full sales quota. Dell used to pack new employees off to boot camp for three weeks to be taught about systems and processors, rules and regulations on selling, and the finer points of Dell's product lines. But that was wasteful: some recruits knew most of it already, others knew nothing. Now the company first tests what people know and then offers part of their training online. It has cut a week off boot camp and two weeks off the normal ramp time.

Managers, too, receive some online training, for example on coaching. An optional one-day old-fashioned class is available at the end of the course, but Mr Coné says that only a small minority signs up for it. "The only thing we can't do asynchronously online", he says, "is to have an individual attempt to display a learned behaviour, and get immediate feedback based on judgment." Dell now delivers roughly 60% of all formal learning online, and hopes to raise that proportion to 90% within two to three years. The main thing to remember, he says, is that online learning is like the microwave oven: it is not a complete replacement for the traditional model, but it does some things better.

Selected, rewarded and trained: the next stage is for employees to learn to work together.

A little knowledge ...

... goes *further* if *you* collaborate

Companies these days bang on a lot about knowledge management. But what, exactly, does it mean? Some interpret it as training, others as managing an online database. One of the better definitions comes from the Yankee Group, an American consultancy: knowledge management involves efficiently connecting those who know with those who need to know, and converting personal knowledge into organisational knowledge. People are wonderful receptacles of valuable ideas and information, but they tend to move on, taking their knowledge with them. The challenge for companies is to find ways to extract and share the stuff.

That is what many of the most interesting new Internet applications are intended to do. "Collaboration" is a powerful word in Silicon Valley. Companies need their workers to share ideas more than ever before, for a variety of reasons. One is the need for incessant innovation and refinement of new products and processes. That requires an endless stream of new ideas. Another is that, just as workers in an old-economy factory work together physically to build a machine, so workers in an office need to communicate and co-operate to build a service.

But sharing has grown harder, partly because workers on the same project may be separated by long distances and time zones. The stimulating chat around the coffee machine, source of bright ideas and quick fixes, gives way to the international telephone call or e-mail interchange. In addition, the employees who collaborate to produce a given service may work for different companies. As tasks become fragmented among different firms, good collaboration tools become essential.

Daily sharing of information goes on in most businesses, of course, and in geographically dispersed companies some of this has been long-distance for many years. Designers at some companies have been based in different time zones and passed work to each other round the clock. But until recently they have used proprietary networks. The Internet makes such round-the-clock sharing available to everybody in a company, or all the people working together on a particular project. It thus enhances global teambuilding, and encourages the emergence within companies of horizontal communities, bound together by a common function or interest. These communities can now easily float ideas with each other, or gossip, or discuss best practice – around the clock and around the globe.

Managing collaboration requires special skills: less emphasis on individual achievement, more on teamwork. Moreover, just as companies can learn lessons from developing online HR services for their own staff that can be applied to running online support for their customers, so the lessons they learn from collaborating within the organisation can be applied to collaboration with other companies. A company that cannot persuade its own staff to work together smoothly and efficiently is unlikely to do better with its suppliers.

Collaboration also requires appropriate pay structures, designed to reward teamworkers rather than lone rangers. But the motives that persuade people to work together are not exclusively financial. One of the most interesting and inspiring models of collaboration, according to Alan MacCormack of Harvard Business School, is the development of open-source software such as Linux, on which thousands of people around the world who have never met work together – unpaid. The model requires a workable kernel (in this case, the initial 10,000 lines of code written by Linus Torvalds) to which people can easily add; a modular design, so that different people need to understand only the part they choose to work on; and a small team at the top to set broad guidelines and select the best ideas. The most powerful development, says Mr MacCormack, is that by users. Their reward is global recognition – "because software code is a universal language, if I make a good patch, the world knows" – and the satisfaction of seeing their ideas discussed (often on slashdot.org, a website boasting of "news for nerds") and adopted.

Could companies inspire the sort of altruism that has gone into developing open-source software? In some other ways, Mr MacCormack points out, corporate innovation increasingly resembles Linux code-writing. The teams that work on it are often geographically dispersed. And design is increasingly modular rather than sequential: people no longer design the engine and then pass it on to a second group to produce the casing, which discovers problems with the engine design just as the first team has moved on to its next project. Besides, innovation is increasingly delivered not by a single company's research-and-development department, but by a network of companies, each working on a different part of the project.

However, unlike Mr Torvalds, companies need to rely on their employees' ideas for making their money. Biotechnology companies long ago found ways to give staff a share of the rewards for their research. Now even IBM has a scheme to make sure that good ideas bring more than a pat on the back. Developing a patent wins a financial reward; so does authorship of a certain number of articles; and consultants get bonuses for creating and sharing good ideas. The company is also working on a way to encourage people to put their ideas into its knowledge database, by rewarding those who create material that is frequently used, as well as those who review or grade the stored ideas in particularly helpful ways. The aim, says Scott Smith, who helps to run the knowledge side of IBM Global Services, will be to create a "self-rewarding content-grading system", a bit like Amazon.com's way of persuading customers to review the books they buy.

Divided but united

Much of the everyday collaboration that goes on in companies is far more humdrum stuff. But when people are scattered, or working for several different employers, simply co-ordinating their joint efforts can be immensely time-consuming. Keeping track of who has done what is essential, though, if only to avoid legal wrangles when things go wrong.

All sorts of new collaboration tools now allow people to work together on a single project. For example, they may set up a shared website on which any of them can post or update material. That does away with the cumbersome business of sending e-mail attachments back and forth, especially irritating for people working with a laptop in a hotel bedroom. GE Capital, for instance, has something called a Quickplace on which a group of staff members working together can store all the documents, plans, correspondence and other details to do with a project. Ford uses a similar collaboration technology to handle due diligence when it acquires a company. The system was developed when teams in Sweden, Britain and America collaborated over the acquisition of Volvo; after that, it was used in the purchase of Land Rover. Staff can use instant messaging for quickly checking particular points. The advantage of such "e-rooms", says Bipin Patel, head of management systems at Ford, is that they are asynchronous (meaning that people can use them when it suits them); they are always up-to-date; and they do not use much manpower.

Such tools are now being developed further by companies such as Firedrop, a Californian start-up that has devised something it calls a "zaplet". This arrives in your mailbox like an ordinary e-mail, but when you open it, the zaplet becomes a window on to a server, or central computer. The information you see, therefore, is whatever is now held on the server, so you always get the most up-to-date version. The zaplet may also allow you to use an application that sits on the server: a spreadsheet, perhaps, or a way of managing a customer database.

Alan Baratz, Firedrop's chief executive, arrived in July 2000 to find the company concentrating on consumer services. He saw a way of turning it into a tool that managers could use in, say, recruitment. At present, piles of applications pour daily into the recruiting department, which sorts them and sends the best to managers, who indicate the candidates they want to see. The department then telephones the applicants and goes backward and forward trying to find a suitable date for an interview. Firedrop's device, Mr Baratz says, allows the recruiting department to e-mail hiring managers just once. Then they can all look at the same application and write in comments, or compare notes on which time slots are free for an interview. With luck, zaplets should be commercially available during 2001.

Lots of consultants and technology companies now hope to teach firms to collaborate better. At Peoplesoft, which has made it a speciality, Baer Tierkel, who is in charge of worldwide marketing and strategy, argues that effective tools must be based on the Internet: its open standards make it much easier for everybody to work with everybody else. Such intercommunication becomes easier with XML, or Extensible Markup Language (see below).

In future, Mr Tierkel thinks, software tools will increasingly allow the sort of information normally available only in corporate back offices to be readily accessible to people in the field: "A customer-services manager might get an alert to say that, given the level of orders coming in, she was going to need more staff; or a salesman might be able to find out, as he was walking into a customer's office, whether that customer was happy with the relationship so far." New tools will also increasingly turn a company's customers and suppliers into one large collaborative network.

For the moment, dream on. Most companies are still discovering how to do online procurement, and how to deal electronically with their customers. Both often turn out to be harder than the enthusiasts would have you believe.

Do you speak invoicing?
The joys of XML
For companies to make full use of the Internet's potential, they need to be able to receive information arriving electronically from a customer or supplier, and pass it through their own systems without having to print it out and manually transcribe data, or change the format. This is what

23

Electronic Data Interchange (EDI) tries, clumsily, to do. Until recently it has not been possible with information that arrives on the Internet.

To understand why, look at the "page source" on your web browser. There you will see how Hypertext Markup Language (HTML) tells your computer how to display a page of material you have found on the Internet. Enclosed between angular pairs of brackets, you will see words such as <HEAD> or <FONT SIZE>. These are called "tags". What you will not see are any tags that tell you whether you are looking at an invoice, or a set of medical records, or instructions for installing a condenser. The absence of such information helps to explain why, when you search for something on the Internet, you receive vast amounts of irrelevant junk. Search engines cannot tell, from the tags on web pages, whether they have found a page on books *by* Charles Dickens or books *about* Charles Dickens.

Since 1999, companies have begun to use a new language to describe web pages, called Extensible Markup Language or XML. It inserts many of the same standard tags as HTML (such as P for paragraph and IMG for image), but it also allows people who create web pages to add more tags of their own. These, unlike the tags that HTML uses, need not be confined to a few dozen standard words. They can, for instance, say that the page provides information on a book's authorship rather than title; or that it is a purchase order; or that it is in Chinese.

But, if the creator of the web page has invented these tags, how will your browser know what they mean? The answer is that the top of the page will carry all the information your browser needs to understand the rules that the originator of the page has drawn up. It is as though each page was a board game which arrived with a set of rules telling you exactly how to play it. To be comprehensible to your browser, the rules must be set out in a standard way. XML is that standard.

Because XML describes the content of a web page in terms of the type of data it contains, rather than the way the data should look, it helps groups of like-minded people to share information. They simply need to agree on a set of tags that meet their particular needs. So a consortium of fishing fleets might agree on a standard way to describe information about fish catches – the number landed, the species, the average size. They could use their own XML tags to store this information. A search engine could then look for data types rather than just words: for all the fleets that landed cod of a certain size on a certain date, for instance, rather than just any website containing the word "cod".

Like HTML, XML is an open standard: anybody can use it without paying a licence fee. It was developed by a working group from w3c, the World Wide Web Consortium, a standard-setting body. Gartner Group, a research firm, reckoned that by 2001 it would be used for 70% of electronic transactions between businesses.

However, individual industries and other groups still need to agree on the set of tags that their particular trade will use. Otherwise, some fishing fleets might store data on catches with a tag called <SIZE> while others might use <WEIGHT> instead. These subsidiary standards, crucial for commercial interaction, are being agreed on in various ways. Some will emerge from standard-setting bodies such as RosettaNet, a not-for-profit consortium that mainly works with companies in the electronics industry. Some will be commercial versions, hoping to drive out rivals and achieve supremacy. Microsoft has an initiative called BizTalk which aims to create common ground. Some of these new standards may be proprietary, although most will probably be open. Agreeing on them will often be a tortuous and acrimonious process. However, once these standards emerge, xml will become the core of electronic commerce.

New life in the buying department
Tons of savings on toner cartridges and toilet paper

As old-economy companies go, few are in more robustly physical businesses than United Technologies, owners of a cluster of firms such as Pratt & Whitney (aero-engines), Otis (lifts) and Sikorsky (helicopters). Yet few enthusiasts for the transforming power of the Internet rival Kent Brittan, who heads supply management. The reason: UTC is one of the world's largest online purchasers.

The idea that anybody in supply management should be enthusiastic about anything would once have seemed a contradiction in terms. Buying departments have long been one of corporate life's dead ends, full of people chasing up invoices and trying to work out how many widgets the company bought last year. No longer. These days, the folk who manage purchasing are the shock troops of the business-to-business business, and those far-sighted enough to have gained an MBA in supply management from the state universities of Arizona and Michigan, the only two places that award them, are on an Otis ride to the top. Mr Brittan even has his own human-resources staff, to augment the "legacy" employees of UTC's purchasing department with people who know their xml from their EDI.

Mr Brittan's purchasing people can deliver something that not many managers struggling to introduce the Internet into established firms can hope to achieve: real and speedy savings. To do so, though, they need to persuade this traditionally decentralised group to accept a high degree of central discipline. That means finding ways to make the Internet understandable and interesting to the multitude of employees who think of it mainly as something to play with at home. So the purchasing department has built its own elaborate website, with news articles, employee profiles, a glossary of financial and engineering terms, and information on corporate training courses. Advertisements in the company's lifts and corridors tell people to click on this corporate portal – which also offers a gateway to electronic purchasing.

Corporate buying online seems at first glance a logical development, on a far larger scale, of Internet purchases by consumers. In fact, consumer buying is mainly online catalogue shopping, with a few advantages such as round-the-clock ordering and more flexible pricing. But much industrial purchasing is far more complex. For instance, many products are made to detailed specification, not bought off the peg; they are purchased by teams, not individuals, so that the decision to go ahead occurs at a different time and place from the actual transaction; and they are generally bought under long-term contracts, specifying all sorts of quality, price and delivery characteristics. Sam Kinney, one of the founders of FreeMarkets, a Pittsburgh company that runs electronic marketplaces, explains in *An Overview of B2B and Purchasing Technology: Response to Call for Submissions*, a paper of exemplary clarity written in 2000, that "these complexities eliminate the possibility that simple B2C business models could be successfully applied to business purchases".

Mr Brittan's task is thus a complicated one. But it is made a little simpler by the fact that purchasing falls into two rough-and-ready categories: direct materials that go into end-products (such as parts or chemical feedstocks), and indirect materials, which may be anything from carpets to lubricants to hotel accommodation for travelling staff. The arrival of the Internet changes both kinds of buying, but many of the quickest hits are in the second category. In many large companies the first kind of purchasing has been online for years, although the systems have been proprietary, inflexible and expensive. The second has floated free. Buying the paper for the ladies' loo can sometimes be done on the say-so of the local building manager, and sometimes needs a sign-off from the buying department.

One way, it tends to be extravagant and hard to track; the other, expensive to manage and infuriatingly slow. When the local manager places the order, a big company may use hundreds of suppliers; "rogue" purchases proliferate; and company purchasing policy becomes impossible to enforce. Nobody can track how many pencils are being bought each year, or where, or at what price, or whether a rise in the pencils budget is the result of a rise in pencil prices or in demand for pencils. When the buying department does the ordering, the company spends money on squads of bored clerical staff that might be better spent on a few of those Arizona State MBAS.

All too often, the business of purchasing costs more than the items bought. When companies pause to look at these systems, they are aghast: SAP, for instance, realised that purchases had to go through four levels of approval; UTC found that it was handling 200,000 invoices for 12,500 different items of office supplies. "Maintenance, repair and operation typically account for 20% of a company's purchases but 80% of its orders," says Patrick Forth, managing director of iFormation, a spin-off of the Boston Consulting Group. "The cost of a purchase order is typically $100. E-procuring costs $10."

One of the fastest ways to save money, therefore, is to use the Internet to try to bring indirect purchases under control. That means, first, putting somebody in charge of the task. Next, it involves negotiating centrally with suppliers; drawing up a single catalogue; and insisting that staff either buy from it or explain why they want something different. Even if a company does no more than that, it makes savings: "If you don't get at least 10% out," says Mr Brittan, "something's wrong." If you cut the number of suppliers, you not only get bulk discounts; you save your buyers' travelling time, and you probably save money and space tied up in unwanted stock.

Some companies find that the largest savings come from curbing those rogue purchases. At IBM, purchases made outside the procurement system accounted for 30% of the total in 1995. The figure is now down to 0.6% of total purchases of more than $45 billion a year. Because expenses claims are online, it is easier to check who steps out of line. If staff are to accept such discipline, they need a system that is very easy to use and very quick. IBM cut the purchase process from 30 days to one, renegotiating the contract with Staples, a large office-supplies company, to speed up delivery.

In time, many other benefits emerge. For example, there may be savings in buying legal or accountancy services. This will be harder than reorganising the purchase of paper for the photocopier, because professional services are difficult to specify. Yet even this may turn out to be possible. SAP, for instance, is trying to define different levels of consultant, because consultancy services are its largest single purchase. If it can do so, the company will be able to start managing its consultancy purchases in the same way as it now manages purchases of PCs.

Moreover, quite apart from the gains that come from aggregation and control, there may be savings in the transaction costs of placing orders, especially if the Internet can link the buyer's computer system directly to the vendor's. Until the middle of 1999, SAP's offices bought locally. Now, employees log on to a standard catalogue, click on an item and fill in an online purchase order. This is sent electronically to a specific vendor, with whom a price has already been agreed. The system confirms the delivery date and issues the credit note, closing the whole deal under a set of predetermined terms and conditions. The enormous saving in staff that such automation makes possible has allowed SAP to cut internal purchasing costs by around 80%.

Such standard catalogues are one of the more important innovations that the Internet has made possible. Its low-cost, flexible technology allows them to be used by everyone in a company who has access to a browser, and to carry illustrations or even videos to show how a particular part fits or a tool is used. Even small companies can afford them. They will transform the management of indirect purchases and become one of the most reliable sources of corporate cost savings.

Direct hits

Some savings also turn out to be possible in companies' purchases of direct materials. But these have always tended to be handled differently. No local manager nips out for a rogue purchase of a few thousand motherboards. Instead, expensive software programs called Materials Requirements Planning track the materials and components that a manufacturer needs in the production process and calculates what replenishment is needed on the basis of production orders from the sales department.

However, such programs are no use when a company designs a product from scratch, hunts for suitable components and suppliers, specifies parts and negotiates prices. Nor can they easily be connected to the programs of other companies, to allow a supplier to understand what is happening in a buyer's plant. The Internet and its associated technologies make both these things possible.

The answer here is not a standard catalogue. Most companies buy custom-built parts and components from suppliers with whom they have worked on design specifications and entered into long-term contracts. Instead, Internet-based software makes collaboration easier, both within and among firms. That, as the next section demonstrates, turns out to be useful at almost every stage along the supply chain.

Trying to connect you

A supply-side revolution

Every day Cisco Systems, acme of the new-economy corporate model, posts its requirements for components on an extranet, a dedicated Internet-based network that connects the company to 32 manufacturing plants. Cisco does not own these plants, but they have gone through a lengthy process of certification to ensure that they meet the company's quality-control and other standards. Within hours, these suppliers respond with a price, a delivery time, and a record of their recent performance on reliability and product quality.

This process, says Cisco's Mr Nuti, has replaced a room full of 50 agents, who would pull together much the same information with the help of telephones and faxes. The operation generally took three to four days. Now, says Mr Nuti triumphantly, "those 50 people are redeployed into managing the quality of components".

Three aspects of Cisco's supply system are particularly significant. One is the use of a form of electronic market to set prices. Online marketplaces of various sorts have proliferated in the past year. One is the exchange of information between buyers and sellers. The Internet's ability inexpensively to increase this flow is altering the whole nature of the supply chain. The third is the extent to which Cisco outsources activities that other companies do in-house. That, again, is made easier by the Internet.

Most companies have moved nothing like as far as Cisco (see Figure 2.2 on next page). But they are beginning to realise the essential steps they need to take. These involve both widening the potential pool of suppliers for any given contract, and deepening the relationship with the supplier that eventually wins it.

The obvious way to widen the pool of suppliers is to participate in an online auction of some kind. Many companies are beginning to put contracts for supplies out to tender online: indeed, GE has done so for several years, though on a proprietary network. By the end of 2000, the company aimed to "e-auction" more than 10% of what it buys, using the Internet as a trading floor. GE thinks that eventually 70% of its supplies can be bought this way.

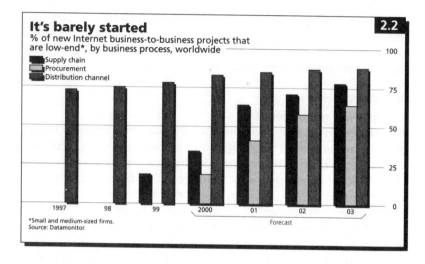

It's barely started **2.2**
% of new Internet business-to-business projects that
are low-end*, by business process, worldwide

- Supply chain
- Procurement
- Distribution channel

1997 · 98 · 99 · 2000 · 01 · 02 · 03

*Small and medium-sized firms.
Source: Datamonitor.

Forecast

One result has been to widen the geographical range of suppliers, says Mr Reiner. For example, the company has developed new capacity to ship supplies from Shanghai, in response to a big rise in bids from Chinese manufacturers. Over time, electronic tendering seems bound to push up the proportion of their supplies that rich-world companies buy abroad, and especially in the developing world. That has important implications. For a start, buying abroad will help to push down prices. "Instead of importing inflation, you import deflation," says GE Capital's Mr Alexander. Moreover, a labour shortage at national level is no longer a problem: "Labour is more fungible than ever before." But casting the net more widely will also increase the need for verification services, of the sort provided by SGS, a 120-year-old Swiss firm that has 60% of the world market for managing trade risk. It has recently launched an online division to protect the interests of buyers and sellers who may never meet.

On the whole, GE has preferred to build its own electronic exchanges rather than use those run by others. However, lots of experiments in online auctions are taking place. As it happens, auction theory has become one of the most fashionable branches of economics, and plenty of academics dream up (and sometimes set up) ingenious auctioneering enterprises of their own. For example, Barry Nalebuff, of Yale University, has launched a company called splitthedifference.com. Buyers and sellers of a given commodity set out their reserve prices; the software then works out the mix of buyers and sellers that delivers the greatest value, and splits the surplus evenly between both sides.

Such ingenious schemes work for standard commodities that can be readily specified. Companies now often put out to tender (in essence, a reverse auction) such basics as the printing of their annual report or their stationery needs. As a result of one such auction, GE Capital switched the publication of its annual report from the United States to Indonesia early in 2000.

But most purchases of direct materials are not of that sort. Even where they are, the bidding process is often preceded by a couple of arduous months of "prequalification", where company and would-be suppliers nail down every variable except price: quality, size, timing, ability to deliver, and so on. This rigorous discipline brings benefits in its own right.

Most companies, moreover, have long-established relations with their main suppliers. Are they right to toss them aside in an auction? Das Narayandas of Harvard Business School has studied five suppliers whose customers went to FreeMarkets, the grand-daddy of electronic business-to-business auction houses, and put the work out to tender. Four of the five customers, he will report in a forthcoming article, "were back knocking on their [old] suppliers' doors three months later". The new suppliers had underestimated, and failed to match, the huge value of customisation in the contract.

At FreeMarkets, the founders agree that such things happen. But, says Glen Meakem, the best auctions do something rather different. They provide the foundation for long-term relationships. In his paper, Mr Kinney adds that "Buyers typically use the auction to determine with whom to establish the market relationship, based on excellent price discovery. But, once the auction is over, production parts are approved and tooling is installed, the working relationship can run for years." That "price discovery" is not to be sniffed at: at FreeMarkets's auctions over the past five years, says Mr Meakem, buyers have ended up paying on average 15–16% less than the previous purchase price.

What am I bid?

Given the frenzy to set up electronic marketplaces, a bit of scepticism is in order. The experience of financial markets strongly suggests that many of the 700 or so e-markets will soon be wiped out or merge, as happened with the multiplicity of regional stock exchanges in the early 20th century. However, whereas some electronic markets will be too puny to live, others have such powerful parents that they worry competition regulators. Covisint, set up (and spun off) by four of the world's biggest car companies, was initially stalled on competition grounds.

In fact, many of these marketplaces were established to provide a common trading standard, so that buyers and vendors can easily exchange information electronically. "It is a convenience for suppliers not to have to build 20 interfaces," says Ron Wohl, head of applications development for Oracle. The bold vision of some trading platforms is to assemble an entire industry, not into a supply chain, but into a network or – to use the most fashionable word in e-business – an "eco-system". For that, common standards are the essential first step.

Enter the eco-system
From supply chain to network

Every quarter, Cisco Systems hosts about 1,000 meetings with the top brass of companies around the world. "It used to be the technicians," says the company's Mr Daichendt. "Now it's usually the CEO." At the height of the Firestone crisis, Jac Nasser brought along the entire board of Ford. The same thing happens at Dell Computer. A procession of chief executives make the pilgrimage to Austin, Texas, to learn how to "Dell" their company.

They want to understand how the Internet can transform the management of their supply chain. The main thing they learn is the importance of sharing information. Suppliers benefit greatly when they can see their customers' production schedules and sales data, because they can then plan ahead for the volume and timing of orders. They can react at once, rather than waiting for news to trickle down. Something of the sort was possible before the Internet came along, but only if both supplier and buyer had installed expensive proprietary technology. The Internet (along with its associated applications) allows such communications to take place among many buyers and suppliers, big and small. It also makes information available simultaneously all the way along the supply chain. Once this happens (and it is only just starting), it becomes more appropriate to think in terms of a supply network than a chain.

The Internet has allowed a further refinement. Dell's suppliers know not only how fast Dell is using their components; they know what finished products customers are ordering. When a customer places an order by clicking on the company's website, the software immediately feeds the order into the production schedule, and can thus tell the customer, almost instantly, when the order will be ready for shipment. Once the order is in Dell's system, suppliers can see it coming and start making the appropriate parts. So the Internet turns the company into a sort of portal through which orders arrive for redistribution among suppliers. Dick Hunter, who is in charge of Dell's supply-chain management, explains: "We are not experts in the technology we buy; we are experts in the technology of integration."

In time, says Mr Hunter, "Information will replace inventory." As an example, he cites the suppliers who make the metal and plastic boxes for Dell's computers, mostly local firms with factories up to 90 minutes' drive away. They have access to up-to-the-minute information on Dell's stocks and its use of their products, and often keep a truck full of boxes waiting on Dell's site. The moment the first is unloaded, they send another truck. In their own plants, they keep less than a day's worth of finished stock. "If our information were 100% right," says Mr Hunter, "the only inventory that would exist would be in transit."

This point is worth pausing to think about, because it has large implications for the business cycle. Lee Price, chief economist in the American Commerce Department's Office of Policy Development, sounds rather like Mr Hunter when he describes inventories as: "A substitute for information: you buy them because you are not sure of the reliability of your supplier or the demand from your customer." But since the late 1980s inventories have been falling sharply, relative to sales, all over American manufacturing (see Figure 2.3). A report for the Commerce Department in which Mr Price had a hand, "Digital Economy 2000", calculates that this has saved American companies some $10 billion a year – a cumulative $115 billion since 1988. Moreover, leaner inventories should reduce the ferocity of any future downturn. In the past, when demand grew a bit more slowly, inventories would often fall, amplifying a mild deceleration into a recession.

But back to Dell. Three things make the company's build-to-order approach easier. First, it is a relatively young company, which began in direct sales, so it does not suffer the conflicts among competing distributors that plague most old-economy companies. Second, Dell is a one-product company. Old-economy firms, with much more complex product lines, find it hard to integrate even their in-house supply operations, let alone those with myriad outside firms. Third, Dell (like Cisco) has remarkably few suppliers: 200 or so in all, with 30 companies accounting for about 78% of its total purchasing. Conventional large computer companies have about 1,000 suppliers. Dell tries to have at least two sources for every component, if only for safety's sake. Many of those sources are on the other side of the planet: it buys more than half its supplies from Asia. What matters is the closeness of the relationship, not

33

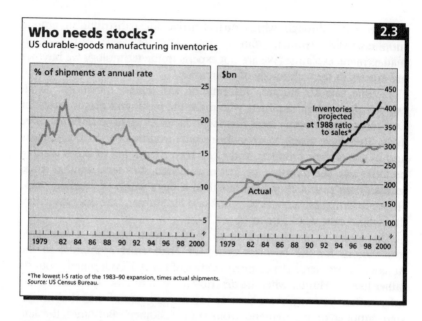

Who needs stocks?
US durable-goods manufacturing inventories

2.3

% of shipments at annual rate

$bn

Inventories projected at 1988 ratio to sales*

Actual

*The lowest I-S ratio of the 1983–90 expansion, times actual shipments.
Source: US Census Bureau.

the physical distance. But as Mr Hunter points out, "It would be very complex to have an intimate relationship with hundreds of suppliers."

The next step is to pass on the information that goes to suppliers to the second tier of companies that supply them. Texas Instruments sells digital signal processors to Solectron, which incorporates them into motherboards that Dell buys. Dell is talking to both companies to see how much of the data it passes to Solectron should also go to Texas Instruments, and is having similar talks with other suppliers. The company dreams of the day when all computer manufacturers who buy hard drives, and all suppliers who produce them, make that information available anonymously on an electronic exchange. That would allow the whole industry a clear view of the balance of supply and demand. It might even reduce the gluts that periodically plague the industry, as lack of information leads many companies simultaneously to take the wrong decisions.

For whom the Dell tolls

What benefits spring from collaborating? Dell makes much of its greater capacity to get technological innovations to customers quickly, and the fact that customers can specify exactly the machine they want. But the real gains are those inventory savings. A company building a product the material cost of which drops 1% every fortnight cannot afford to keep more stock than absolutely necessary. Compaq, says Mr Hunter smugly, may have 30–35 days' worth of inventory in its sales channels. "We have none." In total, the company holds about 140 hours of inventory (measurement in days is now old hat), and hopes to cut even that minuscule number in half over the next two years.

Better still, Dell collects the money from its corporate customers 30 days after shipment (or, for retail sales, on ordering), but pays its suppliers after 45 days. As a result, the company is in the delightful position of having what it calls "negative cashflow", which actually means money in the bank. That benefit will not last indefinitely: sooner or later, competition will make sure it is passed on in lower prices. But getting your customers' credit-card companies to provide your working capital is a trick worth knowing.

No wonder so many other companies hope to do the same. Among the most enthusiastic are the car manufacturers. At present, their customers face a bleak choice. In Europe, most cars are now built to order. In the United States, most cars are built for stock. Plenty of permutations are possible, but the customer sees only what the dealer ordered, two or three months earlier. These stocks of finished products clutter dealers' lots, tying up billions of dollars of cash; and yet customers still complain that they cannot find the car they want. A dealer who guesses wrong needs to persuade customers to buy to shift the stock and cut his interest charges, periodically wreaking havoc with margins.

However, applying Michael Dell's bright idea to Henry Ford's legacy is not easy. For one thing, American car companies do not go in for direct sales but have huge dealer networks. Brian Kelley, who came from GE to run e-commerce at Ford, thinks that dealers are an essential part of any new supply chain. "Most customers planning to spend $25,000 to $30,000 on a new product want to see and test it first," he argues. "Besides, 80% of people who buy a new vehicle have an old one to trade in." And cars need servicing from time to time. But Mr Kelley also sees Ford's dealers as delivery channels for a new venture called FordDirect, launched in August 2000. This allows customers to configure, select, price, finance and order a new car or truck through a website and then pick it up from a dealer.

Ford's strategy of deepening relations with intermediaries provides a model for the many old-economy companies that depend too much on physical distribution channels to want to abandon them overnight. Instead, they use the Internet to give intermediaries additional

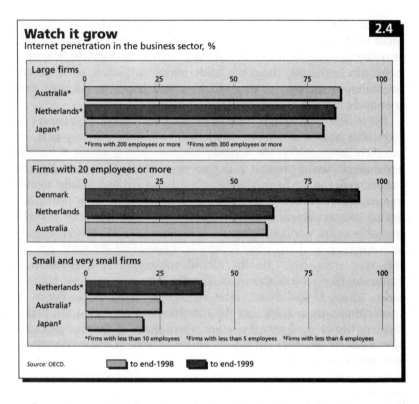

Watch it grow `2.4`
Internet penetration in the business sector, %

Large firms
- Australia* (Firms with 200 employees or more)
- Netherlands* (Firms with 200 employees or more)
- Japan† (Firms with 300 employees or more)

*Firms with 200 employees or more   †Firms with 300 employees or more

Firms with 20 employees or more
- Denmark
- Netherlands
- Australia

Small and very small firms
- Netherlands* (Firms with less than 10 employees)
- Australia† (Firms with less than 5 employees)
- Japan‡ (Firms with less than 6 employees)

*Firms with less than 10 employees   †Firms with less than 5 employees   ‡Firms with less than 6 employees

Source: OECD.   ▢ to end-1998   ▢ to end-1999

information, to bind them into the distribution channel in the way Dell and Cisco have bound suppliers into their supply network. Thus Honeywell, a computer company that has relied heavily on intermediaries to sell its products, has created myplant.com, a website that solves problems for managers of large industrial plants. As a strategy, this may not necessarily be second-best. Physical channels have some advantages over virtual ones. For example, Wells Fargo, which has been offering Internet banking for consumers longer than just about anyone else, still has bricks-and-mortar branches, and finds that they do better at closing sales than anything offered online.

Most of Ford's biggest dealers have signed up for FordDirect; smaller ones, and those in less populated regions, have been much less enthusiastic. But winning dealers' support is only part of the challenge. A bigger problem is that Ford's cars are simply not built like Dell's computers. To take just one example, the colour of a Ford car is determined early in the production process, before the metal is even stamped. That is not the only way to build a car – DaimlerChrysler's Smart car, for its part, has clip-on side panels, allowing a dealer to change its colour in an hour. Eventually, Mr Kelley accepts, Ford will have to refit its plants so that they can build to demand, rather than "to sit on a lot". But, without a way to smooth out peaks and troughs in demand (a virtue of building for stock), capacity utilisation will fall and costs will rise.

The trick will be to make the manufacturing process more modular and less sequential: for instance, the basic platform will be built for stock and then turned into the vehicle the customer orders. Indeed, a change in the manufacturing process is at the heart of true build-to-online-order projects. Frank Piller, an economist at the Technical University of Munich who has made a special study of the way companies customise a basic product line (a process dubbed "mass customisation"), argues that the biggest change is usually in the design and construction of the product. "You need modular production that fits together like Lego blocks," he says.

Ford also hopes to use Covisint, and the common standards that the trading platform will create, to share its forecasts and its inventory information with its suppliers, both the front line and those further along the chain. As Mr Kelley freely admits, "It won't be simple to link the unconnected legacy systems and the internal workings of each of these very large companies." The putative savings, of $1,000 to $3,000 a car, will appear only if all the disparate systems can be joined up. "It will take years to play out," forecasts Mr Kelley.

Between the two extremes of Dell and Ford, many companies will search for middle ground. Hau Lee, director of the Global Supply Chain Management Forum at Stanford Graduate School of Business, sees them moving through four stages. First, there is an exchange of information, such as demand forecasts and sales data that allow better planning. Companies quickly realise that they need to define common standards for things like point-of-sale and inventory information, so that each can interpret the other's material. Next, companies move beyond data to exchange knowledge: for example, when Wal-Mart's Florida stores ran out of mosquito repellent during a heatwave, the company discovered that Warner Lambert not only made the repellent but tracked weather forecasts to spot future peaks in demand. By sharing the information online, both companies could do better.

At the third stage, says Mr Lee, companies exchange the right to take decisions. Often, it is enough for one link in a supply chain to make a move: for example, if Wal-Mart decides to stock more nappies for babies, there should be no need for Procter & Gamble, which makes the things, and for 3M, which supplies the sticky plastic tapes, to have three separate decision-making processes for a single product. So these companies are experimenting with a system that allows one person to reach the decision for all three. The last step is an exchange of work and roles. "The manufacturer becomes a retailer," says Mr Lee, "and retail moves to a support role." For example, companies such as VooDoo Cycles and Cannondale, makers of high-margin sports bicycles, are increasingly taking customers' orders direct and only then building the bicycles. But a costly bike requires much last-minute tweaking before it is fit for the road. Returns by dissatisfied customers are expensive for mail-order manufacturers. And customers picking up a new bicycle may well want to buy a new helmet or some lycra shorts. That is the new role – akin to Ford's repositioning of its dealers – that bicycle retailers may take on. One effect of the supply-chain revolution is thus to change the way companies manage their relations with customers.

The personal touch
Making customers feel special
How do you persuade people not to buy a car-insurance policy purely on price? Progressive, an insurance company based in Ohio, has an answer. If a policyholder has an accident, a claims officer goes straight to the scene, gives him a cellphone and a cup of coffee, pulls out a laptop and, in 95% of cases, hands him a claim cheque on the spot. Some customers say: "I wasn't a member until I was hit by one." The service, not the price, sells the product.

"It creates a 'wow' experience," says Joe Pine, an authority on such things: he published a book (with James Gilmore) in 1999 on *The Experience Economy*. The Internet, he argues, transforms the way companies have to manage relations with customers, partly because it is "the greatest force for commoditisation ever invented". But it also affects companies' relations with customers by cutting the cost of routine transactions, and by giving them new ways to reach and monitor those customers.

For the technology companies that have pioneered many business applications, customer support is one of the first opportunities for change the Internet provides. But the opportunity is to offer a service that is more of a commodity rather than less, by refining ways to deliver help online rather than over the telephone.

Companies will continue to offer telephone help: indeed State Street, a Massachusetts bank which uses lots of voice response to answer calls, is building a new call centre as well as developing the Internet. "Some customers simply want to talk to someone," admits John Fiore, the chief information officer. But the scarcer support staff become, and the longer telephone inquirers have to hold on, the easier it is to encourage customers to look up the answer to their problem online. And there are huge gains to be made from applying the usual 80/20 rule, says Ward Hanson of Stanford Graduate School of Business: if the staff answer only the complicated 20% of questions, their work is far more interesting and productive. ("The grey area", he adds, "is trying to hide the help-desk telephone number from the remaining 80%. I usually go to 'investor relations'.")

More savings are to be had if the customer can be trained to place orders online. "Accepting a simple order on the phone takes about four minutes and costs around $5," says GE's Mr Reiner. "In our higher-tech businesses, it may cost $80. We get 20m telephone calls a year in our appliance business. If the order comes in online, it costs 20 cents." For the customer, too, Mr Reiner insists, it costs less to place an order on the Internet than on the telephone. But just in case the customer does not initially see things that way, GE offers to send out "e-mentors" with its sales staff to visit customers. It also gives sales people a bigger commission on orders that arrive online, so that they share some of the savings. The sales folk themselves know all about working online: in the past four years, the number of sales offices has fallen by half as more of them work on the road, from home or from their customers' premises.

Nor do the savings in online selling come only from lower transaction costs. Dell's Mr Marengi argues that the best thing about moving to online ordering has been to dispose of endless arguments over whether the customer ordered this keyboard or that keyboard. "If the customer puts in the order," he says cheerfully, "that conflict is eliminated."

By exploiting the Internet, companies not only gain opportunities for cost-cutting; they can also create new business opportunities by learning more about their customers (see Figure 2.5 on next page). At present, such information tends to be strewn among many different databases, each attached to a particular product line or sales channel. By integrating the data, companies can present a single, coherent face to customers. That task is easier when customers shop online.

It may be valuable for a customer to have a single view of his trans-actions. "A company may know what it's buying in Boston, but not what its subsidiary is buying in Spain," says Mr Marengi. "Often a company will ask us what it bought globally, because its own internal systems can't tell it." But the seller benefits too. "The web allows companies to draw a graph of a customer's lifetime value," says Mr Hanson. "You can learn

Why companies need to get wired 2.5
% of 60 global companies
Only 48% of firms know about a problem before a customer does
Only 43% offer better service to profitable customers
Only 42% would sell something during a service call
Only 37% know if they share a customer with another division
Only 23% of telephone agents can see customers' web activity
Only 20% know if a customer has visited the website
Source: Forrester Research.

how customers end up in your fold, which are the best and the worst ones, and why some abandon their electronic shopping trolley before they make the final transaction."

One effect of such data has been to teach companies much more about the relative costs of acquiring and keeping customers. All of them promptly reach the same conclusion: "There has been a big shift from acquisition to retention," says Harvey Thompson, who runs customer relationship management at IBM Global Services. The reason is partly that a click of a mouse is the fastest way ever for customers to change providers. But companies now also have the tools to exploit what they know about their existing customers.

Among the first businesses to take advantage of those tools have been financial institutions. Wells Fargo, that experienced online bank, finds that attrition is one-third less for online than for comparable offline retail customers. For customers who make bill payments online, attrition is 54% lower than for offline customers. Online customers, says Avid Modjtabai of the bank's Internet services group, tend to keep higher balances, and seem to be much more likely to buy extra products, than the unwired ones. Simply knowing more about your customers makes it easier to keep them.

One obvious way companies could use that knowledge is to offer different customers different prices and levels of service. So far, most have hesitated to do so – or at least have hidden their attempts more carefully than did Amazon.com, which was savaged in 2000 for quoting different prices for the same book. But many companies are starting to understand that they cannot offer the same quality of service to everyone. They know that the true promise of customer data is to help them to discriminate, in service quality and perhaps in price, and to target their services so that they give priority to the most profitable folk on their books. They also know that this will not be easy to do. "I would not want one of my customers bumping into another and saying we had given them a better deal," says Cisco's Mr Daichendt.

But whose customer is it anyway? As companies tie their databases together, and try to cross-sell products to a customer who sees a single common front, they run up against a new version of an ancient problem: how to motivate one salesman in a company to hand over a customer to another. Without incentives to share customers, the most elegantly reconciled data in the world will make no difference. In most companies, the tyranny of the distribution channel will make customer-sharing a hard problem. "In large companies," observes George Colony, chief executive of Forrester Research, a high-tech consultancy, "tremendous political power has built up around these channels. It takes the CEO to force the breakdown of the walls."

Every company now claims to be, in that horrid but popular word, "customer-centric". In fact, most companies always said they were. But the Internet and its associated technologies allow companies to discover whether customers were aware of it, and if not, to do something about it.

From a commodity to an experience

One force for change will be the discovery of the commoditising power of the Internet. Once buyers can readily shop around online, or aggregate corporate demand, or put out tenders on electronic trading platforms, then companies that sell on nothing more than price will be in trouble, unless they are supremely efficient. What is the alternative?

One strategy, described by Philip Evans, co-author of a book with the ominous title of *Blown to Bits*, is to separate the information-rich part of the business from the commodity part, and sell them separately. He describes a manufacturer of industrial abrasives and drills who decided to split his business in this way. One part now specialises in long runs of standardised products. It has eliminated most of the salesforce, and abandoned research and development. The other part, which is far smaller in turnover but almost as profitable, employs engineers as consultants, solving problems with the "drilling solution". The first part uses the Internet to sell partly through electronic markets; the second, to connect engineers with their customers.

For consumer products, there is Mr Pine's experience-economy type of solution: turn a product or service into an "experience", and you defeat commoditisation. As examples, he cites a company in Minneapolis that repairs computers. It calls itself the Geek Squad, and sends round nerds dressed in white shirts and black ties in new vw Beetles or vintage cars. Or there is Steinway: when a customer acquires one of that company's top-of-the-range concert grands, the company offers to lay on a free concert in the buyer's house, providing a concert pianist, sending out the invitations and passing round the hors d'oeuvres. Mr Pine's own daughter favours American Girl Place, which makes character dolls. It has a sort of indoor theme park in Chicago where small girls and their parents can pay to watch a show about their doll, or pay again for lunch with a special chair for their doll to sit in. What they all have in common is that they add extra value to an easy-to-emulate product by throwing in a corny experience. This produces at least three gains: a higher margin, greater customer loyalty and local jobs.

With a bit of ingenuity, the technology that turns a manufactured consumer good into a commodity can also turn it back into an "experience". Levi, whose famous blue jeans now compete with cheaper copies, offers customers in its Union Square store in San Francisco the chance to be measured by a body scanner. Half an hour later a Levi factory has pulled their vital statistics off the Internet and begun to cut the jeans of their choice. Unfortunately, it then takes ten days to get the finished jeans to the customer. At present, the jeans cost 30–40% more to produce than a standard pair, mainly because as yet the company does not accept online repeat orders. But returns, which usually run to 40% of mail-order sales, are down to single digits. Moreover, the store has found that it learns from its customers when it sells to them this way: for instance, it noticed that those who designed their own jeans wanted them slung low on the hips, months before the average customer stopped buying "high-rise" jeans.

Levi's experience carries several lessons for companies that want to use the Internet to manage customer relations. One is that companies which once thought of every sale as a separate transaction will increasingly make money not from a first sale but from repeat business. That implies creating a continuing relationship with the customer, such as service providers usually enjoy. A second lesson is the importance of being able to involve the customer in development, design and market research. Richer communications make that possible. A third is the need for speed: the Internet, with its round-the-clock, round-the-week availability, raises customer expectations. Lastly, the relationship between factory and retailer changes. The factory may become the retailer's back office. Or, if the manufacturer has a strong brand and an accumulation of customer data (including, in Levi's case, their hip and inside-leg measurements), then the manufacturer becomes a portal for the retailer. Either way, the close contact with the customer fostered by the Internet is the most valuable commercial advantage a business can have.

The shape of the new e-company
Who runs what, and for whom

Two years ago, Nortel Networks, a Canadian company that specialises in building high-performance Internet networks, took a revolutionary decision. It would move from vertical integration to "virtual" integration. Since then, the company has sold 15 manufacturing facilities around the world that make things like printed circuit-boards. The plants have been bought by large manufacturers such as Solectron, sci and Sanmina, which were already selling to Nortel and have now signed new long-term supply agreements with the company.

The benefits, says Chahram Bolouri, president of global operations, come partly in the form of lower costs, because these contract manufacturers have a far larger turnover than Nortel alone would have had. They can also afford to keep track of the fast-changing manufacturing technology of the particular components they produce, and invest heavily in their development. In addition, Nortel gains flexibility: if it has a large order from a particular part of the world, it can more easily arrange production nearby. Most important of all, the company can specialise in what it does really well: it has retained the highest-value part of the manufacturing process at seven "systems houses" worldwide, staffed with people skilled in industrial and test engineering.

The reorganisation has also changed the way Nortel deals with its suppliers. Three years ago, says Mr Bolouri, it concentrated on buying; now it deals with technology and planning. It employs a different bunch of people: fewer paper-pushers, more industrial engineers. They spend much of their time talking, not only to the first tier of suppliers, but also to the second and third, about the main constraints in meeting demand from a particular market or consumer, and how they can be eased. Particular teams concentrate on the needs of particular customers, such as WorldCom or Cable & Wireless.

Thus rearranged, Nortel can move much faster than in the past. In the mid-1990s, when it owned most of its suppliers, an order might take up to three months to fulfil. Today, orders for some products take days, and soon that will be hours. Using a newly created Internet exchange, called e2open, the company can circulate an order instantly to a galaxy of

60 potential suppliers. Mr Bolouri devotes most of his time to recruiting and keeping high-quality talent to manage the supply chain, and to making sure that everyone along the chain is kept constantly up to date on what the company is trying to do.

As the Internet becomes built into corporate life, the economic foundation of the company changes. In an essay on "The Nature of the Firm", published in 1937, Ronald Coase, an economist who later won the Nobel prize, argued that the cost of transactions determined the boundaries of firms, making it more efficient for workers to band together in a company than to operate as separate agents. The impact of the Internet has been to reduce those costs. Because almost everything can be inexpensively outsourced, it is possible to create a company from nothing in no time: to go from idea to product in nine months. Many Internet start-ups are, in the neat phrase of Stanford Graduate Business School's Mr Saloner, "plug-and-play" companies.

Many of the barriers to entry that once protected big companies are therefore disappearing – or at least some parts of established companies are vulnerable to being "blown to bits". One effect, as Nortel's case demonstrates, is a move away from vertical integration, as the value chain is broken up into more specialised firms. In that respect, says MIT's Mr Brynjolfsson, we are seeing the substitution of hierarchies by markets.

Competition may not challenge all the things a company does – just the most profitable parts. Brendan McLaughlin, head of e-business at Cambridge Technology Partners, a high-tech consultancy, has a story about how he told one of his clients, a manufacturer of tapered roller bearings, about a Scandinavian firm that made nothing but replacement tapered roller bearings, and monitored other companies' production lines over the Internet to check when the parts were needed. "Our client's jaw dropped. 'But we make all our money from replacements,' he gasped."

Plenty more such competition lies ahead. At Harvard Business School, Bill Sahlman, professor of business administration, observes: "Our students go systematically, SIC code by SIC code, through industries, looking for ones to revolutionise." Moreover, start-ups are starting to understand their intrinsic weaknesses, and to evolve business models that cure them. Julian Lighton, in charge of corporate networks at the Silicon Valley office of McKinsey, a consultancy, notices that the incubators in which some start-ups begin life are becoming "semi-permanent *keiretsu*", or loose confederations, to share the costs of acquiring and managing customers and talent. One incubator, ICG, has a common recruiting department with 20 staff to help its offspring. "Shared talent management" is the heart of these confederations, because the scarce talent of Silicon Valley prefers to work for a network of small companies that pool job opportunities.

Dotcom or dot.corp?

Big, established companies often find it hard at first to respond to such competition. Not every company is as bold as GE, which in 1999 ran an exercise called "destroyyourbusiness.com" to force managers to consider where they were most vulnerable to unexpected competition delivered by the Internet.

Most old-economy companies initially choose not to re-engineer their whole business, but rather to spin off a new division to experiment. IBM's Mr Martinez sees three possible models. One is that of Reflect.com, a start-up by Procter & Gamble, a consumer-products giant based in Cincinnati, Ohio, which sells customised cosmetics over the Internet from the safe distance of San Francisco. That avoids nasty conflicts with existing distribution channels, and gets the expense (and possible losses) safely off the balance sheet.

A second model is that pursued by Staples, a successful office-stationery business, which has created Staples.com as a separate business, but kept the links close. Staff at Staples have options in the dotcom's tracking shares, and the dotcom folk have options on Staples shares. The two businesses share a building in Boston, to make sure that each learns from the other. Staples's own share price has been hit because the company has had to write off this investment as an ordinary operating cost. One of the great oddities of this revolution is that whereas investments in physical assets can be capitalised and depreciated, investments in intangible assets count as expenses.

The third model, says Mr Martinez, is that of IBM itself, where the company has decided that it cannot afford to spin anything off. The firm itself becomes a dotcom – or rather, as Forrester's Mr Colony quips, a "dotcorp". This is hardest of all to pull off, so not many companies try it.

One trouble with spin-offs is that they waste a company's scarcest resource: good people. "That's why I tell companies to take all the juice and put it in one place," says Mr Colony. Another problem is that spin-offs are odd animals. The business model of the genuine dotcom is usually to grab the money and run. For the purchaser, it is a way of outsourcing innovation: the start-up takes the initial risk, and the big firm buys the experiment that has succeeded. But if a big company spins off its most innovative bits, it may lose the chance to recreate itself.

The alternative, for old-economy companies, will be far-reaching change. As Mr Saloner explains, many companies resist innovation partly because it seems expensive, and partly because they cannot bear to destroy their existing, successful business model. "We are designed to do what we do really well," they say. What they need to remember is that this is a transitional stage. It is good news for business schools, he points out: "The demand for executive education is going through the roof as chief executives say, 'The top 300 people in my business just don't get it.' But these people will be needed again, and they know the business."

Conclusion

There are no easy answers on how to manage this period of dislocation. The e-commerce shake-out brought the downfall of many dotcom pioneers. Economic factors aside, the truth is that these bold and brash new managers did not have the experience or in some cases even the interest to build a solid business in the first place. Chapter 6 outlines some of the lessons to be learnt from their spectacular demise. For old-economy companies, sitting back on the sidelines may not have proved such a dumb decision after all. But the shake-out is not a reason to resist change. E-business is here to stay. For some useful tips on how to become a successful e-manager turn to Chapter 7.

3 Ahead of the game

SOME GOODS AND services are tailor-made for the web because they can actually be delivered over the Internet. Computer software is an obvious example, but increasingly such things as airline tickets, stockbroking services, banking and insurance, and even encyclopedias and newspapers are being delivered electronically. Pornography, the earliest big seller on the web, may rate a special category of its own, but anything with content that can take digital form, which includes most recorded music and film, is especially suitable for the web. Indeed, the economics of the web could pose a big threat to the traditional distribution channels for such products.

Of the material goods, standardised, or "low-touch", items such as books and CDs have sold best over the net so far. "High-touch" items, such as clothes and shoes, as well as many groceries, which consumers often prefer to handle before they buy, have been left behind (see Figure 3.1).

This chapter looks at some of the sectors that have experienced the fastest growth of e-business.

Computing and electronics

The computer and electronics industry has been the most aggressive in Internet adoption, which is not surprising since it created the technology that is changing the way businesses do business. It has charted the new territory of e-commerce for other industries to follow.

The e-business approach to everything – from procurement to human-resources management – has been led by young and innovative companies like Dell Computer and Cisco Systems, which have used their knowledge of the markets they serve and the absence of any baggage to steal a march on older rivals. It was through nifty deployment of its sales to the Internet that Dell finally overtook Compaq Computer as the global number one in the PC industry. Although big companies have been ordering PCs online for years using proprietary systems, the Internet opened up a new sales channel with a far broader reach and more possibilities.

No guide to e-commerce would be complete without the story of Dell. Although the company's performance was hit by the high-tech tumble of 2000 and a slowdown in demand for PCs as other Internet-enabled

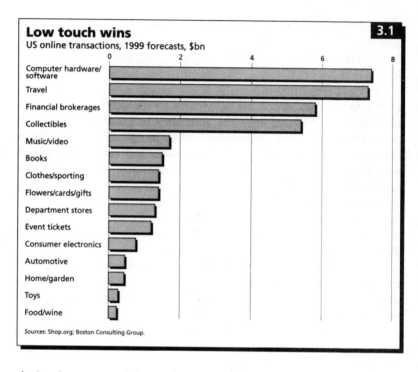

Low touch wins
US online transactions, 1999 forecasts, $bn

Computer hardware/ software	
Travel	
Financial brokerages	
Collectibles	
Music/video	
Books	
Clothes/sporting	
Flowers/cards/gifts	
Department stores	
Event tickets	
Consumer electronics	
Automotive	
Home/garden	
Toys	
Food/wine	

Sources: Shop.org; Boston Consulting Group.

devices began to proliferate, the new models of supply management and lean and mean organisation Dell invented stand unchanged.

The Dell way

The company's factory on the outskirts of Limerick, on the west coast of Ireland, supplies custom-built PCs all over Europe. As orders come into the factory via Dell's website and call centres, the company relays to its suppliers details of which components it needs, how many and when. All the bits and pieces – hard drives, motherboards, modems, and so on – roll up in lorries to big bays at the back of the building, and move off again as complete computers just a few hours later.

Dell gets a lot of attention as a pioneering e-business because it sells millions of dollars' worth of computers from its website each day. Because Dell's suppliers have real-time access to information about its orders via its corporate extranet, they can organise their production and delivery to ensure that their powerful customer always has just enough of the right parts to keep the production line moving smoothly. By plugging its suppliers directly into its customer database, Dell ensures that they will instantly know about any changes in demand. And by plugging its customers into its supply chain via its website, Dell enables them to track the progress of their order from the factory to their doorstep, thus saving on telephone or fax inquiries.

Dell was pretty efficient before it started using the Internet, but now it is able to do even better by creating, as the jargon has it, a "fully integrated value chain". But what exactly does "value-chain integration" mean? John Dobbs of Cambridge Technology Partners, a leading systems integrator, defines it as "a process of collaboration that optimises all internal and external activities involved in delivering greater perceived value to the ultimate customer".

The Internet's universal connectivity has enabled it to create a three-way "information partnership" with its suppliers and customers by treating them as collaborators who together find ways of improving efficiency across the entire chain of supply and demand, and share the benefits. The company's founder and boss, Michael Dell, agrees that the Internet gives customers unprecedented power to seek out the lowest prices, but argues that it can also be used to deepen relationships and ultimately build far greater customer loyalty than before. If you don't create an integrated value chain, he says, don't expect to survive.

The Cisco way

Another company that has embraced e-business with messianic enthusiasm is Cisco, a company that sells about 80% of the routers and other forms of networking gear that power the Internet. It is famous for selling lots of its complex kit over the web (see Figure 3.2 on next page). Customers place their orders through its website, and suppliers know exactly what materials and components they need to ship to the factory by accessing Cisco's "dynamic replenishment" software through a web interface. But Internet applications reach into every part of the company's operation. Susan Bostrom, who heads Cisco's Internet Solutions Group, says: "We live our lives on the browser."

In the early 1990s, Cisco was a young, fast-growing technology company that had the same sorts of problems as similar companies. Faced with apparently unlimited opportunities, it simply could not grow fast enough. The first bottleneck was in after-sales support. The equipment that Cisco sells, however good, does not just run first time out of the box. Networks have to be carefully configured, and each mix of kit ordered is highly cus-tomised. Customers expected continuous support, yet highly trained engi-neers who could deal with the full range of technical problems were hard to find. Besides, they were being submerged by the daily flood of relatively trivial queries.

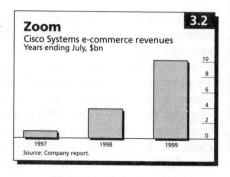

Zoom — 3.2
Cisco Systems e-commerce revenues
Years ending July, $bn
Source: Company report.

The answer turned out to be the web. Cisco decided to put as much of its support as possible online so that customers would be able to resolve most workaday problems on their own, leaving the engineers free to do the heavy lifting. It was an almost instant success, becoming, in Ms Bostrom's words, "a self-inflating balloon of knowledge". Cisco's customers did not just go to the website to get information, they started using it to share their own experiences with both Cisco itself and other customers. More than 80% of customer and partner queries are answered online. And although Cisco's sales have grown exponentially, its technical support staff only doubled between 1994 and 1999.

Another problem the web was enlisted to deal with was inaccurate customer orders. Sometimes the customer was asking for the impossible, sometimes the firm's catalogues were to blame, but whatever the reason, more than one in three orders were coming in wrong, creating chaos for everybody. Customers select from an electronic catalogue, are helped to get their order exactly right and can track its progress online. The whole process of ordering, contract manufacturing, fulfilment and payment is automated.

Mr Carter claims that 55% of orders pass through Cisco's system without being touched by anyone. "We just collect the money," he says. In 1999, he reckoned that Cisco was saving well over $500m a year by using the web; indeed, it could not have maintained its growth rate without it.

The company's use of its own intranet has played an important part in its success. Travel and expenses are dealt with entirely on the web, with reimbursement within two days. Employees can instantly find each other wherever they are in the world. Procurement, employee benefits and recruiting are all web-based. Selling shares in the company – which all employees have – takes just a couple of clicks.

As well as freeing up time for more important things (which at Cisco usually means meeting customers) and saving money, the virtualisation of the business also offers a constant supply of real-time information.

From his desktop PC, Mr Carter can instantly find out who wants to buy what or recruit whom, and get an instant read-out on the net revenue effect of every order.

When Mr Carter joined Cisco from Motorola in 1995, closing the quarterly accounts would take up to ten days. He got it down to two days and halved the cost of finance, to 1% of sales by 1999. Knowing exactly where you are all the time, says Mr Carter, allows you to respond faster than your competitors. But it also means that the 600 people who used to spend ten days a quarter tracking transactions can now be more usefully employed on things such as mining data for business intelligence.

How many of these things Cisco would have been able to do had it been 50 years old rather than 15 is anyone's guess. Mr Carter admits that the absence of baggage was critical, though both the nature of the company's business and its culture helped. But Cisco's new competitors in the rapidly converging market for data networking and telecoms equipment are companies with stacks of baggage, such as Lucent Technologies, Nortel Networks and Alcatel. They would all like to become more like Cisco, but may find it hard to get there.

Travel

The online travel industry is one of the fastest-growing e-commerce sectors. But as the margins grow wafer thin, who pockets the savings?

Before the Internet, travel agents served as useful intermediaries for customers. They could navigate the Byzantine structures of ticket pricing, scheduling and flight availability, removing much of the hassle of organising a holiday or a one-day trip. Moreover, their service was included in the final price of the package and was thus perceived as free of charge by the customer. As such, they were quickly spotted as the unnecessary intermediaries to be replaced by the Internet.

Airlines moved first to cut travel agents out of the picture, hoping they could pocket the huge sums spent on commissions and reach the customers directly. They began their onslaught on travel agents in two ways. The first was by selling seats on their own websites directly. The second was simply cutting the fees they pay to travel agencies. At the same time new dotcom "infomediaries" emerged, pooling information from airline sites and reservation systems and promising better deals for customers, who have clearly taken a liking to the convenience of these offerings. According to Forrester Research, surfers had spent more than $12 billion on online travel purchases by the end of 2000. It says the figure should increase to $30.4 billion by 2003.

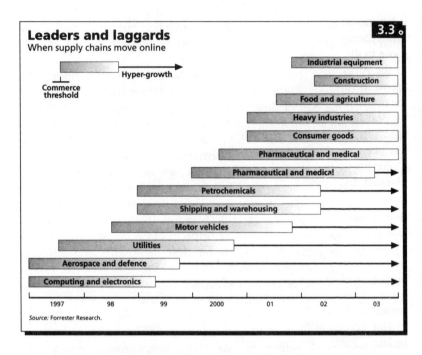

Leaders and laggards
When supply chains move online

3.3

Hyper-growth

Commerce threshold

- Industrial equipment
- Construction
- Food and agriculture
- Heavy industries
- Consumer goods
- Pharmaceutical and medical
- Pharmaceutical and medical
- Petrochemicals
- Shipping and warehousing
- Motor vehicles
- Utilities
- Aerospace and defence
- Computing and electronics

1997   98   99   2000   01   02   03

Source: Forrester Research.

In America alone, consumers booked $6.5 billion of leisure and business travel online in 1999, nearly three times the $2.2 billion booked in 1998. In a study released in April 2000, Jupiter Media Metrix (formerly Jupiter Communications) predicted that online sales of leisure and unmanaged business travel services in America would soar to $28 billion by 2005. And although Jupiter itself called the figures dramatic, the predictions were already lower than earlier growth estimates of online business within the sector. According to a March 2001 study by Nielsen/NetRatings and Harris Interactive, Travelocity has captured the largest share of the online travel market with 18%, followed by Southwest with 14% and Expedia with 11%. Priceline has a 9% slice of the market and Delta has 8%.

So what were the driving forces behind the online revolution in the travel business? The simple answer could be that it is easy to sell plane tickets, which account for the biggest part of travel spending, on the Internet – or so the theory goes. Airlines built their electronic reservation networks long ago, either on their own or in association with other airlines in the market. AMR, parent of American Airlines and 80% owner of Sabre, the leading travel-reservations system used by agents in America, is betting on a web strategy that would move its biggest customers safely into cyberspace via its Travelocity site, cutting out the middlemen. The move to the web has had a devastating effect on travel agents. According to the American Society of Travel Agents (ASTA), the number of travel agents in America had fallen to 27,000 by 1999 from 33,000 in 1994. And the future for local travel agents looks bleaker. A report published in 2000 by Bear Stearns, an investment bank, asserts that 25% of offline travel agents in North America are at risk of going out of business in the next few years.

For an illustration of what is at stake, take Orbitz.com, a travel site planned back in November 1999 by the four major American-based carriers. Continental, Delta, Northwest and United Airlines agreed to form a travel portal selling everything from airline tickets to rental cars and hotel rooms. American Airlines joined in as the fifth partner in March 2000. As well as the five partners, some 30 affiliate airlines will also post their fares on Orbitz, the site maintains. Users will be able to search fares and buy tickets from more than 450 other airlines. The site has garnered more than $100 million in funding and can rely on the massive resources of the airline industry.

Not surprisingly, it has already managed to ruffle feathers in the industry. Following the path of many B2B exchanges set up by industrial groupings, Orbitz has now found itself at the mercy of the market regulators. In February 2000, the ASTA filed a complaint with the US Department of Justice (DOJ), alleging that the new site represents unfair competition for both online and offline travel agencies. Competitors are concerned that member airlines will find ways to offer low-fare tickets on Orbitz while withholding them from other intermediaries. The DOJ has yet to have its say on the matter.

Orbitz dismissed the accusations, arguing that the portal will expand the competitive landscape, not constrict it. Among other things, Orbitz says, the site will inevitably lure some users away from the individual airline sites that Orbitz members will continue to maintain. However, Orbitz has been bogged down by other problems of its own. The site was originally scheduled to launch in September 2000, but this has been put back to June 2001. By the time it does launch, competitors such as Travelocity and Expedia, which have already established strong brand names online, will have moved further ahead in the game.

Who pockets the savings?

There is more bad news for the online travel industry. According to a study by Consumer Reports, a New York-based organisation, consumers are no more likely to find a cheap airfare from an online travel service than from an ordinary telephone call. The study looked at the activities of four well-known sites: Cheap Tickets, Expedia, Lowestfare and Travelocity. Some of the findings were that the lowest fares were not always listed online, the listed fares were not always available and in some cases the top place in the listings was often given to advertisers.

The report, published in the *Consumer Reports Travel Letter* (CRTL), said that the research "came to no firm conclusion on whether travel websites are biased because of deals with airlines". It did say, however, that there was evidence of favouritism. It found that at Travelocity airlines that had advertising deals with the company were listed first 48% of the time, but their fares were not always the cheapest when they occupied the top spot. Lowestfare listed TWA, with which it is linked, as first choice 50% of the time. No other site listed TWA more than 23% of the time.

The study also compared the search results from the four websites with the results from Apollo Galileo, a major computer reservations system used by travel agents. It found that some airlines offering low fares were absent from the online travel sites. Southwest only appeared at Travelocity, and Vanguard was absent from both Expedia and Lowestfare. The report said that the websites gave better results than Apollo Galileo when given a flexible departure time. They also produced equal or better fares when flights were requested weeks or months in advance. But it concluded that although many consumers log on to travel sites expecting to get better fares than those offered by their local travel agent, the low fares listed by the four travel sites were often no cheaper than Apollo Galileo's offerings for the same route.

Customers have found that doing away with the middleman is not always beneficial. Clicking from one airline site to another in search of a low fare can be frustrating and time-consuming. The results are not always guaranteed to please. The rise of new intermediaries is putting plenty of pressure on the big airlines and travel companies. Upstarts like Qixo and FareChase scour dozens of travel sites looking for the cheapest fares for customers and cutting out even more of the hassle. The sites do not book the flights; they simply republish the information. Qixo charges $10 for the service to the travel agency that makes the booking. New York City-based FareChase hopes to grab a percentage share of each transaction. But they may be heading for a court battle; eBay took Bidder's Edge, a site that allowed people to compare auction bids across multiple websites, to court because of its practices. The court ruled in favour of eBay.

Name your own price – if you can be bothered

Priceline.com, a start-up based in Stamford, Connecticut, stole the march on the web discount travel sector in its early days with its reverse-auction model. This allows consumers to name their own prices for products such as airline tickets and hotel rooms. In April 1999, after only a year in business, Priceline achieved a market valuation of $24 billion, which analysts say was largely because it has a broad patent on the reverse-auction concept for e-commerce. Now Microsoft, undaunted by Priceline's patent protection, has said it plans to offer reverse auctions of hotel rooms on its web travel site, Expedia. It is not clear whether Priceline's arguments will hold up in court. The concept of the reverse auction existed long before the Internet. Simply transferring it to cyberspace does not mean it is a novel invention. Analysts say that without the patent Priceline would be just another online retailer.

Investors have become increasingly nervous about the company's future. Many began to jump ship after the company warned in late September 2000 that third-quarter revenue would fall as much as 10% short of expectations. Some have filed lawsuits alleging that Jay Walker, Priceline's founder, who resigned from the board in December 2000, gave misleading statements that encouraged them to buy stock in the company. The company has been hit by the departure of key executives such as Heidi Miller, its chief financial officer, a rising tide of customer complaints and job cuts.

It also faces competition from Hotwire.com, a bargain-fare site backed by seven leading airlines. Like Priceline it offers fares that are cheaper than those found on sites such as Travelocity or Expedia. But, like at Priceline, these offers come at a price, which includes lack of flexibility and a requirement that customers commit to a purchase without really knowing what the journey will entail. In the long run customers may decide that bargain travel is not worth the hassle. Anecdotes abound of Priceline customers stranded at airports hundreds of miles from home having missed non-transferable connections trying desperately to get help from the company's customer-services department.

So where does this leave travel agents, sitting in their offices surrounded by fading posters of exotic faraway destinations? Just like banks, they will not simply disappear. Jupiter says travel agencies will have to become either "broad, mass-market players" or niche players.

Companies that take the mass-market approach will have to find a way to offer broad products and services while catering for distinct segments of the population with targeted products. Companies taking the niche-market approach, however, should focus on targeted products, and by doing so may become a compelling partner for both mass-market travel sites and suppliers.

Banking and financial services

Money is ideally suited for the virtual world of the Internet. For many customers of banks and other financial institutions, cash has long been virtual, represented by a series of numbers on monthly bank statements. The Internet might have been designed for the distribution, monitoring and management of this ubiquitous electronic commodity. But although the concept of money lends itself so freely to the digital world, it is surprising how little the Internet revolution has changed the deep-rooted way of doing things in the financial services sector.

In essence, banks and other financial institutions are merely intermediaries. They stand between lenders and borrowers, savers and spenders. For decades, banks in rich countries have been fretting about how to cope with "disintermediation": lenders dealing direct with borrowers (as many do already in the capital markets), without using a bank's balance sheet to add a layer of cost. The Internet is, potentially, the greatest force for disintermediation the banks have ever had to tackle. Other intermediaries, such as retailers, face the same problem. But money, unlike, say, an item of clothing, is a commodity that can actually be used, transferred and delivered electronically.

Samuel Theodore, of Moody's, a credit-rating agency, believes the banks are currently undergoing their "fourth disintermediation". The first involved savings, and the growth of mutual funds, specialised pension funds and life-insurance policies at the expense of bank deposits; the second saw the capital markets take on some of the banks' traditional role as providers of credit; in the third, advances in technology helped to streamline back-office operations. Now, in the fourth stage, the distribution of banking products is being disintermediated. This process has been going on for some years, with the spread of automated teller machines (ATMs) and, over the past decade or so, telephone banking and PC-based proprietary systems; but the Internet hugely enlarges its scope.

Banks have approached the Internet threat with a varying degree of success and creativity. Broadly speaking, they handle their Internet business in one of four ways:

- "Pure" Internet banking. Few go as far as America's Wingspan, which keeps the offline parent and its Internet-banking subsidiary completely separate. But a number of Internet banks have names that do not even hint at their parentage. Egg (offspring of the Prudential) is the most famous. Whatever its long-term prospects, it has certainly started a trend in Britain for staid old-economy banks to give their new Internet subsidiaries quirky names: Marbles (HFC), Cahoot (Abbey National), Smile (Co-operative Bank) and IF (Halifax). Non-British examples of separate branding include Uno-e (BBVA) and e-cortal (BNP Paribas).

- Online hybrids. More often, banks simply extend their existing brand to the web, either in its most obvious form (wellsfargo.com, bankamerica.com), or in a jazzed-up version. Chase Manhattan, for example, has made an effort to give a distinct identity to its online service, chase.com. In Britain, Barclays sought to capitalise on the familiarity of its brand in marketing its online service ("its new-fangled name is 'Barclays'"). American Express has taken a similar line ("online banking from a company that's been around longer than a week"). The hybrid approach has obvious advantages: it is easy to find the banks' websites, and whatever brand loyalty the bank commands offline will be transferred to the Internet. This matters in a business where familiarity and trust count for a lot.

- Online alliances. One quick and effective way for a bank to secure online credibility, as well as, potentially, to expand far beyond its existing client base, is to team up with a telecoms company, Internet-service provider or portal. At their most basic, such deals are simply arrangements to become designated providers of specified financial services for a popular website. But in 2000 some more ambitious alliances were announced: in Italy, Sanpaolo IMI, a big bank, negotiated an agreement with Tiscali, an ISP. Similar alliances between banks and ISPS were announced in Spain (BBVA and Telefonica) and Germany (Comdirect, a Commerzbank subsidiary, and T-Online, Europe's largest ISP).

- "White labelling". Also called "private labelling", and growing fast, this involves banks' becoming silent partners. They might, for example, provide unbranded back-office services to enable another firm to run a bank. In Britain, Sainsbury's Bank is actually a 55:45 joint venture with the Bank of Scotland. Royal Bank of Scotland (RBS NatWest) is behind another supermarket bank, Tesco's, and also handles processing for first-e, an Internet bank.

The threat to the traditional banks comes from a variety of directions. Internet banks, with their low costs – and their dotcom habit of paying more attention to the acquisition of customers than the turning of profits – have drawn deposits away from offline banks in some countries. The banks' conservatism, on which they used to pride themselves, has become an embarrassment. This has resulted in financial institutions now becoming promoters of change. Commercial and investment banks, fund managers and financial advisers are all vying with each other to present themselves as Internet-savvy, and boasting about their investment in online services.

The Internet brings established financial institutions huge opportunities as well. It enables banks to cut costs and to market their products more efficiently. But, for banks, each of these pluses comes with a minus. Because costs are so much lower for Internet-based transactions, the barriers to entry are lower as well, which implies that margins will come under pressure. And although the Internet makes well-directed sales pitches easier, that is hardly compensation for the precariousness of online customer relationships. (See Figure 3.4.)

Banks have so far rejected the concept of "open finance", a term coined by market analysts under which web aggregators such as portals or financial supermarkets offer their customers products of (often) competing financial institutions and enable them to manage their finances on one site. Many in the industry see portals such as NetCenter, Yahoo! and AOL, and online personal-finance sites such as Microsoft's Money-Central and Intuit's Quicken, as the biggest long-term threat to the banks. These sites have visitors in their millions, and many of them have established a reputation for reliability.

The ideal would be for an individual to be able to deal with all his finances on one easily accessible site. Bank accounts, insurance policies, share portfolios and tax returns would all be available there, completely up to date, and the user could do whatever he wanted without having to leave the site or go through any additional security firewalls. A customer would have a "universal password" which would give him access to all his online finances. Pursuing this ideal are firms such as Yodlee and Vertical One, known as "aggregators" or, more rudely, screen-scrapers. Yodlee's site offers to set up just such a personal balance sheet. But, like Vertical One, it also licenses its technology to other Internet companies – selling "picks and shovels for the gold-rush", as Vertical One's boss, Gregg Freishtat, puts it. By May 2000 it claimed 110,000 accounts and growth of 10–15% a week. Yodlee has a deal with Altavista, one of the biggest portals and search engines.

Web brokers

Investment, along with e-mail and pornography, is one of the "natural" uses of the Internet. So thinks Daniel Leemon, chief strategy officer at Charles Schwab, a San Francisco-based stock-broking firm. Schwab should know. It boasts of maintaining the World Wide Web's lar-

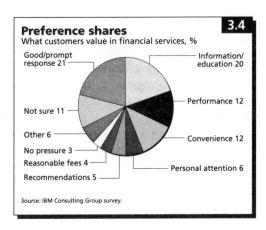

Preference shares
What customers value in financial services, %

3.4

Good/prompt response 21
Information/ education 20
Not sure 11
Performance 12
Other 6
Convenience 12
No pressure 3
Reasonable fees 4
Personal attention 6
Recommendations 5

Source: IBM Consulting Group survey.

gest encrypted site, and of doing more business over the Internet than any other firm, anywhere. Of its nearly 7m customer accounts, more than half are online and "active", in the sense that the holders have visited in the past given eight months. They contain about a third of the $700 billion-plus in assets sitting in Schwab accounts. In 1999, Schwab's stock-market valuation even overtook that of Merrill Lynch, which at the time controlled three times as much in customers' assets.

Schwab is by no means a "pure" Internet broker. It had a large offline business in pre-Internet days, and still has some 415 branches. It also offers its clients both touch-tone and speech-recognition telephone services. But it has been in the forefront of a charge online that has already transformed stockbroking in America, and is rapidly doing so in Europe, Asia and elsewhere. The growth has been phenomenal. E*Trade, for example, an online broker, began Internet trading only in 1996. Now it claims to be the world's "most-visited online investing site". In 1999, its number of customer accounts nearly tripled. By the end of March 2000, it had reached 2.6m.

The online-broking market is now fiercely competitive. It is still dominated by discount brokers, led by Schwab and E*Trade, and including rivals offering even cheaper services, such as Ameritrade, TD Waterhouse and Datek. For years, the big Wall Street firms either snootily ignored the sniper fire from the Internet, or were openly hostile. In 1998, one of Merrill Lynch's bosses famously called online-trading firms "a serious threat to America's financial lives", and reassured Merrill's thousands of brokers that his house would never go down that path. Merrill was soon forced to change its mind and is now together with the rest of the heavy artillery running to get to the front as fast as it can.

But what began as a battle largely about the costs of individual transactions is increasingly moving into the race for the quality of technology and the ancillary services stockbrokers offer. A mind-boggling array of financial data, newswires, advice, gossip, and so on is available on the net at no charge at all. So the brokers are having to expand their services in other ways too. These include, for example, alert systems, which will inform the customer by e-mail, or message to a mobile phone, pager or PDA, when a particular share price has reached a trigger level. The brokers are also competing by offering banking and money-market accounts. Schwab, for example, already provides an electronic bill-payment service. In 1999, E*Trade agreed to buy Telebank, a telephone and Internet bank, and is now offering a current account on which it pays interest, bill payment and (within limits) free ATM use.

In any forecast of likely winners in the Internet-finance stakes, firms such as Schwab and E*Trade are likely to figure prominently. They have the customers, the name-recognition, and the ability to expand energetically into new areas of business.

But it is not just in the US that online investing has taken to the web. From a later starting point, online investing is also showing spectacular growth in other countries. In parts of Europe, for example, it is growing faster than in America, even though far fewer adult Europeans own shares (35m, or 12% of the total, compared with 104m Americans, or 50% of the adult population, according to estimates by J.P. Morgan, an investment bank). In January 2000, Datamonitor, a research outfit, estimated that an average of 466 new online accounts were being opened in Sweden every day, 685 in Britain, and 1,178 in Germany. It forecasts that the number of online-brokerage accounts in Europe will reach 7.5m in 2002. J.P. Morgan puts the total even higher, at 10.5m. It estimates that in 1999 the number of specialist discount online brokers in Europe increased from about 20 to over 50, and the number of their customers more than doubled.

More than half of these were in Germany, where in the last quarter of 1999 the four biggest discount brokers already accounted for 13% of all stockmarket transactions – a proportion not far short of that in America (about 16% by number of transactions). Measured by the number of executed orders, three of the four biggest Internet brokers in Europe are German, led by Comdirect, owned by Commerzbank, and ConSors, 73% owned by Schmidt, a small bank. It seems puzzling that Germany should have taken such a lead over, say, Britain, which has more Internet users (12.5m compared with 10.4m), and, since the privatisation splurge of the

1980s, a much higher level of share ownership (25.1% of the adult population, compared with 7.1% in Germany).

But perhaps the biggest potential for growth in online broking lies neither in Europe nor in America, but in Japan. At present it lags behind not only the rich Western countries, but also regional neighbours such as Taiwan and South Korea. Both those markets are dominated by retail investors and enjoy a strong technological infrastructure. South Korea has also been boosted by an extraordinary bounce-back from economic near-collapse over the past two years. Taken together, these factors have given it the highest proportion of online trading in the world, about 30% of stockmarket turnover.

Virtual threats

Banking and stockbroking are just two of the most obvious examples of threats and opportunities the Internet brings to the financial world. On a completely different level, the changes are being made in the way the markets themselves operate. Indeed, activity in the world of financial exchanges is perhaps even more hectic than among the firms that use them. New "Alternative Trading Systems" (ATS) seem to emerge almost daily, particularly in Europe and America, and new cross-border alliances form or dissolve. Meanwhile, the established stock exchanges are advertising radical remouldings of themselves to cope with the combined forces driving technological advance: globalisation, the growth in Internet-based trading and, in many rich countries, the demographic pressure of older, longer-living populations that invest in stockmarkets more than ever before.

In their domestic markets, Europe's exchanges have so far proved less vulnerable to upstart electronic communications networks (ECNs) than their American counterparts. However, the launch in London in March 2000 of E-Crossnet, a matching system backed by some of the world's biggest fund-managers, caused some concern. Its advantages for users are, first, to cut dealing costs, and second, to provide anonymity, avoiding the "market-impact" costs of large trades (ie, the effect they have on the price).

European exchanges' squabbling has slowed down their efforts to provide efficient cross-border trading. This has opened the door to new competitors, including Easdaq, based in Brussels, Tradepoint, an electronic exchange set up in 1995, and Jiway, a joint venture of OM (which runs the Stockholm exchange) and Morgan Stanley. The fight for a pan-European exchange reached its peak with the hostile bid of OM for the London Stock Exchange in 2000 (which failed after months of uncertainty).

Lagging behind it all are the insurers. In explaining why they have been relatively slow to adopt the Internet, insurers point to the complexities of their products. It is true that many consumers prefer to talk through their insurance needs rather than buy them off a virtual shelf, and also that underwriting rules and criteria vary. But there are two bigger factors that are holding insurers back, particularly in America. The first is that established insurance companies moving online suffer from channel conflict in spades. Most have networks of agents to whom the Internet is a direct challenge. The agents' commissions typically account for 25% of the cost of the insurance, which is precisely where direct insurers hope to make their savings. The second set of obstacles lies in the divergent regulatory regimes between countries, and, in America, between states. These make it more complex to buy insurance than many other financial products.

Cannibalisation (or at least the fear of it) indeed seems to be the word that applies across the sector. If the insurers are fearing it, it is actually even more stunning that many banks were reluctant to promote their online services among their offline customers. Why should they? Offline customers have been the source of the banks' handsome profits by paying concealed charges for all sorts of services they may not use. Trying to make them bank online before they are ready risks antagonising them; it may even open their eyes to some of the competing services available on the web.

For many financial institutions the Internet is a double bind. Embrace it, and you may still find yourself losing business, or at least seeing profit margins dwindle. But ignoring it could be terminal. The pressures for change have become irresistible, but the world in which Internet will underline every financial transaction is still some way off. Many big financial institutions, despite the sniping of the dotcom upstarts, are in fact quite well placed to meet the challenge of the Internet. They have trusted brands, which may have an even greater value in cyberspace than offline; they have customer bases that start-ups can only dream about; they have made huge investments in state-of-the-art technology; and many of them are making profits that will enable them to spend even more. The only risks are their own complacency, arrogance and sluggishness. If they can avoid those sins, the Internet becomes less of a virtual threat than a virtual promise.

Music

Wired for sound

Music is the first part of the entertainment sector to be transformed by the Internet. Unlike films and television programmes, which cannot be widely distributed until high-speed broadband connections abound, music can be easily compressed and sold online. Making money out of it is much harder.

At first it looked as if the new electronic channel might sound the death knell for the music industry. Panic-stricken by cyber-pirates, record companies feared the loss of their treasured intellectual property rights. Internet music boomed and sales of CDs to young people initially declined after musicians, websites, consumers and hardware producers adopted a common standard – a compression technology called Motion Picture Expert Group-1/Level 3, or MP3, which came from an intergovernmental attempt to create standards for interactive television.

Big record companies tried to block MP3 because such files are easily copied, encourage piracy and are hard to make money from. But music fans loved it. MP3 quickly became the most searched-for term on the web – even more popular than sex, according to searchterms.com, a website that ranks search words. Millions of college students began filling their PC hard drives with their favourite songs plucked from the Internet for free. Some colleges were even forced to clamp down because music downloads were taking up most of the bandwidth on their high-speed computer pipes.

The International Federation of Phonographic Industries reckons that around 3m tracks are probably downloaded from the Internet every day, the great majority pirated. A new generation of portable music devices, from wristbands to cellphones, on to which this music can be downloaded, is taking hold in Japan and expanding overseas.

Malcom Maclachlan, a senior analyst at IDC, a market research firm, says:

> Online music is very much a youth phenomenon, which
> will increase in importance over time. Not only are young
> people the backbone of music sales, they also have several
> other upsides. They are heavy users and early adopters of
> technology, they influence the behaviour of those slightly
> younger than they are, and as a group, they keep making
> more money as they grow older. The habits they form now
> will have a huge effect on sales of music and other
> entertainment 5–10 years from now.

According to a survey by IDC, more than 77% of respondents aged under 20 said someone in their household has downloaded songs from the Internet. More than 47% of those under 20 who have downloaded songs said they or someone in their house owns a portable digital music player.

One company that has had a huge impact on promoting digital downloads is Napster, an online service launched in 1999 by an 18-year-old college student. It lets users swap copyrighted music files in the MP3 format anonymously and for free. It amassed 10m users worldwide within ten months of its launch, demonstrating the latent demand for online music (see Figure 3.5). The only way to satisfy the demand so far has been to break the law. Napster is being sued for encouraging copyright infringement by a consortium of the five biggest record labels. In late July 2000, an American judge ordered the site to close down. But an appeal court stayed the injunction, and Napster continued to operate through the appeal process.

Record companies supported by the Recording Industry Association of America (RIAA) argue that such services will damage music sales and harm the industry. But according to research by Jupiter, users of networked music-sharing technologies, such as Napster, are 45% more likely to have increased their overall music purchasing than non-users. The RIAA tried to close Napster down. But other services quickly sprang up to replace it. Services such as Gnutella and FreeNet will be far harder to shut down than Napster, because they operate without a central server.

In October 2000, Napster announced an alliance with Bertelsmann, a global media giant based in Germany, which owns BMG, one of the record labels suing Napster. This alliance shows that Bertelsmann and Napster have realised that co-operation is wiser than combat. They plan to operate the music site on a fee basis. Napster lost its appeal and was forced to install software that prevents users from swapping copyrighted music. It is not clear whether users will be willing to pay for a service that they once received for free. Meanwhile, in April 2001, AOL Time Warner, Bertelsmann, EMI Group and RealNetworks announced a new online music subscription service called MusicNet. It plans to licence its platform to other distribution outlets, including Napster, so long as legal, copyright and security concerns are satisfied. Napster remains, though, a poor way to build a record collection. Tracks play at different volumes; most music files are unobtainable at any one time; and it offers people only what they already know they like. But the technology can only improve in the future and has already been cloned into countless similar applications that can never be eradicated. As Mick Brady, a columnist for

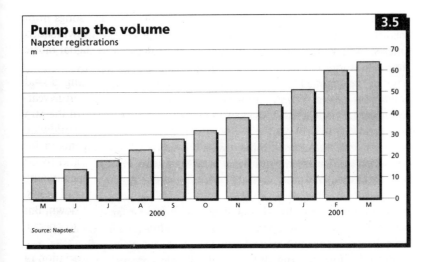

Pump up the volume
Napster registrations
m

Source: Napster.

the *E-Commerce Times*, noted: "Whether Napster dies is irrelevant ... the company is just the front line of the digital download army." What started as a college addiction could eventually become mainstream, as millions of people of all ages download music from the Internet.

Not surprisingly, other big record companies, reluctant to give up their huge margins, have resisted change and attempted to fight off competition from web upstarts. Among them are familiar names such as MTVi and Rollingstone.com, as well as new ones such as Launch Media, musicmaker.com, liquidaudio.com, ARTISTdirect and Listen.com. Big portals like Yahoo! could also present competition.

The record companies are trying to replace the Internet's standard for digital downloads with their own, which would allow them to encrypt their products and thus protect their copyright. The Secure Digital Music Initiative (SDMI) was launched by the big five – Warner Music, Sony Music, Universal, BMG and EMI – and brings together 150 content, hardware and software companies. But it is way behind schedule. Only a few manufacturers have actually implemented any security specifications for portable players of music files. And existing SDMI-compliant devices are cumbersome to use.

In any case, copy-protection alone will not answer the music industry's prayer. In the past, the industry has bundled, in albums, songs that consumers want and those they do not want. In future, it will no longer be able to play such tricks. To get consumers to accept some encryption, it will have to pay closer attention to how people want to buy their music. This may mean allowing consumers to go to a site and make their purchase on a track-by-track basis. A new singles market could emerge, but pricing may prove tricky. For the record companies to recoup the same amount of money for a single as for a full CD, consumers would have to be charged up to $5 per track. Gartner Group believes that consumers would be willing to pay only $0.99–1.99 per track. According to Robert Labatt, Gartner's research director:

> It's an absolutely defining moment because it's the first time that consumers have dictated how they want to relate to an industry, and the recording industry doesn't get it.

In the long term, digital downloads could prove far more profitable for record labels than traditional CD sales. Napster and other services have helped condition a new generation to digital downloading. The number of adults going online to get music content jumped by 48% between December 1999 and March 2000, according to CyberDialogue, a research firm. It is not just music that will be acquired this way. Nearly a quarter of all media products sold online will be acquired by digital downloading in 2004, according to Forrester Research. The company predicts that a new breed of media merchants will emerge to combine books, music, software and video.

But the 80-year-old music industry will need time to adapt. Record companies are understandably nervous about cannibalising their existing distribution channels. If they opened up their entire catalogues for purchase over the web music retailers would naturally be upset. There is also the problem of renegotiating contracts with artists. Then there is the challenge of the technology itself. Despite years of development, a copyright-secure, easy-to-use way of transferring music online is yet to be found. But the big question facing all e-tailers is how to make money on the web.

Record companies could have the upper hand over upstarts. Between them they comfortably control most of the music that has ever been recorded. By moving online they will save the costs of manufacturing and distribution. According to a breakdown by *Billboard*, a publication covering the music and entertainment sector, distribution, shipping and store mark-up account for more than $9.50 of the retail price of a typical $17 CD. Sending a song over the Internet costs next to nothing. If record companies claimed just half of that $9.50 themselves, they would clear nearly eight times their current profit, now just 59 cents per album.

Savings can also be made on stocks because the virtual world offers unlimited storage space. The costly business of dealing with CDs that flop is also avoided.

But the record companies have a serious disadvantage: not many people like them. Artists feel ripped off by them. The vast majority of musicians make little or no money on CD sales. Customers also feel cheated by them, typically paying $17 for a CD that invariably contains only one track they really want to hear. The bad-boy image of the record companies may not have mattered much before. But in the new era, Internet businesses are increasingly about building a community of loyal customers

With so much bad blood, artists may decide to go it alone and use the Internet to promote themselves and bypass the record companies altogether. A small but significant group, ranging from David Bowie to rapper and producer Chuck D to singer Aimee Mann, is using the web to go straight to fans. Some artists may create their own labels in cyberspace and independent labels have the chance to proliferate. A website called MP3.com has signed up more than 10,000 bands which use the service to distribute or promote their works. Many star-struck newcomers, however, may still prefer a big fat cheque and a shiny limo to the hassle of becoming an entrepreneur.

One likely model to emerge is a subscription service where consumers will pay to receive their choice of music and added extras such as concert tickets, memorabilia or bonus songs. Universal and Sony have announced that they intend jointly to develop subscription services for audio and video music. EMI, which already allows consumers to download albums and singles, has also announced an online subscription service. There are other encouraging signs. Warner Music Group and BMG entertainment have both dropped lawsuits and instead signed deals with MP3.com, which will now be allowed to distribute music from their catalogues online, in return for royalties. All five of the largest record labels have invested in Listen.com, a website that helps fans to find legitimate sources of downloadable music.

But these initiatives are mere toes in the water, and the longer it takes for record labels to dance to the Internet beat the harder it may be for them to convince customers that they have to pay for music downloads (see Figure 3.6 on next page). According to Jupiter, the most important deciding factors for consumer adoption of subscription services will be guaranteed file quality and virus protection. If, in addition, the music labels can put their songs online in a format that is more organised and

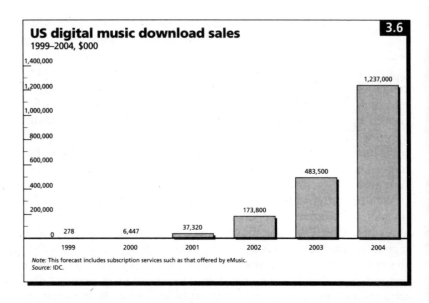

US digital music download sales
1999–2004, $000

3.6

Year	Value
1999	278
2000	6,447
2001	37,320
2002	173,800
2003	483,500
2004	1,237,000

Note: This forecast includes subscription services such as that offered by eMusic.
Source: IDC.

more appealing than their illegal competitors can, fans may be willing to pay something for that privilege.

For music lovers the Internet is a dream come true. Prices will come down and new as well as old recordings will become easier to obtain. It is not just the college students who are in heaven. At the click of a mouse, the massed ranks of the middle-aged, who have neither the time nor the inclination to hang out in record stores, will be able to download their old-time favourites. Record shops will need to do something fresh to hang on to their customers – transforming themselves into cafés or music clubs, for example.

As technology improves and high-speed broadband connections proliferate, music could become one of the most valuable products to make the move from the physical to the virtual world. Jupiter reckons that the online music market will secure approximately one-quarter of the total American music market by 2005.

Digital-rights management systems now being developed may prove a better way to protect copyright than the SDMI. InterTrust has the most advanced and capable technology, protected by at least 12 patents. It has the backing of Universal Music and Bertelsmann; Pricewaterhouse-Coopers, one of the big five accounting firms, has signed up to use the technology for its clients. InterTrust's may indeed become the main operating system for the new market, and could yet come to govern the distribution of all digital content over the web, including films, news and books.

To use the InterTrust model, a record company (or, indeed, anybody who has digital content) has it packaged into an encrypted file known as a "Digibox", which comes complete with rules about use, access and payment methods. These can be as flexible as the content provider wants to make them: three free plays followed by a charge, say, or a fixed price for the whole thing, or a system that charges a small amount for every replay.

Liquid Audio, Xerox and Microsoft are also devising their own digital-rights management systems.

Books

The name Amazon has become synonymous with e-commerce. It is one of the few Internet brands recognised the world over. It is the most visited e-commerce website in America, and one of the top two or three in Britain, France, Germany and Japan. Now it is trying to stretch its brand, which to most people is linked to books, to cover anything that can be sold online.

At first glance, Amazon seems ill-suited to being the giant of the web. Its headquarters, an Art Deco building that once housed Seattle's Pacific Medical Center, is imposing, but the desks within are still made out of old doors. The staff are still a touch, well, geekish: after all, the firm is only five years old. And Amazon has often been quite cautious. It was only in mid-1998 that it ventured beyond books to CDs and videos. David Risher, senior vice-president, smugly notes that: "Within four months of going into CDs, and within six weeks of going into videos, we were the top-selling sites for both products."

What is Amazon's appeal? It is seldom the cheapest place to shop on the web. Firms such as Buy.com have set up with the explicit promise of undercutting it. But thanks to its large investment in warehouse distribution centres, Amazon has the best reputation in the business for fulfilment and delivery. Its patented "one-click" technology makes shopping delightfully simple. And by pioneering consumer reviews of books and other products, and using its database to make recommendations, it has built a sense of community among users: 66% of sales go to repeat customers.

No doubt other firms can and will imitate most of this (patenting one-click shopping seems as far-fetched as patenting wallets, and is under court attack). Yet Amazon founder Jeff Bezos is betting that his reputation for customer service, combined with first-mover advantage, will let him build an unassailable lead. Customer-acquisition costs, he believes, can only get higher. He talks of being the world's most "customer-centric" company, delivering from what it likes to call the "earth's biggest selection" of products.

Will it work? There is no denying Amazon's success so far, as it has expanded to greeting cards, toys and gifts. It has made useful small investments in other firms, including drugstore.com, homeGrocer.com, an online grocer and Gear.com, a sporting-goods seller. It has launched an auction site and zShops, a portal-cum-marketplace that other online sellers use to hawk their wares.

And yet none of this quite adds up to becoming the Wal-Mart of the web, for two reasons. First, Wal-Mart's true strength has been its ability to squeeze suppliers. It is hard to associate Mr Bezos's firm with similar ruthlessness. More important, Amazon seems to suffer more than any other firm in e-commerce from a congenital lack of profitability (see Figure 3.7). The year 2000 marked the end of the stockmarket's infatuation with dotcoms, especially in the business-to-consumer field. Amazon's announcement of record losses in the fourth quarter of 1999 was softened by the claim that it was at last making profits on books alone – perhaps vindicating its view that losses taken to build market share can turn into profits later. But the firm has also, for the first time, shed staff. And the stockmarkets are increasingly sceptical about it.

Amazon may still be one of the best-quality Internet retailers (and shares) around. But in the longer run its problems raise the all-important question for the industry: how long will investors in any firm that sells on the web be ready to wait for profits?

It is also facing a serious challenge from Borders.com, which usurped Amazon as the top online bookseller, according to a November 2000 report by Forrester Research. Borders achieved a ranking of 66.83 to finish just ahead of Amazon.com (66.76) and Barnesandnoble.com (now bn.com; 65.46). Buy.com came in fourth at 55.52.

Tom Rhinelander, a senior analyst at Forrester, said: "While Borders.com only won by a tiny margin, the win demonstrates that Amazon.com's advantages over the competition are diminishing." The report said Borders's attention to detail in handling customer orders has helped it unseat Amazon. It also said that Amazon is slow to respond to phone calls and inventory information is "vague", although it did say that it offers features such as express shopping. Turning to bn.com, Forrester said its site offers excellent search facilities but customers are

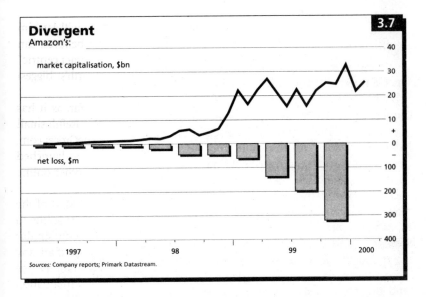

Divergent

3.7

Amazon's:

market capitalisation, $bn

40

30

20

10

+

0

−

net loss, $m

100

200

300

400

1997   98   99   2000

Sources: Company reports; Primark Datastream.

often irritated when they realise they cannot cancel orders without contacting customer services.

Both Borders.com and bn.com have been integrating their Internet businesses with their bricks-and-mortar operations. Borders said its plan would be completed by the end of 2000. Bn.com said it is in the process of installing Internet access points in the 551 Barnes & Noble stores and will be providing consumers with more options for collection, purchase and returns. Meanwhile, analysts have also questioned whether Amazon's strategy of diversification is wise or whether it will be spreading itself too thinly.

E-books

According to an Andersen Consulting report published in 2000, e-books will account for 10% of the publishing market by 2004. By 2005 the total revenue from e-books will reach $1 billion–3.4 billion. In January 2001, bn.com announced the launch of a new e-publishing division and said it would offer authors a higher royalty rate than other publishers. But technical problems abound in the emerging market for electronic books. Readers trying to access horror author Stephen King's book were confronted with all the usual glitches affecting e-shoppers when they log on to the Internet: connection problems and difficulty in accessing pages or finding them slow to download. Much like the record companies, traditional publishers are reluctant to go digital because of copyright concerns. Authors worry that they will lose control of their distribution rights.

When Mr King began publishing extracts of his novel *Riding the Bullet* on the Internet, some took it as a clear sign that consumers are ready for e-books. As further proof a new literary prize for the best book to be published in electronic form was awarded at the Frankfurt book fair in October 2000. The backers of the $100,000 prize are the computer software companies, such as Microsoft and Adobe, that are trying to prod publishers into getting the e-books business off the ground.

As *The Economist* stated in an article in October 2000, the business faces the usual chicken-and-egg problem that always confronts new devices for delivering content – from televisions to today's DVDs. Consumers are not going to buy the devices unless the content is available; and it is not worth producing the content until consumers have bought lots of devices. As a result, there are probably fewer than 1,000 titles now available for downloading from electronic bookshops, and probably no more than 20,000 of the reading devices – the Rocket eBook and the Softbook Reader – on consumers' laps. Hence the computer firms' willingness to finance a fat e-book prize. They want to give publishers an incentive to digitise more of their books, in order to boost the market for reading software and devices.

Some big companies are spending serious money. The three main competitors in the software-and-devices business are Gemstar, which produces electronic programme guides for digital television; Adobe, a software company; and Microsoft. Gemstar believes there will be a market for specific book-like electronic devices; Adobe and Microsoft think that the market is in software to make books easier to read, which will be used on multi-purpose computers.

In January 2000, Gemstar bought the two companies that make devices for reading e-books, Nuvomedia and Softbook Press, both of which were struggling. Those companies' Rocket eBook and Softbook brands have now been abandoned, but the two second-generation devices, made under licence by Thomson Multimedia and launched in October 2000, the black-and-white REB 1100 ($300) and the full-colour REB 1200 ($700), are descendants of those earlier models. Gemstar is offering an end-to-end solution: reading devices, software and a library of compatible e-books.

Microsoft and Adobe are sceptical about the market for electronic-book devices. "We just don't think consumers in large numbers are going to be interested in spending that sort of money on dedicated hardware," says Mario Juarez, Microsoft's marketing manager for e-books. Microsoft and Adobe both make software that can be used on PCs and laptops; Microsoft's Reader software, which was launched in August 2000, comes pre-shipped on the PocketPC, Microsoft's version of the Palm Pilot. Adobe is working on producing a version for hand-held computers.

Retailers are becoming interested, too. Bn.com has established an online e-bookstore, and in August 2000 Amazon announced that it was planning to do the same, offering e-books using Microsoft software.

Publishers are proving harder to excite. They worry that e-books could prove expensive and complicated to create. They put the cost of translating a previously published paper book into electronic form at up to several thousand dollars. They also see new difficulties arising, such as the need to renegotiate agreements with authors. But so far, they do not see any revenues.

Nobody is giving out figures on how much consumers are actually spending on those few books that are available for commercial download, but the sums are reckoned to be tiny. That may partly be because publishers have set prices high, despite the fact that the manufacturing and distribution costs of e-books, compared with paper versions, are almost negligible.

In addition to the Frankfurt prize, the software people say, they are doing a lot to help the publishers. Microsoft, for instance, has been running advertisements in the *New Yorker*, promoting particular e-books.

But even if the devices, the software and the content are all available, industry folk accept that consumer resistance will be hard to overcome – much harder, for instance, than persuading people to buy music online. Young people take to new technologies easily, but book readers tend to be older people who are not enthusiastic buyers of gadgets. Further, bookish people have an emotional relationship with the titles on their shelves. They regard crisp paper between cardboard covers as more than a content-delivery device. For many dedicated readers, the idea of abandoning paper books might just feel uncomfortably close to burning them.

Conclusion

The Internet is still in its infancy. What sells well on the web is not predetermined forever. Technological change is increasing the possibilities all the time. The distinctions between "high-touch" and "low-touch" items are blurring: catalogue experience suggests that consumers will buy clothes without trying them on, and the Internet may yet offer "virtual" fitting. One striking example of the web's ability to deliver the most unlikely goods is Omaha Steaks. The company already has a strong catalogue business selling raw steaks by post that it is transferring to the web. Many adventurous online merchants now reckon there may be no such thing as a product that is unsuitable for being sold on the web. Chapter 4 looks in detail at customer behaviour on the Internet.

4 The customer is king

THERE ARE PLENTY of glib phrases about the importance of the customer in the offline world, such as "the customer is king" and "customers are our greatest asset". But often in the traditional marketplace the less the customer knew the better from a company's point of view. Lack of general information about what the market had to offer meant customer ignorance could be exploited to gain competitive advantage. Companies fixed their prices based on their perception of the value of products and services to the customer. Customers were loyal out of necessity, not out of choice. The Internet has changed all that. Now customers are in the driving seat. Armed with the same or similar information as companies and the ability to compare products instantly online, they are becoming price-makers not just price-takers. The online shopper is not passive or naive but armed and dangerous.

Power to the people
According to C.K. Prahalad and Venkatram Ramaswamy, professors at the University of Michigan Business School, in their article "Co-opting Customer Competence" (*Harvard Business Review*, January–February 2000): "The customer is the agent that is most dramatically transforming the industrial system as we know it." John Hagel, a McKinsey consultant, also reckons the Internet is bringing a fundamental shift in power from sellers to buyers. He says: "This is going to create the greatest wealth transfer we've seen since the Industrial Revolution."

How should companies respond to this challenge? Messrs Prahalad and Ramaswamy say in their article that companies should view customers as a new source of "competence". The knowledge and skills they possess, their willingness to learn and experiment, and their ability to engage in active dialogue should all be exploited by firms for competitive advantage. They say this should be done by:

- engaging customers in an active, explicit and ongoing dialogue;
- mobilising online customer communities, which can exercise a powerful influence on the market;
- managing customer diversity;
- creating a personalised shopping experience with the customer.

For example, an online florist might let the customer discuss ideas with experts and other customers before making a purchase. In the business-to-business sphere the collective knowledge of suppliers, manufacturers and partners can also be tapped to add value to the company.

Not surprisingly, technology companies such as Microsoft and Cisco have proved good at this game because they understand the electronic wizardry that has made e-commerce possible. More than 650,000 customers tested a beta version of Microsoft's Windows 2000. They shared ideas on how to improve the product and helped detect early glitches. The value of the collective R&D investment was estimated at more than $500m in time, effort and fees. Cisco's customers help solve problems encountered by other customers through an online service that allows open access to the company's information, resources and systems. Thus companies are able to understand more about the products they are creating and more about the customers they are selling to.

John Hagel reckons companies that succeed in getting privileged access to information about customers, so-called "infomediaries", will drive the next wave of value on the net. The battle for driving customer traffic to a website will move on to the battle for customer profiles.

So who are these new kinds of customers exploring the realms of cyberspace? According to an August 2000 report by Jupiter Media Metrix, women are now slightly ahead of men in online use. The survey of 55,000 Internet users found that 50.4% of current web users are women. Internet use among women grew by almost 35% between May 1999 and May 2000, compared with 22% for all users. The report found that by far the fastest-growing segment was teenage girls, and there was also steady growth among women aged 55 and over.

Does this mean that companies should cater for specific gender markets? The answer is no. Sites such as women.com and iVillage, which tried to cater exclusively for women, have not done well. In December 2000, women.com cut 85 jobs, 25% of its workforce, in an attempt to reduce expenses and achieve profitability. In July 2000, iVillage said it was quitting e-commerce, selling its iBaby division and closing two other e-commerce lines, iMaternity.com and PlusBoutique.com. It now provides content for women and is trying to make money through advertising and sponsorship deals. Anya Sacharow, an analyst at Jupiter, said: "It's no longer enough to think of women as the target audience." She said that to reach the women's market sites must pursue deeper relationships based on interests, personal identities and affinities. Besides, the leading Internet sites are the same for both men and women: America Online

(AOL), Yahoo!, Lycos and Microsoft.

Teenagers are as challenging online as they are in the real world. They spend far less time online than adults and have concentration levels lasting just nanoseconds. This makes attracting their attention difficult. They also have limited purchasing power. According to a Jupiter consumer survey of more than 1,500 teenagers aged 12–17, only 15% of those questioned actually buy online. Most (49% in this survey) use the Internet to research goods and services that they eventually buy offline. These purchases are usually more expensive and include computer games and software. When they do purchase online, teenagers generally buy low-priced items such as CDs, books, videos and clothing. Jupiter's advice to e-tailers is to use their online presence to "educate, communicate, and reaffirm brand value and drive teenagers to offline sources for purchase".

Pensioners may seem unlikely online shoppers. However, research in America and Britain points to the lightning speed with which senior citizens, with time on their hands, are adopting the Internet. Forrester Research reckons that by 2005, 3.2m over-55s will be online in Britain. The most dedicated users will log on to the Internet six or seven days a week. Across the Atlantic, a report by Greenfield Online, an Internet research firm, points to the increasing number of over-55s who are spending more time shopping in cyberspace than general users. Among their favourite e-commerce activities are gambling, looking for special offers and visiting online pharmacies.

Shop till you log off

Rather than looking at gender or demographics, Melinda Cuthbert, chief executive of ShopTok.com, which supplies customer-services applications for e-business, thinks it is important to understand a customer's motivation. She says in the *E-Commerce Times* that there are six basic types of online shoppers:

- **"New to the net" shoppers** are still trying to grasp the concept of e-commerce and will typically use the web to research the market and make small purchases in safe categories. The net "newbie" will need a simple interface, an easy checkout process and lots of encouragement to buy online. Pictures of products will help convince these shoppers to complete sales transactions. Communicating with other shoppers will help guide them around a particular site and gain confidence.
- **Reluctant shoppers** are nervous about security and privacy issues

and prefer to use the Internet to research the market, rather than to buy. Clearly stated security and privacy policies will help them feel more comfortable. Immediate online customer support will help dispel concerns, and online discussions with more experienced shoppers will provide encouragement.

- **Bargain shoppers** are looking for the lowest price and will use comparison-shopping tools extensively. Retailers must convince them that they are getting the best price and do not need to continue searching online or offline for a better deal. Sale-priced items listed on the site or made available through an operator are attractive to these shoppers.
- **Surgical shoppers** know exactly what to buy and where to go on the web before logging on. Typically, they know the criteria on which they will base their decision, seek information to match those criteria and purchase when they are confident they have found exactly the right product. These shoppers benefit from quick access to insights from other shoppers' experiences and real-time customer service from knowledgeable operators.
- **Power shoppers** shop out of necessity rather than pleasure. They develop sophisticated shopping strategies to find what they want and do not want to waste time looking around. Sites that have excellent navigation tools and offer lots of information on the available products, such as customer experiences, expert opinions and customer service, are attractive to power shoppers. They want instant access to information and support, and expect highly relevant product recommendations that match their criteria.
- **Enthusiast shoppers** use shopping as a form of recreation. They purchase frequently and are the most adventurous shoppers. It is important to cater for their fun-loving nature by offering them engaging tools to view the merchandise, personalised product recommendations and community applications such as bulletin boards and customer feedback pages.

According to Ms Cuthbert. the most important factors that appeal to all customers are easy-to-use websites and a way of communicating with other customers. It sounds easy. So how come so many companies have got it wrong? The web is littered with "ghost sites" of e-tailers that failed to calculate the long-term investment needed to maintain, improve and update their websites. Customers returning to sites with queries, for information or to make fresh purchases want to see something new each time. Changing the window dressing is just as important in the virtual world as it is in the real one.

Are you being served?

However, by trying to be all things to all people sites become slower to load and more complicated to use and customer service is compromised. A survey by Gartner Group of 50 top e-tail sites failed to identify any company that qualified for "excellent" or "good" ratings in customer service. It concluded that most sites pay "little more than lip service" to customer relations. Almost all companies surveyed included a frequently asked questions (FAQ) section on their website. Gartner says a more proactive approach is needed to help resolve customer problems online.

According to a report by Datamonitor, poor online service cost e-tailers $6.1 billion in lost sales in 1999. It says that an industry-wide failure to resolve the problem could lead to at least $173 billion in lost revenue by 2004. Shoppers filling up online carts and then clicking away before completing their purchases cause the biggest headache for companies. The report says that some 7.8% of abandoned online transactions could have been salvaged and converted into sales if e-tailers had provided better service.

In October 2000, a survey of 9,500 online shoppers by BizRate.com revealed that 55% of respondents who abandoned their carts did so before they reached the checkout. Another 32% abandoned their carts at the point of sale, either when entering their billing and shipping information or after the final calculation of the sale. The study found that problems with the checkout process accounted for over 40% of all failed sales. Shoppers most commonly abandoned apparel items, but they also left behind computer-related goods, books, music CDs and videos. According to the survey, 31% of respondents abandoned their carts because they had changed their minds, although many of the abandoned items were purchased later from offline or online competitors. More than 40% said they had abandoned their carts because of expensive shipping and handling charges. Another 21% said they had given up because of slow-loading pages.

This is bad news for customers but good news for software companies selling customer relationship management (CRM) products. AMR Research reckons the market for such products will grow to $16.8 billion by 2003, compared with $3.7 billion in 1999. However, most CRM software solutions target a specific part of the online selling or customer-care process and often do not work together effectively. A report from Yankee

Group, a technology research and consulting firm, says an integrated approach is needed. Customer service must integrate seamlessly not only with the company's existing website, but also with the company's entire operations, online and offline. And there is more high-tech wizardry on its way to help manage customer relations. Voice-Over Internet Protocol (VOIP) will allow customer-services agents and consumers to communicate through their computers using microphones and speakers.

One strategy being adopted already is real-time communication, where customers use the Internet to communicate with agents who will help resolve problems and guide them around a site. This option is much cheaper and more effective than staffing a call centre. Lands' End, a catalogue retailer, which embraced the Internet early on (launching a site in 1995), was one of the first companies to begin using this method in September 1999. It offers several services including an online chat with a customer-services agent. The agent can help solve problems and make shopping recommendations, opening up web pages on the customer's browser to display products. Customers with a second phone line can ask a Lands' End agent to call them while they are still connected to the Internet. The financial benefits of this are not yet clear, however.

Customer acquisition

The huge up-front investment in site development and process design needed to launch a successful e-business often tempts companies into a frenzy of indiscriminate customer acquisition to offset costs. On the Internet, the doors are open any time, any place and anywhere. This makes attracting as many potential buyers as possible even more appealing. However, allocating vast sums of money on banner ads and TV commercials with little investment in building communities and promoting referrals probably amounts to building long-term losses into the customer base. Instead, companies must stop and think what kind of customer they want to attract. It is not the quantity but the quality of customers that counts.

Many e-tailers are spending more than $100 to acquire a new customer. In their article "How to Acquire Customers on the Web" (*Harvard Business Review*, May–June 2000), Donna Hoffman and Thomas Novak say that some companies are spending over $500 per customer. As the directors of eLab, an e-commerce research centre, pointed out in the *Harvard Business Review*, for most companies the results are "suicidal". The average customer acquisition cost is higher than the average lifetime value of their customers. The authors cite CDnow as a successful online model for customer acquisition. It uses a mixture of online and offline channels, including advertising and strategic partnerships. But like other successful e-tailers, the lion's share of its customers come by word-of-mouth, or in Internet parlance word-of-mouse.

Meg Whitman, chief executive of eBay, reckons that it costs her company less than $10 to acquire each new customer when they come recommended by friends and family. And because they cost so little to acquire they generate profits much earlier. They are also cheaper to maintain. Rather than calling eBay's technical support desk, they often seek advice from the people who referred them in the first place, and they are often more loyal.

It is often thought that online customers are fickle and will disappear to the nearest competitor at the click of a mouse. But studies have shown that the Internet can be a very "sticky" place, in both the business-to-consumer and business-to-business spheres. According to Frederick Reichheld, author of a forthcoming book, *Building Loyalty in the Age of the Internet*, the rewards for retaining loyal customers are huge. He reckons customers must stay on board for at least two to three years for an online firm to recoup its initial investment. Yet his research shows that a large percentage of new customers – up to 50% in some sectors – leave before the first three years. He says the five primary determinants of loyalty are not technological bells and whistles, but rather old-fashioned customer-services basics, such as quality customer support, on-time delivery, compelling product presentations, convenient and reasonably priced shipping and handling, and clear and trustworthy privacy policies.

The first few legitimate, recognisable brand names have emerged from the chaos of the virtual world. AOL, Amazon.com, Yahoo! and Netscape were once obscure names; now they score in the 50% range in unaided brand-recognition surveys. They have shown that a brand can grow and secure customer loyalty on the net. As today's generation of computer-savvy youngsters matures, that power will only increase. Rather than diluting the power of brands the Internet actually strengthens it. Brands act as signposts, guiding the customer through the jungle to a familiar site. With nothing to pick up or touch and hundreds of similar-sounding sites to choose from, it is quicker and easier to find something you know than to surf through the waves of dross that swamp the Internet. Choice is great but choosing is difficult.

Seth Godin, head of direct marketing at Yahoo!, is someone else who thinks the Internet offers a breakthrough in marketing efficiency. It is cheap and fast and can convey highly targeted information. Ineffective ads can be quickly identified, changed or dropped, minimising wastage. He says that rather than forcing a message on large numbers of people through traditional advertising channels, online companies should entice customers with simple introductory ads. These ads do not need to sell the product; instead, they ask permission to say more by setting up a dialogue with interested customers – so-called permission marketing.

Besides, expensive television commercials are becoming less effective (though rarely less expensive) because network audiences have shrunk. Yet many dotcoms still see the American Super Bowl, the biggest advertising event of the year, as the perfect launch venue. Some 130m Americans and 800m viewers worldwide tune in to the game where a 30-second spot costs $2.2m. Gartner Group says an e-commerce company should make the Super Bowl the start of a major advertising campaign, rather than the central focus of its advertising strategy. It cites Monster.com as an example of a site that has successfully used the event to advertise itself.

Some companies become blinded by their own marketing hype. Boo.com spent huge sums on advertising itself when it launched in seven languages in 18 countries. Its site was so high-tech that only users with enough bandwidth could get it to work. Cynics joke that the purpose of a dotcom is to transfer money from venture capitalists to advertising agencies. But the days of wild extravagance are over for dotcoms. High marketing costs were initially justified in the race to stake out a territory in cyberspace. Now, venture capitalists hungry for profit may insist that companies find better ways to spend their money than lavish launches and advertising campaigns.

There is also a growing recognition among marketers that the new tactics they have used to attract customers' attention so far have not worked. Interstitials, ads that just pop up on the screen, are seen as annoying interruptions to the online experience. Spending on banner ads has dropped as companies conclude that computer users are ignoring them. Here, too, the customer is in charge. After years of being force-fed TV adverts it appears that in cyberspace the hard-sell does not work and customers only tune in when they want to hear the message. Companies are increasingly turning to tailor-made ads based on personal tastes and preferences, using one-to-one marketing to elicit information about individual customers. There are dangers here too. An unsolicited e-mail suggesting an array of gifts for your baby's forthcoming first birthday may be a little too personal for many mums to accept.

Mass customisation

Such information can be used to produce individually tailored products at affordable prices for huge numbers of consumers. This means focusing on what customers want, rather than what the company can produce. "As in so many areas," notes Ward Hanson, author of *Principles of Internet Marketing* and a professor at Stanford Business School, "the Internet allows the democratisation of goods and information."

Mass customisation is easier for goods that can be digitised. But in addition to services such as banking, stockbroking, communications and online information, products that cannot be digitised are increasingly receiving the all-yours treatment too. And as the revolution spreads to manufacturing, firms are finding they need to change their entire production process. The first manufacturers to tailor products to particular customers have, not surprisingly, been selling to other businesses. "Mass customisation is more prevalent in business-to-business, because the customer can attach a dollar value to it," says Mr Pine. The simplest approach is to design a product that buyers can customise themselves.

The manufacturer that has done most to apply this approach in the consumer world is Dell Computer. To the customer, the company's most striking feature is a website that allows the buyer to design an individual computer and then track it through to delivery. But Dell also shows that when you get mass customisation to work, some remarkable things start to happen.

First, the need to hold stocks of parts, partially finished and finished goods falls sharply: inventories at Dell fell from 31 days of parts at the end of the 1996 financial year to only six days today in 2000, says Paul Bell, who runs Dell's operations in Europe. Much of Dell's production, up to the point of final assembly, is outsourced. That makes it essential for suppliers at every link in the chain to be plugged in to good information about what customers want, and when. "If all our suppliers are guessing," says Mr Bell, "you end up with inventory, which is the physical embodiment of bad information." Mind you, this process can also bring an opposite problem: delays when Dell runs out of a particular part.

Speed and good communications are thus essential if mass customisation is to work. Get them right, and another prize is yours. In Henry Ford's day, Ford made the car and the customer paid for it. In Michael Dell's day, the customer pays for the computer and then Dell makes it.

Delivering the goods

Getting the right product to the right place at the right time is a challenge for any company. As often with an unglamorous back-office business it is the fulfilment and distribution end that has proved the hardest part of e-commerce.

Indeed, in late 1999 a huge explosion in Internet retail sales was overshadowed by terrible tales of delivery snarl-ups. Toys "R" Us and Wal-Mart announced as early as the second week of December that they could no longer guarantee delivery of website orders by Christmas. Consumers started to scream when they found they were unable to cancel or amend orders; many made it clear that they would have liked some real live human contact to sort things out. Some observers thought things were so bad that frustrated customers might abandon their efforts to shop on the web, and that e-commerce, instead of growing by leaps and bounds, might start sliding downhill. They were right. It is now clear that the one thing that has counted a lot in the e-commerce shake-out is fulfilment, not price.

The early e-commerce pioneers concentrated on the end of the action that they reckoned to understand: website design and snazzy marketing. Many outsourced the whole tiresome business of order checking and distribution. In its early days, even Amazon relied wholly on Ingram's book-wholesaling operation. Consumer electronics sites left the business to Micro, another big wholesaler and distributor. Everybody used United Parcel Services (UPS), Federal Express or the post for delivery.

Yet two things soon became clear. One was that shipping costs were (and remain) one of the biggest deterrents for consumers considering online purchases of physical products. The second was that traditional warehouse and distribution centres were not well suited to the business of e-commerce fulfilment: if it is to work properly, it needs newly designed systems. Both these things have combined to undermine some of the economic advantages of online shopping.

Perhaps this should not have come as a surprise. Physical shoppers, after all, handle their own order fulfilment, by choosing the goods and paying for them at the checkout, as well as their own delivery, by personally taking them home. And they do all this at their own expense, in both time and money. Merely to replicate this system efficiently, down to the individual consumer, is demanding enough; financing it, whether by absorbing the cost or by adding it to the bill, makes it even harder. It might have been better had e-commerce firms given more attention to this end of their business first.

Ironically, the delivery problems encountered by pure plays (companies with an online presence only) were one of the things that led many traditional retailers to assume that they could do better. Ironically because, here as elsewhere, many quickly found that their own distribution systems, geared to moving goods on pallets from warehouses to shops, proved a disadvantage, not a benefit. Wal-Mart, for example, has the most highly praised distribution system in the world: even the tyre pressures of its lorries are calibrated so that, when fully laden with pallets, the vehicles will be at exactly the right height for the unloading docks at Wal-Mart stores. But such a system is unable to cope with individual orders that have to be delivered to people's homes. So Wal-Mart has had to outsource its website distribution to two rivals: Fingerhut, a distributor that now belongs to Federated Department Stores, and Books-a-million.

Catalogue retailers such as Lands' End and J. Crew are a different matter. Their warehouses were already aimed at delivering individual orders to people's homes. Adapting their order-taking to the web has not been simple, but distribution has certainly been far easier than building new warehouses from scratch. This remains the biggest reason for expecting the catalogue businesses to emerge as a success story of the web.

For the rest, is outsourcing the answer? Sometimes it can be. It certainly seems to work for long-distance deliveries by road. ups has been one of the biggest beneficiaries of the e-commerce boom: the company reckons it is handling around two-thirds of all goods ordered online. It has also developed a sophisticated (and very popular) website-cum-tracking service that allows consumers to check exactly where their order is at any time of the day or night. It has edged out its biggest rival, FedEx, which realised too late that its main business, document delivery, was being disintermediated by e-mail.

But although actual delivery can be outsourced, many e-commerce firms are finding that it is risky to do the same with picking and packing, because a contractor working for many web merchants will never be able to give all of them priority, especially when the pressure is on during the holiday season. So more and more e-merchants have decided to follow the example of Amazon and build their own giant automated warehouses.

Logistics and delivery are also crucial to understanding the nascent online grocery business. Like the physical supermarket business, it was initially small and highly localised. Some of the most striking experiments have taken place in Boston and San Francisco.

Boston has several Internet grocers in fierce competition with each other. One, called HomeRuns.com, an offshoot of Hannaford's, a supermarket chain, is testing the notion that offline and online can work well together. So far, it seems to be doing well. In October 2000 it began offering its services in Washington DC. In March 2001 it announced improvements to its service, including a revamped website that offers faster and easier ordering. Another, called Streamline.com, founded in 1993, appeared to be on the right track when it set out to provide its mostly suburban middle-class clientele with a lock-up fridge in an outbuilding. This allowed Streamline staff to deliver and unpack the weekly grocery order even when a customer was not at home. Despite occasional complaints, Streamline acquired a dedicated clientele willing to pay a subscription and a premium price for its goods. But it developed cashflow problems and in September 2000 sold off some of its assets to a rival, Peapod.com. Then in November 2000 it was forced to shut up shop altogether, having failed to secure an infusion of capital or find a buyer. Peapod was also on the brink of bankruptcy by the end of 2000 but was rescued by Ahold, a Dutch grocery giant.

A real battleground for the online supermarket has been guaranteed delivery. Kozmo.com, a firm that began operating in New York and San Francisco, tried to guarantee delivery of basic snacks and other groceries (along with a selection of videos, CDs, books and games) within an hour of an order being placed. But its experiment failed and in February 2001 it shed the dotcom part of its name, moving away from the Internet and back to old-fashioned catalogue and call-centre sales.

A far more ambitious bid to guarantee delivery within a selected 30-minute window was made by Webvan in San Francisco. Webvan's boss, George Shaheen, caused a stir in 1999 when he quit his position as boss of Andersen Consulting for the Internet start-up. He had grand ambitions for his new firm. At the time, he said that Webvan aimed to be everybody's grocer, saving its customers both time and money. Mr Shaheen envisaged it as becoming the "last mile of e-commerce", with people talking of "webvanning" rather than "fedexing" things. The company spent more than $1 billion on building a string of state-of-the-art warehouses all round America. After that, it planned to move abroad.

But the company ran up significant losses from the start. In September 2000 it began laying off staff, and during the first quarter of 2001 it introduced a number of cost-cutting measures. In February 2001, Louis Borders, the company's founder, announced that he had resigned from the board of directors for "personal reasons". In April 2001, Deloitte &

Touche, the company's auditor, said in the annual report, "There can be no assurance that [Webvan] will be successful in its efforts to achieve future profitable operations, generate sufficient cash from operations or obtain additional funding sources." The company also faced the prospect of being delisted from Nasdaq.

Online grocery shopping seemed like paradise for the "time-poor, cash-rich" consumers of the 21st century. But there is something to be said for touching fruit and vegetables and checking if the meat is lean before buying after all. Another big problem is that the type of shopper likely to use an online grocer is rarely at home. It may be all right to leave a delivery of books or other non-perishable goods with a neighbour, but who wants boxes of fresh produce hanging around the house? Apart from chocolates and flowers, delivering to work is out of the question. As for the strategy adopted by some companies, who would have enough trust to let someone open the door and pop the things in the fridge, even when it is in a garage or cellar?

This is not to say that there is no market for ordering supermarket goods. But the companies that will excel are probably those with bricks-and-mortar and brand names that people trust. In America, Safeway and Kroger are moving aggressively online. In 2000, Kroger took an equity stake in the online retail industry exchange, GlobalNetXchange, founded by Sears and other big retailers. It aims to cut purchasing costs and speed up the supply chain while moving cautiously into online selling. It is a strategy that could well pay off if the online grocery business takes hold.

In Britain, Tesco, a large supermarket group, has in Tesco Direct what it now claims to be the biggest online grocery business in the world. It employs teams of people to pick the items on their customers' web-transmitted shopping lists from the shelves of the nearest supermarket, and teams of drivers to deliver the orders at agreed times. But the company has had a number of teething troubles, and there are doubts about the profitability and the scalability of its web business.

As companies improve their logistics networks and get better at delivering the goods, the online grocery industry is expected to grow. For now, the jury is still out on whether grocers have a future in e-commerce. It will take time to establish whether online shops such as Webvan really can replace the supermarket trip, or merely supplement it. Even if they can provide the wired and short-of-time with everything they need, online shops are never likely to take more than a smallish share of the market. According to Jupiter, the business will net $2 billion in 2001, yet online grocery sales account for less than 1% of grocery sales in America.

However, some goods and services companies have the best possible answer to the nightmarish logistics of e-commerce: deliver over the Internet itself. For if you do that, you can eliminate most of your physical rivals altogether. A lot of computer software is now digitally downloaded by the user. The next businesses to head this way are music, films and books.

Growing pains

The Christmas 2000 shopping season showed that e-commerce is not dead in the water as some have concluded from the high number of dotcom flops. The sector is alive but still suffering from growing pains.

Overall Christmas sales matched the most optimistic prediction, coming in at $10 billion. Taken in context, though, this is still less than the money that flowed through the tills at Wal-Mart alone. E-tailers succeeded in attracting more customers than in 1999. A report by PricewaterhouseCoopers said that 80% of Internet users shopped online for gifts, compared with 69% during the 1999 season. But studies also show that e-commerce is still bedevilled by the same problems it has suffered from the outset, most notably in the areas of delivery and fulfilment. According to a report by Accenture (formerly Andersen Consulting), 67% of deliveries were not received as ordered and 12% were not received in time for Christmas.

The number of abandoned shopping carts shows that e-tailers are still having a tough time closing sales. A study released in late 2000 by A.T. Kearney said four out of five transactions were not being completed, causing losses of $3.8 billion in online sales. Many of the reasons remain the same as before. Top of the list is frustration, closely followed by the fear of having to part with detailed personal information, including credit-card numbers, before being able to make a purchase. Other factors which put off would-be customers are sites that are hard to navigate, making basic information about sales prices, gift certificates and returns policies difficult to find.

These results prove that many e-tailers are continuing to ignore the old lesson of making things simple. They opt for snazzy sites, hoping to grab customers' attention by standing out from the crowd. Instead, as study after study has shown, what most customers want is clearly displayed information and visuals together with a quick, easy payment process.

Companies that are mastering the art of online selling are still uncommon, with many of the same names appearing in the Christmas 2000 season. Not surprisingly, Amazon remained the clear online leader.

There were some changes, though. Other star performers included J. Crew, Wal-Mart and Sears, showing that traditional retailers are now making their mark in cyberspace. Books, CDs and computer equipment continued to head the list of the most popular products sold on the web.

Conclusion

Cyberspace is not the biggest self-service supermarket in the world but is more of a global village, where all the old-fashioned, corner-shop values of trust and loyalty apply. Internet shoppers are not necessarily fickle nor are they looking for the lowest price. What they do want is convenient and hassle-free shopping. They want sites that are easy to use and they are unforgiving when things go wrong. Successful companies know that e-commerce is not about how many prospective customers or "eyeballs" they attract. The real challenge lies in persuading visitors to stick around long enough to buy something and then come back for more. Understanding customer needs and matching expectations will distinguish the winners from the losers in the online world. In the Internet era the customer really is king.

5 More perfect competition

THE ARRIVAL OF the Internet auction is one of the biggest things to have happened in e-commerce so far. At the consumer end, eBay has come to dominate the market. Buyers and sellers meet to take part in fiercely competitive auctions for everything from Beanie Babies to baseball cards and fine art. In the business-to-business (B2B) sector hundreds of other new exchanges have sprung up such as Ventro, which started life as an online marketplace for the life-sciences industry called Chemdex, and eSteel. These bring together firms and their suppliers to auction, negotiate or simply compare prices. It is in these markets that analysts predict the biggest business will be done in future. According to Forrester Research, 71% of business buyers and sellers will at least have tried their hand at online marketplaces by the end of 2001. It reckons that the value of transactions via e-marketplaces will increase from $54 billion in 2000 to $1.4 trillion by 2004, surpassing trade between individual companies. Because of the web's ability to bring together vast numbers of buyers and sellers in one place from all around the world and generate different pricing mechanisms, some say it moves the economy closer to the textbook model of perfect competition. Is the Internet really an electronic Utopia? Will fixed prices become a thing of the past? Or will the novelty of Internet auctions and other buying techniques such as aggregation wear off?

The right price

From a Turkish bazaar to a Tunisian souk, most of the appeal for tourists is in haggling over prices. Until 100 or so years ago, most trading happened this way throughout the world. Prices moved up and down continuously, and it was easy for buyers and sellers to check up on each other's activities. But not everyone likes to haggle, especially when it comes to essentials, such as food and household goods. It is time-consuming and can be nerve-racking.

In the 17th century the founder of the House of Mitsui, Hachirobei, discovered that fixed prices were a big attraction for Japanese housewives, who were tired of having to bargain for basic items. His decision to set prices was one factor behind Mitsui's rise as one of Japan's most successful industrial conglomerates.

In 1890 Fred Kohnle, an American inventor, came up with a machine that could print a price tag and fix it to an object. Suddenly it became possible to label hundreds of items with a single price. Department stores and customers loved it. Kohnle's invention simplified shopping and helped speed up the growth of the retail industry in America.

But such a general shift in pricing tactics meant that much of the early transparency was lost. For the most part, it was a sellers' market. Sellers set the prices, based on their perceptions of what the goods or services were worth or, as was often the case, on how much they thought buyers would be prepared to pay.

Now the Internet has sparked a fresh revolution in pricing. Online auctions and other forms of exchanges have pushed aside stickier prices and ushered in a new era of "dynamic pricing", where goods are priced according to whatever the market will bear at any given moment. In this great, electronic, worldwide bazaar no prices are ever fixed for long, all information is instantly available, and buyers and sellers spend their lives searching for the best deals. But much like the tourists in a North African souk, the appeal of online exchanges, particularly in the consumer market, owes a lot to the novelty effect. Critics charge that they are not so much a new marketplace as a new form of entertainment. (See Figure 5.1 on next page.)

Consumer-to-consumer exchanges

eBay: from flea market to e-market

The experience of eBay would suggest otherwise. Its runaway success has even taken seasoned theorists on the network economy by surprise. "eBay was a blind spot for us economists," says Hal Varian, dean of the School of Information Management and Systems at the University of California at Berkeley. "We don't think in terms of flea markets."

Indeed, there are many remarkable things about the company, not least the fact that it is one of the few leading Internet businesses to make a profit – something it has done from the start. Founded in 1995, when Pierre Omidyar hit upon a way to help his wife build her collection of Pez dispensers, eBay has forged one of the greatest developments in e-commerce: the online auction. In the process, Mr Omidyar has come up with an e-business model that other Internet entrepreneurs would die for because it turns a profit faster than any other one.

What began as a Silicon Valley start-up is now a firm Wall Street favourite. The California-based business has captured an estimated 85% of the American market and has seven global sites in different languages.

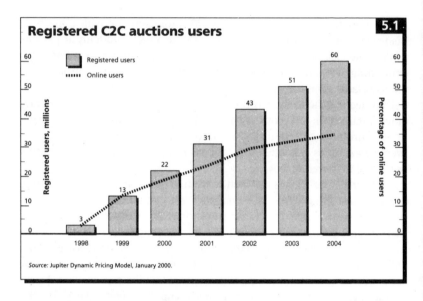

Registered C2C auctions users `5.1`

Source: Jupiter Dynamic Pricing Model, January 2000.

Along with Amazon.com it is considered to be one of the bellwethers of e-commerce. It has an astonishing record of growth and in April 2001 announced earnings that exceeded analysts' expectations. eBay said its net income for the first quarter of 2001 was $21.1m and that consolidated net revenue for the following two quarters could be up to $10m–15m higher than expected. It expects its gross margins to remain above 80% during 2001. The company said it attracted over 7.2m new users during the quarter, making a total of 29.7m registered users. The company aims to reach $3 billion in net revenue by 2005, an annual growth rate of almost 50%.

So what is the key? Remarkably, eBay generates nearly $500m in revenues by letting its 15m or so registered users do most of the work themselves. It does not hold inventory, move goods, or transfer payments. Instead, it lets users post and haggle over roughly 4m items for sale in 4,320 product categories, spending, on average, $166 per second. Most of its revenue comes from straight fees. eBay charges a listing fee of $0.25–$2 based on the merchandise value, and an additional success fee of 1.25–5% if an item is sold. The more valuable the merchandise, the greater is eBay's take. Gary Bengier, the company's finance director, is proud that eBay has found a way to drive revenue with very little capital. He says, "How many companies can say their business model is characterised by the things they don't have to do?"

The aim of Meg Whitman, the firm's chief executive and a former Disney and Hasbro marketing executive, is for eBay to remain profitable while growing aggressively. "I have this philosophy that you really need to do things 100%. Better to do five things at 100% than ten things at 80%," she says, advice that many over-ambitious dotcom founders would do well to heed. eBay has shown that in the new economy it is possible to move fast, do things well and be profitable all at the same time.

Not surprisingly, many dotcoms have tried to follow eBay's example. Even Amazon, widely seen as the crown prince of consumer e-commerce, began holding auctions in direct competition with eBay. In May 2000 it announced that it had increased the number of items listed for auction or fixed-price bid to 2m, or about half of what eBay lists. Competition is also hotting up from Yahoo!, and more recently from a network of auction sites run by FairMarket.

eBay has also had its fair share of problems, from technical glitches that have involved a 24-hour outage to disputes over intellectual property. In a battle over so-called "deep linking", where websites allow users to search for products across a variety of online auction services, eBay filed a suit against biddersedge.com in December 1999 and barred AuctionWatch.com from using its site. The dispute highlighted the problems connected to the growing use of "shopping bots", which are used to trawl various websites for the lowest price on a product or auction item. In February 2000, the US Justice Department launched an investigation into eBay to determine whether its efforts to block price-comparison search software from its site were anti-competitive. At the height of the battle Rodrigo Sales, CEO of AuctionWatch, told the *E-Commerce Times*: "It strikes to the heart of a much bigger issue. The foundation of the Internet lies in freedom of information. eBay's actions are not only contrary to the best interests of consumers, but have the potential to set a dangerous precedent that could threaten the evolution and growth of the web."

Even if eBay wins a court victory, it is likely to be both temporary and incomplete. A new technology is already on its way which eBay will find difficult to stop either legally or technically. The new operating system from Apple will include a piece of software that eliminates the need for deep-linking websites, by allowing individual users to search for items across most e-commerce and auction sites.

Fraud is a potential problem affecting all types of auctions and eBay is no exception. In May 1999 a seller tried to auction a painting purporting to be the work of the late Richard Diebenkorn, an abstract expressionist. He was then accused of bidding for the item himself. eBay eventually cancelled the auction. But the company has come up with an elegant solution to such problems. Regular sellers can establish a reputation for reliable delivery and quality through a rating and comment system based on the experience of customers. Once again, eBay lets the users do most of the legwork. Buyers who are unhappy about a purchase can use the Feedback Forum to voice their complaints. These comments are then included in the seller's profile, which is posted on the site for other users to read. This has helped build a loyal community of buyers and sellers. Amazon has achieved similar results by allowing users to post their own book reviews. So successful is eBay that some 50,000–100,000 sole proprietors now earn a living by hawking items on the site. It is ordinary buyers and sellers, though, who generate the bulk of the trading on eBay.

Keen to expand its user base and remain profitable, the company has made its first foray into the burgeoning b2b market. eBay's Business Exchange enables small businesses to bid for new, used and refurbished office equipment. The company has also begun conducting fixed-price sales. A number of large companies, such as Sun Microsystems, use the site as a distribution channel. eBay has also ventured into other new areas. In March 2000 it agreed to work with AutoTrader.com, the world's largest used-car marketplace, to create eBayMotors, a co-branded automotive auction site. It has also begun tapping the real-estate market through a relationship with zipRealty.com, an online real-estate brokerage. In July 2000 it spent more than $300m buying Half.com, which sells used books, cds, movies and video games at discounted prices.

This move has taken eBay back to the old-economy notion of fixed prices. It seems the company may be treading the same path as Mitsui did four centuries earlier. Maybe haggling will once again go out of fashion, causing eBay to lose some of its initial cult attraction. Ms Whitman says that Half.com's fixed-price trading is one of the keys to the future expansion of eBay. Fixed prices may offer some stability in these turbulent times of the Internet era. eBay is hedging its bets, and seeking growth, by moving into new markets, including Ireland and Switzerland. Getting well established abroad is high on the agenda. It aims to be in ten countries by the end of 2001 and 25 by the end of 2005. It is also trying to establish a strategic network of partners in cyberspace.

Business-to-business exchanges

The bulk of the trade in e-marketplaces is likely to be conducted in the business-to-business arena. According to AMR Research, 29% of all commercial transactions, worth some $5.7 trillion, will flow through the Internet by 2004. In a report published in October 2000, *The B2B Opportunity: Creating Advantage Through E-marketplaces*, Boston Consulting Group says that American companies will be able to generate financial benefits equivalent to 1–2% of sales from e-marketplaces by 2004. By 2010 the consultancy reckons this figure will rise to at least 6% of sales, or roughly $1 trillion. How will this happen? In the same way that eBay has enabled individual collectors to meet online and exchange Beanie Babies, so B2B marketplaces will make it easier and cheaper for companies to get together and do business with each other.

E-marketplaces are essentially a development of the Electronic Data Interchange (EDI) systems that companies have been using up to now. These new Internet-based exchanges do not require the expensive proprietary software or hardware of EDI systems. Moreover, they operate in real time, which means that information can be updated constantly rather than through periodic data transfers. Thus commercial transactions are much cheaper than those mediated by EDI and also potentially much more valuable. And the barriers to entry are much lower, making it much easier for large buyers to scour broad communities of sellers to achieve low prices.

Saving lots of money is obviously part of the appeal. Larry Ellison, chief executive of Oracle, reckons it costs 100 times less to process a purchase via the web than it does through EDI. But greater efficiency in the supply chain is also a huge factor, which explains the boom in B2B marketplaces because it means faster time to market, quicker access to new suppliers and customers, and speedier entry into new markets. But some large companies, such as Wal-Mart, are fearful of the new exchanges that bring together many buyers and sellers. Having successfully applied the technology to their own supply chains, they are watching upstarts use the marketplaces to gain similar advantages for far less money. Moreover, coveted business relationships are suddenly up for grabs.

Around 750 B2B marketplaces were spawned by the end of 2000, many of them based upon auctions. Their evolution can be roughly divided into three main phases.

1 The first type, the private e-marketplace, was set up in the late 1990s by large firms such as General Electric and Wal-Mart, which spotted the benefits to be gained from moving their buying and selling online. They cut down the paperwork, made the procurement process more efficient and made huge savings in time and money along the way.

Boston Consulting Group reckons that B2B online purchasing will reach $4.8 trillion in 2004, or about 40% of total purchasing. Corporations like Cisco, Dell, FedEx and Intel use the Internet as their main platform for doing business. Merrill Lynch reckons these direct sellers will grab 75–80% of B2B revenue by 2003.

2 Next came the upstarts, independent firms that hoped to cash in on the B2B market by serving a specific industry or specialising in products or services used by several industries. Examples include IronPlanet.com, which links buyers and sellers of used heavy equipment, and Ventro. The company, originally called Chemdex, was renamed when it started moving into other industries such as medical supplies and fluid-processing equipment.

3 During the third phase industry giants came together to form various consortiums. The first to make the headlines on February 25th 2000 was Covisint. It was formed when General Motors, Ford and DaimlerChrysler abandoned their stand-alone efforts and joined forces to create the world's largest virtual market, which will buy $240 billion worth of parts from tens of thousands of suppliers. They were soon joined by Toyota, Renault and its Japanese affiliate, Nissan. But the launch was delayed until September 2000 due to technical problems, regulatory reviews and administrative squabbles. Then came a flurry of press releases by the largest companies in almost every major industry, announcing their own collaborative B2B projects. On February 28th 2000 America's Sears, Roebuck and France's Carrefour announced a retail consortium, called GlobalNetXchange, that will bring together $80 billion worth of annual purchases.

For a while it seemed as though B2B exchanges really would be the next big thing. Analysts gushed about the limitless opportunities. But many B2B pioneers, like their B2C counterparts before them, quickly became disillusioned. The founders of many independent exchanges discovered that the streets of cyberspace were not necessarily paved with gold. When prices of tech stocks dived in April 2000, they had to scale back operations or shut down altogether. Many e-marketplaces had decided to go public early to gain first-mover advantage. The hope was that an initial public offering (IPO) would bring in additional capital as well as publicity, thus attracting more buyers and sellers. In many cases this failed to happen. Despite going public, customers, revenue and profit proved as far away as ever.

So far, the first type of e-marketplace set up by individual companies may turn out to be the safest bet. All the participants can benefit from the greater efficiencies generated by the Internet. Besides, these companies usually have earnings, deep pockets and plenty of customers to support their B2B plans. As more and more companies recognise the gains to be made by moving their business operations online, these marketplaces will proliferate.

Exchanges founded by individual dotcoms probably run some of the greatest risks overall. The potential is bigger, but gaining critical mass is harder. They have no established buyers or sellers to bring to the party nor do they have endless supplies of cash. Many have realised that without a solid base to branch out from an IPO may turn out to be a wasted exercise. Attracting participants is also difficult because many companies fail to see why they should go out of their way to slash their own margins and are wary of compromising their existing business relationships. Moreover, many potential customers have turned out to be competitors. As the pure plays tried to establish themselves, traditional companies were joining forces to set up their own exchanges in all kinds of industries from plastics to paper. The battle for individual public industry marketplaces is turning out to be much more fierce than originally thought.

As for the third kind of exchange formed by industry giants, there is good reason to believe they will succeed. The founders have a vested interest in the exchanges because they bring them such a huge volume of transactions. Several industry exchanges, including e2open.com, which serves the computer, telecom equipment and consumer electronics industries, and the one set up by Boeing and others, will determine equity stakes for the founding partners based on who uses the system most for their procurement needs. With so much at stake, rewards for the top job are high. According to Jeff Christian, chief executive of Christian & Timbers, an international executive search firm, in mid-2000 compensation packages for Internet-exchange CEOs were running between $500,000 and $1m, plus 5–10% equity in the new entity.

But it may still be too soon to tell whether the upstarts or the traditional companies will win the battle for e-marketplaces. When large companies join forces to do business together it raises inevitable concerns about monopolistic behaviour. The fear is that sellers could misuse the powerful network effects that create a thriving online marketplace to create cartels and permit price-fixing. Big buyers could also gang up on suppliers, either through collective purchasing or simply through the increased buying power created by an efficient market. The

Federal Trade Commission has already held a two-day hearing on the antitrust implications of B2B exchanges. It is also looking into at least three of the most prominent exchanges: those being set up by the largest American car companies, airlines and aerospace firms. The Department of Justice has also begun its own investigations.

It is indeed possible that the exchanges themselves could turn into monopolies because buyers and sellers alike will be interested only in using the biggest around. *The Economist* has said: "Companies that own such a winning exchange in one market might be able to leverage that power to expand into other markets (a big car maker, for instance, could use its buying power in car parts to dominate related 'horizontal' markets, such as steel or glass). Big buyers or suppliers that own exchanges could have access to information on deals that might give them unfair trading advantages. They might also gain unfair advantages by subsidising their own business with the transaction fees of competitors who use the exchange." ("A market for monopoly", June 15th 2000.)

However, roughly half of all industries have no dominant buyers or sellers. Upstarts may have a natural advantage here because they are neutral and appeal to all parties. But they are burning money fast. All these worries may lie in the future. For now there is a more pressing problem facing many B2B exchanges: finding a chief executive.

Covisint, the highest-profile exchange, faced exactly this problem following a conditional go-ahead given by US antitrust authorities in September 2000. It appointed its first CEO, Kevin English, a former Wall Street executive with no automotive experience, in April 2001. According to a report by Russell Reynolds Associates, an international executive search firm, the right candidate to head a B2B exchange needs to be a strategist, deal-maker and diplomat who has a thorough knowledge of the particular industry sector and a flair for e-commerce. The CEO also needs experience in building successful alliances between companies that have often been fierce competitors. Sounds like a tall order? Many companies have decided that the chances of finding the perfect candidate in such a tight labour market are very slim indeed.

Some exchanges, such as GlobalNetXchange, have opted for an insider for the job. In July 2000 it announced that it had chosen Joseph Laughlin, Sears's senior vice-president for corporate finance and business development, to be its new CEO. Retailers in the exchange account for $175 billion in annual purchases from more than 50,000 suppliers, partners and distributors worldwide. Transora.com, an online supplier exchange set up by 49 consumer-goods makers, including Procter &

Gamble, Sara Lee and Coca-Cola, also chose the same recruitment strategy. In July 2000 the exchange announced that Judith Sprieser, head of Sara Lee's food division, would be its new CEO.

But opting for an insider can also pose problems. Many founding partners hope to purchase supplies through the exchanges. If a CEO from one of the member companies is appointed, others may view it as an unfair advantage. Indeed, governance is one of the toughest issues facing the new exchanges. Many believe that choosing a neutral candidate is the only way to bring member companies together and encourage them to co-operate. Some industry-led marketplaces have asked Big Five consulting firms to step in and oversee negotiations during the start-up phase. Andersen Consulting was invited to help work out a business plan and look at potential candidates for the top job at the B2B aerospace and defence industry exchange announced by Boeing, Raytheon, Lockheed Martin and BAE Systems.

Rather than search in vain for the perfect candidate, the best advice is probably to settle on someone with a solid management and business background and carefully select the people that will supply the right skills and experience to create a winning team. According to Joseph Laughlin, chief executive of GlobalNetXchange: "You need an understanding of e-commerce and technology, but you don't have to be an expert. You've got to surround yourself with experts."

However, in such a new market finding the right people does not necessarily spell success. Despite the initial fanciful figures about how much the B2B market is worth, analysts are now producing more sobering statistics. Estimates vary, although most observers seem to agree that most industries will support only one or two major marketplaces. Based on its survey of 500 buyers, sellers and marketplaces and interviews with 30 B2B companies over a three-month period, Boston Consulting Group puts the figure at up to three.

Many B2B business models are destined to fail. Increased competition will force those that depend on transaction fees to reduce their fees and thus threaten their survival. Financial markets give some indication of the volume needed to generate significant transaction revenue. In 1999, the New York Stock Exchange made $8.9 trillion in transactions but earned only $75.2m in profits – less than one one-thousandth of 1%. This means that marketplaces must be able to serve large markets to have a chance of earning significant revenue.

Some marketplaces have given up charging transaction fees altogether in the hope that this will attract more users. They are trying to make money on other value-added services such as finance and logistics. But this involves more capital and a higher level of risk because it requires investment in fixed assets such as warehouses and trucks. Boston Consulting Group reckons that this additional revenue stream will also be limited.

According to the consultancy, the lion's share of revenue will eventually come from collaboration services, where companies integrate their business processes, sharing information about design specifications and inventory levels, for example. The consultancy reckons that by 2005, collaboration services could represent 40–50% of the total revenue of successful marketplaces.

Some of the more savvy Internet exchanges have spotted the potential of trading contracts rather than commodities. This could turn out to be a much more lucrative game. Only a small fraction of commodities, such as chemicals and steel, can be traded on public spot markets, which quote up-to-the-minute prices. An estimated 80–90% of all business goods and services are actually traded through extended-term contracts, often lasting for a year or more. So as many exchanges were desperately trying to attract business, many big firms were ignoring them and continuing to negotiate contracts with each other as before.

One of the first companies to focus on contracts was FreeMarkets, which designs and runs "reverse auctions" (where the price falls over time instead of rising) for many industries. But it is a complicated process because everything contained in the contract, from the specifications of the product to performance guarantees, needs to be codified so that bidders can compete fairly in an auction. Companies such as Perfect.com and Commerce One are writing software that will help automate bidding across industries, but the sheer complexity of the task means progress has been slow.

According to The Economist ("The container case", October 19th 2000), the more manageable option is to work with a single industry. But even here, few b2b exchanges have had the money, industry knowledge and resources to succeed. One of the exceptions is GoCargo, an exchange for the container-shipping industry, which is expanding from a relatively small spot market to a far larger contract market – and learning just how complex that is.

At first blush, containers look as commodity-like as airline seats. After all, the containers themselves are standard-sized, sealed units. Nobody cares much about how the boxes get from here to there, just how much it costs to send them. Even better, American prohibitions on private-rate negotiations for container space were lifted in 1999, opening the market to deal-by-deal auctions. No wonder Eyal Goldwerger, a consultant with Boston Consulting Group scouting for a B2B idea in 1998, settled on containers and founded GoCargo. If ever there was a product perfect for online trading, this seemed to be the one.

Even so, the exchange faced an uphill struggle. Around three-quarters of the world's $50-billion container business is still done under service contracts, most of them negotiated the old-fashioned way, through relationships, brokers, sales calls and the like. This is partly because the industry, like its ships, is slow to turn. But other problems go deeper. For one, the sea is usually only part of the journey for a container. It will also probably go on a truck and a train, and typically passes through customs twice. Shippers usually want an end-to-end solution; although paying a logistics firm or freight forwarder to provide it may cost them a bit more than they would pay in an open auction, the overall savings on hassle often make it worthwhile.

Nor are all freight carriers as alike as they might seem. Some have better reliability records than others and some can handle bigger shipments, for instance. Where carriers are alike is in their suspicion of any marketplace that might cut their prices by treating their service as an undifferentiated commodity. And on the shipper's side, long service contracts have the additional advantage of locking in availability and price over a set period.

Although GoCargo started by auctioning spot capacity, Mr Goldwerger quickly saw that old-style service contracts were not about to disappear. So he built a staff of 60 multilingual industry specialists and traders, based in New York, who could codify terms, certify shippers and carriers, and otherwise make this handshake business safe for Internet trading. (To respond to the carriers' concerns about becoming commoditised, GoCargo included ways to help them stand out from the crowd by including in the auction criteria such elements as rated quality of service.) As GoCargo got better at this, it started to turn into a real business: contracts now amount to nearly a third of the exchange's total volume (see Figure 5.2) and should have reached half by the end of 2000. The site was boasting more than 12,000 members at the end of 2000 and conducted more than 5,000 live auctions during 2000, providing it with enough liquidity to start compiling real-time market trends and indices.

Another example is Logistics.com, which auctions transport contracts of all kinds, from trucking to air and sea. Yossi Sheffi, its boss, reckons such contracts are among the hardest to bring online. One of the biggest problems is "conditional deals": a carrier will agree to move containers in one direction only if it can find someone who will pay it to bring them back again. Unless online auctions accommodate this kind of problem, they will be ignored.

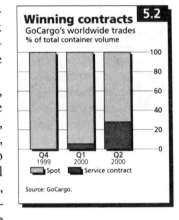

Winning contracts 5.2
GoCargo's worldwide trades
% of total container volume

Q4 1999 · Q1 2000 · Q2 2000
■ Spot ■ Service contract

Source: GoCargo.

In a few other industries, such as steel, B2B exchanges are also starting to make some headway in trading contracts, having realised that spot markets, though easy to enter, are usually too small. The hope is that contracts will gradually become more standardised, allowing them to be traded like commodities themselves. Perhaps. But if the industry has shown anything in its first, dismal couple of years, it is that this will take far longer than those early, breathless business plans suggested.

Some analysts predict that when necessary e-marketplaces could eventually perform the role of temporary corporate departments. When a company needs a team for a specific project, it can use an e-marketplace to find the partners to supply the necessary products and services. When the project is completed, the team dissolves again. This could have an impact on mergers and acquisitions. Companies can benefit from collaboration without the hassle of a full-scale merger, for example. However, industry leaders such as Dell and Wal-Mart are concerned that e-marketplaces may become the main centres of power and are reluctant to join them for this reason.

Another likely trend is corporate spin-offs. One example of a company that has already gone down this path is Eastman Chemical. It decided to spin off its logistics operation into ShipChem.com, which will help chemical suppliers to arrange shipments. By spinning off non-core activities, companies can concentrate on what they do best.

As the number and types of auctions continue to proliferate, "combinatorial auctions" may be the next big thing. These allow businesses to bid for many things at the same time. This is particularly useful in markets where different goods are complementary, such as radio licences – the more you have of these the better. Computerised Market Systems is developing a range of complex auctions that will tell the bidder in seconds if his bid would succeed, and, if not, what to do to win.

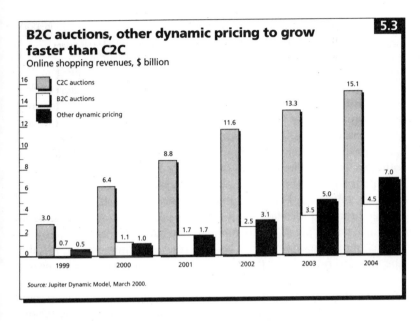

5.3

B2C auctions, other dynamic pricing to grow faster than C2C

Online shopping revenues, $ billion

- C2C auctions
- B2C auctions
- Other dynamic pricing

Source: Jupiter Dynamic Model, March 2000.

Much of the debate on which kind of e-marketplace will survive has focused on type; for example, the dotcoms versus the consortia. But according to Boston Consulting Group the landscape is likely to be much more complex. Companies will not rely exclusively on one marketplace but on several. "Companies will pick the set of relationships that best suits their individual strategies," it says. The survivors of the B2B shake-out will include a handful of giant exchanges and a large number of small niche players.

A not so perfect market

So where does this leave prices? Will the advent of the online auction give economists the first glimpse of a perfect market outside their textbooks? Probably not. Prices are likely to become more efficient but that does not necessarily mean they will all get lower or fluctuate in accordance to supply and demand. First the good news. The Internet does offer an excellent way of comparing prices and collecting information on new products, or on recent bids, for example (see Figure 5.3). In the offline world this is costly and time-consuming. For online auction fans controversial sites such as AuctionWatch and Bidder's Edge automatically trawl hundreds of sites then list the ongoing auctions for particular items.

Price and product comparisons have been made easier for consumers by the development of "shopping bots", computer programs that search many websites for the best deal. Websites such as DealPilot.com enable buyers quickly to compare products, prices and availability. As e-commerce grows, and as people start to use it more to buy bigger-ticket items such as cars and white goods, the role of comparison-shopping agents could become far more significant. But will consumers really be getting the best deal? It will be important to understand in the online world as in the offline one whose side the intermediary is on. The best indicator will often be payment or ownership.

Experience has shown that although some shoppers remain price sensitive, others use brands as the signposts to navigate their way. No change here then. Old-fashioned concepts of trust, reliability and good customer service are still important in cyberspace. A trusted brand may be even more important online because consumers have to pay up-front. They need to be sure that the company will be able to deliver the goods. Consumers are willing to pay a premium to shop at sites that they trust. But even that does not guarantee a fair price. Amazon.com, the biggest name on the web, has been caught fiddling with its prices. In September 2000, customers found that the e-tailer was offering different customers different prices for the same DVD. Amazon quickly admitted that it had been testing prices. It said that although it would continue to test prices, customers charged higher prices would be refunded the difference at the end of every test. But not many people like being used as guinea pigs, especially if they have not given their permission in the first place.

In the offline world many companies engage in dynamic pricing. The airline industry is a good example. Customers seated in the same row may all have paid different prices for their tickets. This is because of different conditions attached to tickets bought in different ways or at different times. If you buy a ticket three months in advance it usually costs less than one purchased minutes before take-off. In Amazon's pricing test, however, there were no differences; some people were simply charged more than others.

When customers use shopping bots to hunt around on the net they still often buy from a market leader, even if it does not offer the lowest prices, according to research by Michael Smith and Erik Brynjolfsson of the Massachusetts Institute of Technology's Sloan School of Management and Joseph Bailey of the University of Maryland. For such reasons, price dispersion continues to exist in cyberspace. Economists usually see this as a sign of an inefficient market.

In a perfect market where products are identical, customers are perfectly informed, there is free market entry, there are a large number of buyers and sellers and no search costs, and all sales are made by the retailer with the lowest price. This means that all prices are driven down to marginal cost. The Internet enables customers to find information more easily and obtain a fuller picture of market prices at much less cost than traditional shoppers can. This would suggest that price dispersion should be narrower in cyberspace than in conventional markets. But this does not seem to be the case.

So far e-tailing has not produced universally lower prices. According to an October 2000 report by the University of California, Los Angeles (UCLA), "Surveying the Digital Future", 58.4% of online buyers think that online prices are as high as offline ones. The figure rises to 75.4% for online users who do not buy on the web. Among those users who do not shop online 58.3% think there is no difference between offline and online prices.

Nor do online auctions offer a perfect form of commerce. Apart from price-fixing and fraud, there is the problem of winner's curse. This is where inexperienced and ill-informed participants overbid for items on sites such as eBay. Paul Klemperer, an Oxford University economist who specialises in auctions, explains the concept to students by auctioning off a jar of pennies. The hapless winner is always the one who overestimates the real value of the jar by the greatest amount, and ends up overpaying the most.

Economists say there is only one situation when winner's curse is not a problem: when there is no objective measure of value. For example, the price of a Van Gogh painting or a rare Spice Girls doll is probably a matter of private taste and opinion. When it comes to most auctions, especially business ones, there is also a great variation in bids. This is because in online auctions as in offline ones, some people may be better informed than others. For example, when bidding for a rail-operating franchise or a radio-bandwidth licence the value is likely to be the same for everyone, but it is not immediately obvious what its market value is at a given time. Online auctions may be most useful when there is uncertainty about the price. They offer a more efficient pricing mechanism but certainly not a perfect one.

Conclusion
The Internet is not the electronic Utopia that the Internet's hippy founders dreamed of. Sellers may love auctions because they are a cheap

way to reach a large pool of buyers. But what about the buyers? eBay's experiments with fixed pricing suggest that for them some of the novelty of online haggling is beginning to wear off. Why waste the time and energy bidding for office supplies or kitchen sinks when the chances are you can buy them from a reputable store for a reasonable price anyway? Amazon's Jeff Bezos thinks fixed prices are here to stay. He says, "Would you want to negotiate the price of the *New York Times* every time you bought it?" The battle for the business exchanges will continue to heat up. But most will capture little of the value they helped to create.

6 Dotty dotcoms

THERE WAS A time, not so long ago, when the word dotcom was revered. It heralded the dawn of a new golden age where dreams would be fulfilled and millionaires made in a day. Enterprising young men and women hurriedly laid out their ambitions in beautifully bound volumes designed to impress the moneymen on the other side of the mahogany desk. In these textured paper tomes they promised such things as "a worldwide Internet portal" or "the perfect global market brand vehicle". How times have changed. Now any eagle-eyed investor would flip past the hyperbole in search of the magic words "path-to-profitability" (P2P), or put simply, "how this business is going to make money". Many dotcoms are finding it hard to raise the money to get off the ground, and many of those that did get established have run out of money and been forced to close their virtual doors, unable to get second-round financing. What happened? Why did so many dotcoms turn out to be dotbombs? And what does the future hold for this once star-spangled sector?

An unhappy affair

No one likes to miss a good party. In the late 1990s everyone was dancing to the Internet beat. "It's like Woodstock," said Rudy Puryear, the former head of Andersen Consulting's e-commerce practice, at the time. You had to be there, man. Like hundreds of others from banks, law firms and consultancies he left his job to join in the fun. Other high-profile departures for dotcoms included Heidi Miller, chief financial officer of Citigroup, who joined Priceline.com, an online reverse-auction site for airline tickets and consumer goods; Jonathan Axelrad, one of Silicon Valley's top lawyers, was snapped up by Idealab!, an Internet incubator; George Shaheen, Andersen Consulting's boss, joined Webvan, an online grocer. PricewaterhouseCooper's e-business unit lost more than half of its consultants. Even McKinsey, the doyen of strategy consultants, experienced a string of defections.

The Internet became a huge magnet, attracting more and more talent and resources. What started as a hippie dream quickly turned into a gold rush. Like the chip boom of the 1970s and the PC explosion in the 1980s, it began in Silicon Valley and reverberated around the world. The catalyst this time was Netscape's public offering in 1995.

Internet start-ups became the new darlings of the stockmarket. Share prices soared. Suddenly, everyone wanted to add the prestigious dotcom suffix to their company name. Traditional firms began converting to the Internet; those that could not manage a complete transformation into an e-business spawned their own dotcom subsidiaries instead. Many firms, though, were motivated as much by the need to attract and retain talented workers as by a plausible business strategy.

But as with other stockmarket infatuations like the one with biotech companies, for example, this one too was short-lived. When the bubble burst after Nasdaq's record close on March 10th 2000 it pounded the whole e-commerce industry, heaping special scorn on e-tailers, business-to-business trading hubs and incubators. At their peak in February 2000, shares in QXL, a pan-European online auction company, were trading at 778 pence on the London Stock Exchange. By April 2001 they had slumped to just 5 pence. Interactive Investor International, a UK-based financial advice site set up in 1995, went public in February 2000 on the London Stock Exchange and Nasdaq. By April 2001 it had been delisted from Nasdaq. Its stock was trading at 20 pence per share at the time compared with 120 pence in June 2000.

As *The Economist* reported in its issue of November 26th 2000, 60 big Internet firms have seen their share prices fall by 90% or more from their peaks, and hundreds more have fallen by more than half. In times like this, many rush to distance themselves from the "irrational" behaviour of the markets. Just as their firms' prospects were never as wonderful as those multibillion-dollar valuations implied a year or so ago, they say, nor are they as poor as their slumping shares now suggest. "It wasn't real then and it's not real now," argues Glen Meakem, chief executive of FreeMarkets, a business-to-business auctioneer that has gone from golden calf to plain brown goat in the market's eyes.

The first part is true, anyway. Those dizzying 90%-plus plunges are from heights reached only briefly, sometimes just for a few weeks in March 2000. Some of the firms trading at a tenth of their peak are still above their prices at the initial public offering. That said, many web firms had assumed that they would be worth more than they now are. And though in some cases a firm can ignore its share price and focus on its business, there are many places where the virtual world of capital markets and the real world of companies' day-to-day operations intersect, sometimes painfully.

Although all publicly traded firms feel pressure from their shareholders to show healthy returns, Internet companies are particularly exposed to the equity markets. This is partly because they tend to be young, unprofitable and dependent on capital infusions to grow. By the same token, their youth, and the youth of the markets they were entering or creating, suggested great growth potential, which is why their shares were valued so highly in the first place.

This disconnect between the cash that firms did not have, and the equity valuations they did, created a dotcom business culture that made equity the currency of the realm. Internet firms paid their employees in part with shares, as they did their suppliers. Their executives were big shareholders and bought other companies with stock, not cash. When the shares were worth a lot, this worked well. Now that they are not, the costs of an equity culture are showing.

The most obvious cost involves stock options. For employees hired during 2000, options have become virtually meaningless, since the "strike" price at which they can be exercised is far above the current market price, placing them deep "under water". Since options were a big reason why people were willing to work the long hours for low pay that many dotcoms required, the market correction has left many firms struggling to hold on to staff.

As a result, firms with depressed shares, from tiny dotcoms to Microsoft, have had to increase their cash salaries, reset strike prices and issue new options. For instance, USinternetworking, an applications service provider, has allowed some employees to trade in their existing, overpriced options for options repriced to current market conditions, at a ratio of two to one. Interestingly, however, many beaten-up firms report that attracting new employees with stock options works as well as ever; at today's strike prices, the options offered by many firms seem a bargain.

Even at November 2000 share prices, many employees who joined before their firm's IPO are still above water. Those who have suffered most are the founders and top executives, who tend to have more of their wealth tied up in options and equity. In one spectacular reversal of fortune, Michael Donahue's stake in InterWorld, a software firm, dropped in value from $448m before the shake-out to less than $12m in 2000. Shelby Bryan, the chief executive of Internet Capital Group, a business-to-business holding company, was once worth nearly $100m. Now he is not even a millionaire.

Even harder hit are those who jumped to the Internet from traditional business. For instance, George Shaheen left the top job at Andersen Consulting to run Webvan in 1999. Webvan then went public and promptly nosedived, sending the value of his compensation package from $285m to $2.7m today. And pity poor Heidi Miller, who left a top job at Citigroup for Priceline, a bargain-finding Internet firm that is now down 90% from when she joined, while Citigroup is up. On November 9th 2000 she packed her bags, disenchanted with her new firm.

The sharp fall in share prices has also had an impact on mergers. For deals within a single industry, a depressed share price may not matter much, since both partners will have dropped by similar amounts, maintaining the same relative difference in valuation between buyer and seller. But for cross-industry deals, relative changes in valuation can turn a buyer into a seller. Cash then becomes king. With the capital markets closed, those firms that do not need money find easy pickings among those that do.

The lucky companies that raised all the money they needed to reach profitability before March 2000, such as Amazon and AskJeeves, are in prime position, able to conserve their equity for a time when it will be worth more. But for those that need more cash now, the price can be high. Buy.com and Webvan may go the way of Pets.com, Furniture.com, Bike.com and Mothernature.com, all of which went bust in November 2000, if they cannot raise the millions of dollars needed to become profitable. eToys, once seen as an e-commerce champion, filed for bankruptcy in February 2001.

"The lesson is to raise money when you don't need it, because it won't be available when you do," says Karl Jacob, founder of Keen.com, which managed to raise $42m in October 2000 thanks to Mr Jacob's Microsoft pedigree and blue-chip backing. Bankers reckon that most of the venture capital now going into previously funded Internet companies is in "down rounds", or valuations below those at which previous investors bought in. This means that those investors are taking a loss, which will soon start to show up in lower returns throughout the venture-capital industry.

Part of the problem is that the favoured dotcom door to capital – the IPO – has temporarily slammed shut, and along with it the preferred exit for venture capitalists. New Internet-related listings are at their lowest in years. Those that do make it are usually forced to cut their offer price. And the whiff of desperation produced by this tends to send the shares tumbling immediately after listing – a phenomenon bankers morbidly describe as a "death spiral".

Rather than sell themselves cheap and risk the agony of a falling price, many firms are choosing to pull their IPOs (see Figure 6.1); cancellations now exceed new listings. Compared with delay, this has the advantage of

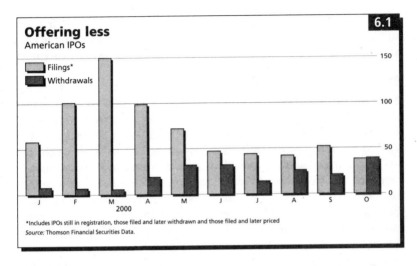

Offering less
American IPOs

6.1

Filings*
Withdrawals

150

100

50

0

J F M A M J J A S O
2000

*Includes IPOs still in registration, those filed and later withdrawn and those filed and later priced
Source: Thomson Financial Securities Data.

freeing the firm from the mandated "quiet period", during which it is
prohibited from marketing itself in anything but the simplest ways, and
allows it to change its business without having to refile reams of legal
documents. But cancellations are risky. Digital Entertainment went bust
soon after pulling its share offering in February 2000; other firms, such as,
iOwn, AltaVista and Techies.com, have had to endure large-scale layoffs
after their listings were pulled.

Worse even than no IPO is a listing that goes horribly wrong. Firms
whose share price falls below $1 for more than 30 days risk being delisted,
a fate from which few return. Dotcoms now on the brink include
PlanetRX and theglobe.com, which was one of the earliest Internet
stockmarket stars.

For most Internet firms, the main task is to spend less and try to claw
their way to profitability. In late 1999 (before the stockmarket correction),
dotcoms tended to operate on the assumption that growth was
everything and more money would be available when it was needed.
Now many have to assume that they may never raise money again until
they are ready to go public, or are bought. Suddenly, cash "burn rates" are
the hottest indicator of health, and they are worrying: on September 30th
2000, some 36 of America's listed Internet firms had less than six months
of cash left, according to Pegasus Research. Some 85 were on track to burn
out within a year. A report by Goldman Sachs said that by mid-2001, only
12–14 of America's 22 publicly traded consumer e-commerce companies
are likely to be around. The projected winners include Amazon.com,

which was predicted to end the year 2000 with "just under $1.2 billion in cash"; eBay, the only profitable e-commerce company, and bn.com, which the report said will not need additional capital soon.

The blame game

When the chips are down it helps to have someone to blame. So a whole host of people took the rap when the fortunes of dotcom companies nosedived. Consultants (always a popular target when things go wrong) got it in the neck with the usual grumbles about "hot air" and "exorbitant fees". Stockmarket analysts were denounced for fuelling the speculative e-commerce bubble. Baby-faced entrepreneurs, once the heroes of the hour, were disgraced for profligate spending on over-ambitious and badly thought-out plans. Somewhere on the list of miscreants, too, were the venture capitalists accused of recklessly throwing money into businesses that had little or no chance of turning a profit.

In Silicon Valley there is a sense of déjà vu. Get-rich-quick games have been played before. Jim Breyer, managing partner of Accel Partners, a leading venture-capital firm, says: "The region has to learn the lesson of excess over and over again." This time round, though, things were more extreme. The business model for start-ups was often not to have a business model – except, perhaps, for a profitable "liquidity event" (public offering). Venture capitalists gave start-ups the cash to collect as many "eyeballs" as possible, to create a lot of hype and then to go public after a year or so, guaranteeing their investors returns of 1,000% or more.

Investment decisions were often made out of a mixture of greed and fear. No one wanted to miss the boat on the next eBay. Theoretically, venture capitalists like entrepreneurs are supposed to be in the business of building and developing sustainable companies as well as bearing the greater burden of risk along the way. But by making an early and often incredibly lucrative exit they shift most of the risk on to the public markets. In the past, venture capitalists typically conducted due diligence on a company before they made an investment. But in the Internet bonanza due diligence often followed the letter of intent.

Bulging portfolios meant that the venture capitalists spread themselves too thinly with less time for mentoring and monitoring, at a time when start-ups needed more support than ever. The entrepreneurs who gave birth to them were still wet behind the ears and faced all the problems of setting up a new company, such as planning, budgeting, managing growth and recruiting the right people. Some of the early spectacular collapses had more to do with mishandling such basics than Nasdaq's slump.

When Boo.com, a spendthrift sports-goods e-tailer, opened its electronic doors in November 1999 it quickly became a symbol of the bold and brash dotcoms. Six months later it became one of online fashion's first victims, the butt of industry jokes and a leading example of how to screw up at a dotcom, big time. Boo described itself as "the first truly international e-commerce site". Based in London, it had offices in New York, Munich, Stockholm, Paris and Amsterdam. The website was available in seven languages and multilingual staff handled queries and requests at its customer call centres, offering free returns to those who were not satisfied with the goods. Its website featured flashy, cutting-edge technology, such as 3D photographs and a zoom facility that allowed customers to focus on different parts of a product and dress mannequins in different outfits.

But by February 2000 the company was in serious trouble. Key staff headed for the door, including Patrik Hedelin, one of Boo.com's three founding members, and Dean Hawkins, the chief financial officer, who left to join Chello Broadband, a Dutch Internet service provider. Its fancy website technology proved to be giving customers too much of a headache. It worked only with high-speed Internet access, something most Europeans do not have. Nevertheless, the company put on a brave face and ploughed on, announcing a marketing partnership with CDnow and another pact with Yahoo!. Time was running out. Boo.com had burned through the $120m worth of initial capital it had raised, spending lavish sums on advertising in glossy magazines like *Details*, *Mademoiselle*, *Glamour* and *Vibe*.

The company said it hoped to receive an emergency cash infusion from its high-profile backers, including Louis Vuitton Moet Hennessy (LVMH), a luxury goods group, Goldman Sachs and J.P. Morgan, investment bankers, and the Benetton family. But it was too late. With no buyer in sight, Boo.com filed for bankruptcy in May 2000 after frittering away $135m. Ernst Malmsten and former model Kajsa Leander, its Swedish founders, said their biggest mistake was not having a strong financial controller in place. Insiders said senior managers were treated to five-star hotels and first-class airline tickets. The company was eventually bought by Fashionmall.com, based in New York, and relaunched in October 2000 as an online community and portal aimed at fashionable 18–30 year-olds with expensive tastes.

Clickmango, an online health-care business promoted by Joanna Lumley, a British actress, became another dotcom casualty in September 2000. The British health site's weekly sales had reached the glorious heights of £2,000 ($3,000), a small fraction of the £25,000 it was spending every week to stay in business.

On the other side of the Atlantic where the e-commerce boom had begun the shake-out was even more intense. By November 2000 the stream of dotcom closures turned into a flood, which swept away companies that appeared to have their markets cornered such as Pets.com, Garden.com and Furniture.com. According to a study by Webmergers, a company based in California that tracks mergers and acquisitions, one-third of the 131 dotcom closures in 2000 took place in October and November that year. Most of them were in the business-to-consumer (B2C) sector and most, 35%, were based in California, the cradle of the Internet revolution. The report said that a further 11% of closures were of companies based in New York and 8% had a European base. However, the report said that despite the seemingly high number of dotcom closures, only a small percentage of the total number of dotcoms in operation had shut down. Webmergers estimated that in November 2000, about 10,000 Internet firms were still in business.

Most of the companies that closed were stuck in the same cash crunch. When Nasdaq's correction began in March 2000 it was back to business basics. On Wall Street this new mood of realism was expressed in phrases such as "path-to-profitability", "Internet infrastructure" and "track record". The attraction of the Internet sector began to wear off and venture capitalists instead put money into companies developing optical telecommunications equipment, wireless technology and software. The newly fledged dotcoms burnt through their start-up cash to establish the business and capture a share of the cybermarket, only to find that second- or third-round venture-capital funding failed to arrive. In some cases, investors decided that it was easier to shut up shop rather than try to convince other buyers to come to the rescue. Buying companies to capture talented staff became less important because as more closures took place, more high-tech staff entered the marketplace and were quickly snapped up again.

Yet there was a positive side to the downturn. Some venture capitalists have a saying: "in a tornado even turkeys fly". The weak companies fell at this first real hurdle, leaving the more robust ones to battle it out in the next round of the e-commerce challenge. Their task is to keep up staff morale and to avoid the self-doubt that comes with a blighted share price. Even the once-giddy venture capitalists are pleased. Start-ups can no longer put their business plans up for auction, and their valuations have therefore dropped significantly. But venture capitalists have not stopped investing altogether. Far from it: in the second quarter of 2000 they put almost $7 billion into Silicon Valley technology companies – a new high at the time.

The shake-out also helped identify some of the items that customers, for now at least, do not want to buy online. Take furniture, for instance. Furniture.com did not overspend on a lavish launch or a sumptuous office in a fashionable area. Instead, it seemed to have a sensible, down-to-earth approach, choosing to locate in suburban Framingham, Massachusetts. It was a pure play but it had warehouses and delivery schemes in place. Furthermore, it had a steady stream of potential customers; the site drew about 1m hits a month. The company shared some of the problems of the early dotcom casualties, including delivery glitches, a cash crunch and unhappy customers. But its main problem was getting enough people to buy the goods in the first place. People were visiting the site to get ideas and compare prices, but they were not making a purchase.

Other companies fighting for a slice of the furniture market have also landed on the scrap heap, including Living.com, which briefly enjoyed the backing of Amazon, and HomePortfolio.com. According to Forrester Research, only 4% of furniture sales will be online by 2005. This is a tiny amount compared with software sales and music. It is predicted that more than half of software sales and nearly half of music purchases will be made online by then.

Cars are another commodity that people seem not to want to buy on the web or at least not yet. When Maryann Keller, head of the automotive business at Priceline.com, left her job she said the company's experience with selling cars online had been a failure. She also said that the Internet might never prove to be a viable channel for purchasing high-cost goods. In Brazil, though, it is a different story. General Motors (GM) reported that it sold over 8,000 Chevrolet Celta cars there via the web between mid-September and early December 2000. The company said that more than 80% of its expected 25,000 sales of the car in that country would take place online during the first part of 2001. Most of the online purchases have been made at kiosks located at GM dealerships around the country. The facility allows shoppers to customise, finance, purchase and track the progress of their new car as it is being assembled. They can do exactly the same from home, but GM found that customers appear to be more comfortable walking into a showroom to do it.

House buying is also an activity that is unlikely to be transferred to the web any time soon. Estate agents initially rushed to the Internet to advertise their property portfolios and services, but it seems that for now at least the Internet will remain little more than an electronic shop window. Prospective buyers are increasingly likely to do their research online first but the actual negotiations will, unfortunately for the buyer, still involve some old-fashioned sales schmooze.

A question of ethics

When closing the virtual doors for good some dotcoms have behaved responsibly, managing to leave enough money in the bank to cover their debts. But generally such examples have been few and far between. Many simply switched off the lights, leaving customers and suppliers in the dark. Writing in the *E-Commerce Times*, Keith Regan gives the example of ShopLink, a company that operated mainly in New York and southern New England, running errands for people who, as the phrase goes, are "cash-rich and time-poor". When it hit the wall the CEO simply e-mailed a letter to customers and posted a copy on the web page, announcing the company's closure and instructing anyone with any outstanding dry cleaning or prescriptions to collect to do so themselves. The letter supplied the names and addresses of the companies ShopLink had used. It also informed customers that as a security precaution they should change any garage door access codes previously supplied for delivery purposes. The letter noted that there would be no one available to answer customer calls.

A flippant disregard for customers is one thing, but in the scramble to make money some dotcoms have dabbled in more questionable practices. In the old economy where profits mattered, creative accounting was usually taken to mean sprucing up the bottom line. The activities of some dotcoms have brought a new meaning to the term.

In one well-known case, Joanne O'Rourke Hindman, the former CEO of iVillage, a women's website, filed a suit against the company, claiming she was dismissed after questioning what she called the company's "marginal and even inappropriate" accounting practices. She alleged that the company was recognising revenue prematurely, in some cases even before the letters of intent were signed. The company dismissed the claims as "groundless" and a spokesman said that neither the Securities and Exchange Commission (SEC) nor the company's auditors had raised any objections to iVillage's financial statements.

According to a March 2000 report by *Fortune* magazine "New Ethics or No Ethics", Priceline.com is a company that has boosted its figures by reporting the entire sales price paid by a customer when in reality it keeps only a small percentage of that amount. The company has defended its strategy, saying that, unlike a travel agency, it has assumed the full risk of ownership as the "merchant of record" and it can determine the size of its spread. Travel agencies do not own the tickets they sell and operate on a fixed commission basis. The SEC has so far supported this logic, although critics have called it a borderline practice.

Some online media companies have reported their barter deals as revenue – a practice that underwriters have encouraged to boost revenue and justify a higher valuation. According to GAAP (Generally Accepted Accounting Principles) rules barter transactions should be recorded at "fair value", but the rules do not specify how this should be determined. If a company has no history of earning cash for the same advertising space how can a figure be confidently worked out? According to a survey by PricewaterhouseCoopers for the Internet Advertising Bureau, barter accounted for 6% of all Internet advertising in the second quarter of 1999. Jupiter Media Metrix said the real figure could be as high as 15%.

Juggling with marketing costs has proved an even more popular game for some Internet companies. Freebies, discounts and other gimmicks are often used as a way to attract customers, but what is the impact on the bottom line? When AOL was distributing free diskettes it tried to hide the costs as a marketing expense. It said at the time that because subscribers usually signed up for at least two years it was fair to consider the cost of acquiring them as an investment and record it as if it took place over two years. This made the company look profitable on paper but led to more than $350m in deferred costs. The company eventually decided to go back to charging acquisition costs when they occurred. But the practice has continued elsewhere.

Amazon.com, Drugstore.com and the late eToys are among the online retailers that have been playing games with fulfilment costs, the expenses associated with warehousing and packaging. Traditional retailers usually record this expense on their income statements as cost of goods sold. But some online retailers prefer to put fulfilment costs into selling, general and administrative expenses. The practice does not affect the bottom line, but it does make gross margins look at lot healthier than they otherwise would. It also enables companies to disguise some of their huge operational costs.

In 1999, the SEC asked the Financial Accounting Standards Board (FASB) to find a way to standardise the way companies keep their books. But the FASB concluded that it was too complicated to create a universal standard because companies were accounting for their expenses in so many different ways. It said that companies could record fulfilment costs as the cost of goods sold. Alternatively, they could choose to put them somewhere else on the income statement. This being the case, companies should then provide a breakdown of the exact costs in a footnote. Amazon.com, Drugstore.com and eToys said then that they do not plan to change their accounting practices.

Some dotcoms stand accused of juggling other figures too, namely the number of visitors to their websites. The figures play a vital role in assessing a company's value and are used to work out advertising charges. Online firms that can demonstrate that their users spend a long time viewing their sites will be able to charge more for advertising. A report by PricewaterhouseCoopers in November 2000 said that every dotcom company it examined had either overstated or understated the number of site visitors. It said this resulted from the lack of an industry standard for measuring web traffic rather than deliberate mistakes. The study showed that different companies define the figures in different ways. Some included visits from automated comparison-shopping sites. Others counted repeated attempts to download the same page as multiple visits. PricewaterhouseCoopers said ABCelectronic should be recognised as the standard body for measuring Internet traffic. It is mostly used by the advertising industry at present.

Not all dotcoms were out to hoodwink their customers or their investors. But Internet executives have had a powerful incentive for inflating the figures with accounting techniques, most of them perfectly legal at the time. Even a slight increase in reported revenue could give a massive boost to market capitalisation and all the benefits that brings for stockholders. And there was no established method for valuing an Internet company.

Warren Buffett, an investment expert, said that if he were a business school professor he would quiz all his students on how to value Internet companies. He said he would fail everyone who did not leave the answer-sheet blank. Investors initially argued that online companies could not be measured by traditional methods used for valuing bricks-and-mortar companies. Some venture capitalists said they used similar methods to the ones used for valuing real estate where key considerations are location and the price of similar properties in the same area. Estate agents are well-known for pushing up the prices of property to receive a bigger piece of the cookie when it crumbles.

So the dotcom phenomenon became known as the dotcon. Some founders had their eyes on the exit as soon as they entered the door. They had no interest in building a profitable company. They saw themselves as investors rather than entrepreneurs. Their focus was on the IPO. They would cash out and then jump on to the "next big thing". Venture capitalists even have a name for such companies: burgers – made to be flipped. Some CEOs have been criticised for unloading their stock in a scramble to cash in with scant regard to ordinary investors.

In America, the process of pumping up the value of stock with press releases and then watching investors push it even higher became known as "the K-tel effect". Philip Kives, CEO of K-tel, a company that produces music compilations, did just that, selling off $41m worth of stock when the price skyrocketed between May and June 1998 after he had announced a new Internet strategy. The company was left facing a shareholder class-action suit, charging that Mr Kives and other company executives withheld information about the company's financial situation.

Handing out friends-and-family stock to key customers and industry representatives is another dotcom practice that has been questioned. This is something technology companies do all the time. In ordinary circumstances, it may make perfect business sense to reward people who have helped the company and who may be valuable in the future. But during the Internet bonanza things look a little different. For example, when a company awards such stock to a customer who has helped it look good on paper by signing a lucrative contract a few months before a successful IPO, the ethics are a little murkier. Usually friends and family means just that and the sums involved are not enough to go out and buy a second home. But in these particular circumstances customers, suppliers, vendors or other industry bigwigs could turn around the stock on the day of the IPO and sell in the open market for a quick profit.

Concern has also grown about the composition of dotcom boards. Compared with traditional ones the differences are striking. According to a study of 39 Internet companies by the Investor Responsibility Research Centre, a non-profit corporate governance organisation, dotcom boards are much smaller than those of a typical s&p 500 company, comprising seven directors as opposed to 11. Many big-name dotcoms have small boards. Amazon has six directors, with two company executives. Yahoo! also has six, including three executives. Dotcoms also have a smaller percentage of non-executive directors, about one-half compared with two-thirds on a traditional board.

In another study on Internet boards, carried out in 1999 by the US Board Services Practice of Spencer Stuart, an international executive search firm, one-quarter of executive directors are aged under 40, almost unheard of in old-economy companies, and only 6% fall into the over-55 category. Even the "grey hairs", the non-executive directors on the board, are comparatively young. Their average age is 51, some ten years younger than their counterparts on the boards of s&p 500 companies, according to the survey. There are far fewer non-executive directors on Internet boards. They are not necessarily made up of the founders, owners or managers of the company; more often these seats are taken by venture capitalists. There is also a lower ratio of non-executive to executive directors. Cyberspace has not proved to be the cutting edge for women to show off their managerial skills – only 18% of the Internet companies surveyed had a female director.

Critics say this amounts to a corporate governance disaster. Shareholders will increasingly want to have their say if things continue to go wrong in this nascent sector, as many analysts are predicting. Dotcom CEOs speak with great bravado about creating new value by breaking old rules. This is fine provided the old ones are obsolete. It does not mean reinventing the wheel. Bricks-and-mortar companies have had at least two decades of experience in corporate governance issues. Some of the lessons they have learnt are invaluable. Here are some questions for dotcom CEOs who risk throwing the baby out with the bath water to ask:

- Is a "mean and lean" board the best for my company? Many argue that it is. Razorfish, an Internet consulting firm, has an eight-member board made up of five executive and three non-executive directors. Jeff Dachis, the CEO, says dotcoms need small boards that can move fast. He reckons they should consist of "aggressive, bright people who 'get it' rather than people with a corporate background who may be more interested in preserving the status quo".
- How will I staff my audit and compensation committees? Small boards often have difficulty staffing their committees. New listing requirements by the New York Stock Exchange and Nasdaq mean that public companies need to have three non-executive directors, including one with financial management experience, on their audit committees. Many dotcoms have only two non-executive directors on the entire board. Often they do not have anyone qualified to sit on the audit committee. Mr Malmsten immediately lamented the lack of a financial controller when his company, Boo.com, went under.

- ◪ How independent are the non-executive directors? If the venture capitalists do not have the time for the careful monitoring and mentoring, who else will be there to offer advice when things go wrong? How impartial will their advice be?
- ◪ What about the "grey hairs" on the board? Are they really old fuddy-duddies who don't "get" the new economy, as Mr Dachis says, or do they have seasoned business experience to offer? Many of the 30-something dotcom entrepreneurs have had no experience in running their own business. It may be fashionable to pretend otherwise, but in many respects an Internet business is just like any other start-up. Examples such as Boo.com show that even the trendiest businesses need to get a grip on the basics.
- ◪ Do Internet boards have to be the "men's clubs" of yesteryear? Most of the early Internet companies were founded by techies and venture capitalists, both fields in which men far outnumber women. It is therefore not surprising to find so few women on the boards. Things may be different in the future if there is a change from executive-dominated boards to ones comprising a more diverse group of non-executive directors.

But before coming down too hard on the entrepreneurs, what about the other people who fuelled the Internet frenzy? Research analysts are not as independent as some might think. Investment banks and consulting firms, such as Jupiter, sell their services to many of the companies that their analysts cover. Such basic conflicts of interests are not new, but the Internet mania exacerbated the problem.

Anthony Noto, an analyst at Goldman Sachs who is widely respected for his views on the dotcom sector, came under fire in the *Wall Street Journal* for listing the financial health of Internet companies. The three-tiered list, which separates companies that are in the pink from those with financial problems, turned out to be top heavy with Goldman Sachs's underwriting clients. Research by Matthew Hayward, a professor at London Business School, shows that companies get higher ratings from analysts at firms they bank with than others. The Internet has created an even more alarming trend: some analysts own stock in many of the companies they cover.

The wild fluctuations of Nasdaq clearly show the herd mentality that has so far governed the Internet sector. Unfavourable remarks from a well-respected analyst such as Mr Noto can drastically affect a company. Institutional investors may know how to read between the lines of such reports or can simply pick up the phone to ask for the straight story on a company. Good analysis with supporting data may not be enough even for careful readers. Besides, most dotcom decision-makers conditioned to working at Internet speed usually go by the bullet points. Analysts need to be more open about their financial relationships with the companies they choose to support or condemn.

Consultants

For most industries that run into trouble, the only sure winners are consultants. Cleaning up other people's messes – or at least promising to – is usually one of the few recession-proof businesses around. But not with the Internet. As dotcoms plummeted in 2000, their consultants fell even faster. The share prices of many of the top 15 listed Internet consultancies dropped by 90% or more during the year, making even e-tailers look good. Among them they laid off more than 3,200 people in the last three months of 2000, including 380 at Xpedior on December 5th. On March 26th 2001 Xpedior filed a request for its shares to be delisted on Nasdaq. Several others face Nasdaq delisting, if bankruptcy does not come first.

The reasons for this demise are familiar, but rarely seen to such a degree: reckless overexpansion, profligacy, poor management, lack of focus and hype. Some of the consultancies never outgrew their trendy web-design origins, even as demand shifted to serious corporate strategy and database programming. Too many staked their fortunes on dotcoms and ended up swallowing unpaid bills and worthless equity. Others assumed that there would always be more business than they could handle and waited too long to build a marketing and sales staff.

"Roll-ups", such as ixl and marchfirst, which were formed by the merger of mid-sized firms and the acquisition of smaller ones, became case studies in failed integration and culture conflicts. Worse, these companies spent as if they were actually worth the many billions that their share prices fleetingly implied. The story of the half-tonne dot on the "i" that fell off ixl's huge sign at its magnificent Atlanta headquarters will haunt the firm for the rest of its (probably short) life. It cut 350 jobs in September 2000.

But as with shake-outs in the rest of the dotcom world, the cloud has a silver lining. What was once a baffling industry, with dozens of firms all promising e-business transformation and transcendental strategic thinking, is now reduced to a rather more digestible shape. Naturally, several losers will go bust; then there are the struggling firms that need time to stabilise before they can take on another big project; and atop

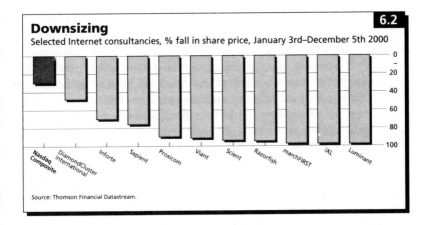

Downsizing   6.2
Selected Internet consultancies, % fall in share price, January 3rd–December 5th 2000

Source: Thomson Financial Datastream.

this pile are a few relatively solid companies whose main crime is being in the same business as the likes of IXL.

How to tell them all apart? Sadly, a glance at consultants' share prices (see Figure 6.2) does not inspire much confidence in any of them: even the best lost more than half its value during 2000. But in many cases this says more about the absurd hopes of investors, dazzled by the growth of web-consulting, than about the industry itself.

At the start of 2000, marchFIRST alone was worth nearly $13 billion, not much less than the consulting arm of PricewaterhouseCoopers, one of the big five accounting firms, which was valued at about $18 billion in September 2000 when Hewlett-Packard made a play for it. Not bad, considering that marchFIRST was losing more than $100m a quarter and sinking further into the red with each day. In April 2001, marchFIRST filed for Chapter 11 bankruptcy protection after selling some assets and laying off staff.

A better indicator of success is how far consultancies have managed to distance themselves from their dotcom origins. An analysis published in December 2000 by Greg Gore of W.R. Hambrecht, an investment bank, shows that the shake-out in the business has divided it into two groups, which he dubs "Tier One" and "The Rest". Tier One firms, which include DiamondCluster International, Sapient, Scient, Proxicom and Inforte, during 2000 shifted their business more than the others to big traditional firms that tend to contract out big projects and pay their bills on time.

But cosying up to the *Fortune* 500 is not enough to save the consultancies. In March 2001, Sapient said it would cut its workforce by 720 people, or about 20%. In December 2000, Scient announced plans to

123

cut 25% of its workforce, or 460 jobs. And in March 2001, Proxicom said that it would cut 227 jobs, or 19% of its workforce. The dotcom crunch has affected old bricks-and-mortar firms, too. With fewer venture-funded start-ups threatening to put them out of business, big traditional companies feel in less of a panic to do something. So they are spending less on web-strategy consultants, and doing more work internally (it is also a lot easier to find dotcom refugees who are only too happy to have a little job security these days). Revenue growth from such customers, which should now be the bread and butter of the business, rose by only 4% in the third quarter of 2000, reckons Mr Gore. That is not terrible by traditional consulting standards, but far below the Internet consultancies' aspirations a year earlier.

Meanwhile, the technology industry has grown up. Projects that once needed to be hand-crafted by outside experts can now be bought as off-the-shelf offerings from firms such as Ariba and i2. The flashy web designs that were the hallmark of "nose-ring" New York firms such as Razorfish, which announced 400 job cuts, a reduction of about 25% of its workforce, in February 2001, are now seen as slow and confusing; Yahoo!'s credo of fast, functional and boring has won the day. Nokia chose Razorfish to design the front end of its first website, but when the time came to build the back-end links to the rest of its business it chose NerveWire, which is run by former consultants with Cambridge Technology Partners, an older, more conservative company.

Mr Gore expects most of the companies in the bottom half of the industry to fail before they can turn around. As for the rest, the future may be brighter than their share-price falls suggest. There is still plenty of work to go round. Moreover, for all their advantages, the big five traditional consultancies are seen as unwieldy; and they suffer from a reputation for pitching a partner's grand strategy to clients, then leaving them with ill-trained junior people to do the work. There is a place for specialised consultancies that focus on just a few industries. None of them, however, should expect to be worth $13 billion again any time soon.

Conclusion

Like all fairy tales this one, too, begs a happy ending. Some investors have struck it rich. But most were paper millionaires who watched their fortunes slip away. Many discovered that instead of a pot of gold the receivers were waiting for them at the end of their rainbow. One thing is certain: things are likely to get much worse before they get any better. So what are the management lessons to be learnt?

7 Winning the war for talent

HOW TO RECRUIT and keep the best workers is one of the biggest challenges facing many firms. What can they do about it?

In a Dilbert cartoon strip the character pokes fun at the management axiom "people are our greatest asset". In the world of e-commerce, finding the right people is crucial. This starts right at the top: the companies that do well have innovative leaders who are willing to take risks. It applies at all levels. According to research carried out by Andersen Consulting and the Economist Intelligence Unit, some 80% of executives say that by 2010 attracting and retaining the right people will be the most important strategic consideration for companies.

Jeff Bezos, chief executive of Amazon, says one of the biggest constraining factors for his company over the past four years has been "having enough smart, hard-working, talented, passionate people to execute our vision". Michael Dell of Dell Computer says that finding and retaining the right people is a top priority.

Organising for the e-economy

Perks and loyalty bonuses aside, nothing is more appealing for the typically young, creative, well-educated and driven people who make up the ranks of the e-economy than being part of a successful team. And what that boils down to is good management. Boo.com seemed to have it all – money, talent and ideas – but it collapsed because it was a badly managed business. So before embarking on a new recruitment strategy, it is worth thinking about what sort of organisational structure will "free the entrepreneurial spirit in your company", as Gary Hamel, a management guru, put it in his article "Bringing Silicon Valley Inside" (*Harvard Business Review*, September–October 2000).

Many companies, especially large ones, still structure their business on a pyramid model, with the employees at the bottom and the boss at the top. Fritz Lang gave an early glimpse of this top-down world in his silent film epic "Metropolis". Hordes of workers dressed in similar shabby clothes scuttle around below ground while their bosses live in luxurious skyscrapers. Similarly, life in a large firm can be a dehumanising experience as the experiences of the cartoon character Dilbert clearly show. Working days are spent in petty battles with fellow cubicle inmates or trying to make sense of the latest management craze.

By contrast, the 21st-century company is more likely to look like a web that links partners, employees, external contractors, suppliers and customers. The management structure will be flat, allowing the free-flow of ideas, capital and talent. What about titles? Many dotcoms decided to do away with them altogether, in the belief that this will conserve creative energy by encouraging co-operation and preventing turf wars and promotion battles. Often the changes are more cosmetic. It is still clear who owns the company and therefore who calls the final shots. Other online companies have spawned new titles such as "chief talent scout" and "director of consumer delight and loyalty", a position created at Reflect.com.

In theory, traditional companies should have a lead over start-ups because they have strong brands, an established customer base and existing logistics systems. But decades of entrenched culture often means the organisational challenges are even greater. One role that deserves special consideration in the age of e-commerce is that of the IT manager.

The IT manager – geek or visionary?

A decade or so ago many companies decided to deal with the terrifying topic of "machines and men" by creating a new post: chief information officer (CIO) or IT manager. The hope was that this newfangled executive would respond to day-to-day technical problems and plan ahead for the coming technological revolution. The revolution is now in full swing. IT is no-longer the exclusive domain of the company geek or nerd. In the so-called new economy everyone from CEO to line manager is expected to speak and understand the language of technology. So where does this leave the CIO? Who should be responsible for IT strategy in the new economy?

Far from being obsolete, Michael Earl, a professor of information management at London Business School, reckons that the role of the CIO is being enhanced by the Internet ("Are CIOS Obsolete?", *Harvard Business Review*, March–April 2000). CIOS often initiated the first e-commerce projects and were invited to join business-strategy task-forces. They were charged with, among other things, acquiring Internet start-ups and hunting for joint venture partners.

According to Mr Earl's survey of 90 CIOS from around the world, more than 75% said they were on the board or on the executive committee of their organisations. Most CIOS said their powers had increased in recent years and they received stronger support from senior management.

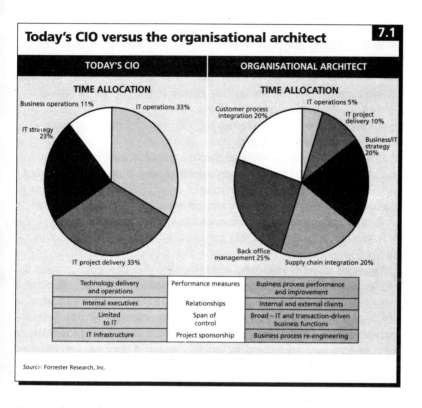

Today's CIO versus the organisational architect 7.1

TODAY'S CIO	ORGANISATIONAL ARCHITECT
TIME ALLOCATION	**TIME ALLOCATION**

Today's CIO:
- Business operations 11%
- IT operations 33%
- IT strategy 23%
- IT project delivery 33%

Organisational Architect:
- Customer process integration 20%
- IT operations 5%
- IT project delivery 10%
- Business/IT strategy 20%
- Supply chain integration 20%
- Back office management 25%

Technology delivery and operations	Performance measures	Business process performance and improvement
Internal executives	Relationships	Internal and external clients
Limited to IT	Span of control	Broad – IT and transaction-driven business functions
IT infrastructure	Project sponsorship	Business process re-engineering

Source: Forrester Research, Inc.

Companies such as BP, J.C. Penney and Johnson and Johnson have moved their CIOs into the ranks of senior management. Reporting lines are also shifting to reflect this change. In many companies the CIO has traditionally reported to the chief finance officer (CFO). Increasingly, they are reporting directly to the CEO.

According to research by Forrester, at least two other factors besides the Internet are changing the role of the CIO: globalisation, and a new generation of technology-savvy managers who do not need lengthy explanations about computer basics. Forrester sees a new enhanced role emerging for the CIO as an "organisational architect". This "catalytic" CIO will help shape the technology agenda in the boardroom, using IT to make it easier to do business with the company and to re-engineer the back-office functions, says Forrester. (See Figure 7.1.)

Will CIOs be the new CEOs or chief operating officers (COOs) of the future? It is possible. Technologists with poor communication and management skills are facing an increasingly bleak corporate future.

What is called for in the new economy is a combination of skills, including a firm grasp of technology. As Jack Rockart, director of the Centre for Information Research at MIT's Sloan School of Management, puts it: "All good CIOs today are business executives first and technologists second." Some leading examples include the following.

- Dawn Lepore, CIO at Charles Schwab, who led the company's move into online trading.
- Gary Reiner, CIO at General Electric, who manages information technology and the company's procurement programme, working with suppliers to get them online.
- Peter Solvnik, CIO at Cisco, who manages the company's online sales and supply chain. He spends half his time developing relationships with external partners.

The roles of other company executives are also changing to meet the challenges of the 21st century. The CFO is expected to be more than just a bean counter. Many of the more mundane accounting tasks can now be performed by software programs. At Oracle, a company that develops such programs, employees fill in expense reports over the intranet, saving time and money and speeding up the payment process. Larry Carter, Cisco's CFO, along with John Chambers, the CEO, has exploited technology to developed the "virtual close". This means the company can close its books in one day. It can also generate hourly updates on revenue, product margins, discounts and bookings.

Using technology to do the job will allow the CFO to concentrate on the wider issues of building the business. This may include acting as a venture capitalist, funding innovation inside and outside the company and acting as a deal-maker with strategic partners. Thomas Meredith, Dell Computer's former CFO, moved on to become managing director of Dell Ventures, responsible for millions of dollars of investment.

The new CFO may also be called upon to be a corporate strategist and a risk manager. Being able to explain the company's finances to Wall Street and in front of the television cameras will be additional strings to the CFO's bow.

Knowledge management is often seen as another fad and a sure way to run up a fat bill from a consultant. Yet few executives would disagree that talent, expertise and other human resources are invaluable to a company. So appointing someone to harness knowledge might not seem such a daft idea. It involves setting up an internal job market, and matching the right people with the right project at the right time. New hires may expect to have several careers at a company and will want to find a company flexible enough to allow their personal development. Alan Kantrow, chief knowledge officer at Monitor Group, a management consultancy, says: "We aren't building organisational citadels. Like nomads, we pitch tents and fight battles, then fold up tents and move on."

One post that is probably destined for the dustbin is that of COO. It used to be seen as a crucial role that freed the CEO from the day-to-day running of the company to focus on broader strategies. But it is beginning to fall out of favour. Some consultants say it is another needless layer of bureaucracy that separates the CEO from the business. At General Electric, Jack Welch prefers to appoint CEOs to run each operating unit.

What about the CEO? What will it take to be a successful leader in the e-economy? Certainly technophobes need not apply. The CEO will be expected to grasp not just the rudiments of IT but also the implications of the Internet and how it can be used for competitive gain. Esther Dyson says that only committed Internet users can be truly effective online providers. She advises recalcitrant CEOs to take the plunge, "getting their feet wet and their hands dirty in the world of online commerce". Globalisation means the modern CEO should expect to learn foreign languages and to understand how to operate in different business climates.

However, mastering these skills will not guarantee a job for life or even the current average tenure, which is nine years. In future CEOs may not last half that time, especially if they are given performance-related pay. CEOs of dotcoms have had a particularly tough time. They may have had the vision and mustered the resources to get the business off the ground, but when the going gets tough investors may want a new pair of hands to steer the company towards profit. Even if the company is doing well, great visionaries do not always have the skills or interest to handle an established company. This sounds frightening, and it is. If the pace of change continues at anything like its present rate, Andy Grove, CEO of Intel, will be right in thinking that only the paranoid will survive.

Churning at the top

As *The Economist* reported on March 15th 2001, corporate bosses are being hired and fired like never before, and many more will go as the economic slowdown in America bites. Why is it proving so hard to find good leaders these days?

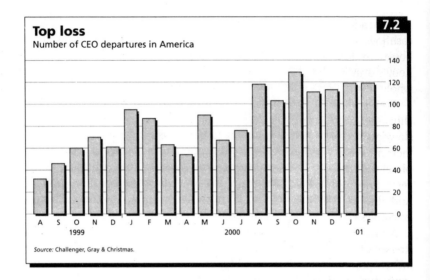

Top loss
Number of CEO departures in America

7.2

Source: Challenger, Gray & Christmas.

In summer 2000, the venerable *Harvard Business Review* published an article, "Don't Hire the Wrong CEO", by Warren Bennis and James O'Toole, two American academics, about a phenomenon they described as "CEO churning". Corporate bosses, they alleged, were coming and going at an unprecedented rate. They had not by then seen half of it. Since the article was published, the rate of churn has increased sharply.

In February 2001, 119 CEOs left their jobs at sizeable American companies, according to data compiled by Challenger, Gray & Christmas, an outplacement firm based in Chicago. That was 37% more than in the same month a year earlier. According to Challenger, departures in the last six months of 2000 were over 40% up on the first six months of the year (see Figure 7.2).

As the economic slowdown in America continues, more and more heads can be expected to roll. Investors (and the boards that represent them) will become less patient with bosses who cannot produce results that exceed those of the previous accounting period. Their patience will be the more frayed because few of them (or of the bosses themselves) can remember anything like it. It's a rare chief executive who was in the job a decade ago, the last time America and Europe experienced recession.

The impact of disappointing results is already visible. A rising proportion of the CEO departures are coming from dotcom companies. Many of them were enticed to the job with the carrot of shares or share options. When the dotcom stockmarket bubble burst, some of those high-fliers headed for nests where they could command a more reliable cashflow. In Europe, four of the leading Internet companies lost their bosses in February 2001 alone, while in America in March 2001 Tim Koogle announced his resignation as CEO of Yahoo!, a bellwether for the whole sector.

Even so, dotcom disappointments account for only a small part of the churning – 20% in America in February 2001. Writing before the economic slowdown had even begun, Mr Bennis and Mr O'Toole maintained that there are two more fundamental reasons for the phenomenon: in the first place, the job of the CEO has become much more demanding in recent years; and second, companies are getting worse at choosing their bosses. Add that to an across-the-board recession, and the churning of chief executives could soon begin to have a distinctly rancid flavour.

A number of changes in the business environment are adding to the stresses of the top job, and increasing the fall-out rate. The flattening of the corporation, for example, that was such a feature of corporate restructuring in the 1990s, left those in charge with a wider span of control. Instead of typically having four or five people reporting directly to them, bosses have come to have a more demanding eight or nine.

At the same time, globalisation has forced chief executives to travel more in order to keep in touch with their far-flung empires. Chris Jones, the 45-year-old chief of J. Walter Thompson, a global advertising agency, resigned in January 2001 after suffering a life-threatening DVT (deep vein thrombosis) on a flight from New York to Geneva. Long-haul fliers are thought to be particularly susceptible to DVT, and CEOs of global companies cannot easily avoid long-haul flights.

Wayne Sanders, the CEO of Kimberly-Clark, a paper maker, has tried to reduce the risk to him by delegating much of his travel to his number two. In February, he told the *Wall Street Journal* that the turning point came on the first day of a 15-day trip to Asia. At one in the morning, he found himself exhausted, unable to sleep, sucking a Snickers bar and thinking, "I'm in trouble."

The need to be on top of every new development in information technology is also putting new strains on bosses, most of whom were brought up in the pre-computer era. Some companies are trying to circumvent the problem by appointing a leader who is already IT-literate. Tom Glocer, the 41-year-old who was due to take over in July 2001 as the boss of Reuters, for example, used to write simulation software when a lawyer in New York. Few geeks, however, yet seem to come with the full range of talents considered essential for the leader of a large corporation.

The spate of mega-mergers in recent years has also added to the churn. When two companies become one there is room for only one boss. Despite initial devotion to a harmonious future together, one or other usually gets the elbow. On January 24th 2001, for example, John Mack, a former head of Morgan Stanley (who became joint head of the firm created by the investment bank's 1997 merger with Dean Witter) resigned – leaving the top job to his co-chief, Dean Witter's Philip Purcell. In such cases, the dear departed soon come into the sights of headhunters and disaffected boards elsewhere.

Moreover, the period immediately after a merger is particularly stressful and can give the final push to a CEO teetering on the edge of resignation. Jacques Bougie, the 53-year-old head of Alcan, resigned on January 10th, only a few months after the Canadian company had bought Algroup, a Swiss aluminium maker. Mr Bougie said that he wanted to "return to activities I have put aside".

As stockmarkets have declined, however, the financing of M&A deals has become less attractive. As a result, their number has fallen sharply in 2001 and their modest impact on the rate of CEO churn will have correspondingly diminished.

Bad choices

It is the job of companies' boards to choose new leaders, and several things prevent them from getting better at it. For a start, the board invariably includes the old CEO, a person whose motives for choosing a successor can rarely be entirely pure. The more successful (and powerful) the CEO, the more influence he has in making that choice, a formula that can lead to disaster.

Take Coca-Cola. A few years ago, when Roberto Goizueta, the company's much admired leader, knew he was dying of cancer, the board chose Doug Ivester, his number two, to succeed him. Mr Ivester had been Mr Goizueta's chief financial officer and also, say Messrs Bennis and O'Toole, "emotionally inept". When hundreds of Belgians were poisoned by the company's products in 1999, it took Mr Ivester a week before he decided to cross the Atlantic and show that he cared about customers.

How could the company have chosen such a wrong 'un? The two American academics believe it was because the directors were keen to honour the dying man's wishes, and Mr Ivester was his "fair-haired boy". In any case, Mr Ivester lasted less than 18 months in the job.

Mr Bennis, a professor at the University of Southern California's Marshall School of Business, says that when they have to choose a new leader, boards "typically go into a kind of collective trance, rhapsodising about 'leadership' and the big need for it without ever taking even the first steps to define what they mean by the term". If pushed, they refer to quantifiable things – paper qualifications, for example, or breadth of experience. Those who appreciate that great leaders must have immeasurable qualities as well tend to turn to outside headhunters for help.

Boards are further hindered in making good choices by two well-embedded misconceptions. The first is the enduring idea that leaders are somehow born and not made: that genetic make-up counts for more than training and experience.

The second was most famously raised in an article by a Harvard professor, Abraham Zaleznik, in 1977 in which he argued that, "Because leaders and managers are basically different, the conditions favourable to one may be inimical to the growth of the other" – ie, long experience as a manager is poor training for a leader. Over time, this encouraged boards to look outside their own organisations for CEOs more than they might otherwise have done.

Zaleznik's point may have been valid in the 1970s when firms were full of managers who did little more than sift information. It is not so true today. The corporate restructuring of the 1990s has squeezed out most such jobs. Corporate managers now have responsibility for bits of their group's profit and loss at a much earlier stage in their career. No longer is their experience "inimical to the growth" of a leader, if it ever was.

In any case, some of the most successful leaders of recent years have had no working experience outside their own organisation: Jack Welch of GE, for instance, (*Time* magazine's "CEO of the 20th century") joined the company in 1960 and was due to retire in 2001; Sir Brian Pitman, who led Lloyds TSB at a time in the 1990s when it was one of the best-performing companies in Europe, joined the bank in 1952 and never worked anywhere else.

More disruptive to the search for good leaders is the widespread belief that they are born (and/or bred), but not made. This belief leads to extensive efforts to find the "qualities" that all great leaders have in common. History books are trawled for hints, with kings, war heroes and explorers popularly held up as role models.

Robert Scott and Sir Ernest Shackleton, for example, have come to represent two (metaphorical) poles of the "born" leader: Scott the inflexible, distant type who would stop at nothing; Shackleton the charming enthusiast who cared first and foremost for his men. Scott was more popular in the ruthless corporate world of the 1980s, while Shackleton is more the man for today – hence the publication in March 2001 of a book by Margot Morrell and Stephanie Capparell called *Shackleton's Way: Leadership Lessons from the Great Antarctic Explorer*.

These characters from history go in and out of fashion. Early in 2000, Joan of Arc was in; later in the year it was the turn of Elizabeth I, the 16th-century unmarried queen of England who has just been celebrated in two management books: *Elizabeth I, CEO*, by Alan Axelrod, and *Leadership Secrets of Elizabeth I*, by Shaun Higgins and Pamela Gilberd. The fact that they were women has probably pushed Joan's and Elizabeth's cause in an age when corporate leaders are exhorted to expose their "feminine side".

Timid and shy

New theories about the necessary and sufficient qualities of great leaders appear at regular intervals. The latest comes from Jim Collins, co-author of *Built to Last*, a best-selling business book of the mid-1990s. His new book (*Good to Great*, due to be published by HarperCollins in autumn 2001) was trailed in an article, "Level 5 Leadership: The Triumph of Humility and Fierce Resolve", in the *Harvard Business Review* in January 2001.

Mr Collins set out to see whether those companies that made an unexpected transformation from being quite ordinary to being great had anything in common. He scoured databases of corporate results going back to 1965 and found only 11 companies that, on his definition, went through such a transformation. They included Kimberly-Clark, Gillette and Abbott Laboratories.

These firms he then put under the microscope to see what characteristics (if any) they shared. And the only thing he could find was that they had all had leaders who possessed "a paradoxical mixture of personal humility and professional will". All of these leaders were men, and all were a rare mix of "timid and ferocious; shy and fearless". Almost all of them were appointed from inside their organisations.

One of Mr Collins's heroes is Darwin E. Smith who, in 20 years as CEO of Kimberly-Clark, turned an insignificant paper company into a world market leader. "Shy, unpretentious, even awkward", Darwin Smith "seems to have come from Mars," writes Mr Collins. After the bruising from the likes of Hugh McColl, the former marine who browbeat Bank of America into its current mess, and Al "Chainsaw" Dunlap who pulped Scott Paper while laying off thousands of employees and pocketing $100m for himself, the boards of corporate America may be yearning to hear Mr Collins's message: Go search out the meek, for they shall inherit the corporation. Would that it were so easy.

For a start, Mr Collins has excluded a large part of the corporate world from his analysis. The computer industry is too young to register, so there is no mention of its big (and highly successful) egos. And the finance industry is not represented at all.

Mr Collins says, however, that there have been leaders in both industries to support his case. John Morgridge, the man who turned Cisco Systems from an ordinary company into a great one, was, he says, "a quiet, reserved, shy and understated man", as was John Whitehead, the partner who helped make Goldman Sachs great in the late 1970s.

Mr Collins has confined himself to America, because nowhere else are there sufficient data to make a comparable analysis. But Europe's understated ways might have provided him with more examples of his leader "type" than America. A couple of European companies that went from good to great during the 1990s may have had such leaders: Nokia, the Finnish mobile-phone phenomenon, and Aegon, a Dutch insurance company. Aegon's boss, Kees Storm, is a self-effacing Dutchman whose humility, *The Economist* once said, "almost amounts to disdain for the latest fashion", while Nokia's boss, Jorma Ollila, preaches the cause of *nöyryys*, a Finnish word meaning "putting teamwork before individual effort".

Leadership school

There are, of course, some things that corporate leaders do unquestionably have in common. CEOs remain, as they always were, overwhelmingly white, male and over 50. And so do the people who select them. A study of outside directors in Britain, published by PricewaterhouseCoopers in January 2001, reported that even today "almost all non-executive directors are white, male and in their 50s". It is no surprise that people like to choose people like themselves.

In addition, Mr Bennis claims that the vast majority of successful company leaders have remained happily married to the same woman all their lives – although this is far from being without exception. There is a long list of colourful bounders and playboys who have both run and built great companies.

Henry Ford II, the man who revitalised the family-car business after the second world war, ensured that his management methods did not get in the way of his jet-setting lifestyle. And Charles Edward Merrill, founder of Merrill Lynch, was a notorious philanderer known to his friends as "Good Time Charlie". He was so busy having a good time that he did not start the firm that bears his name until he was 54, by which time he was on to his third marriage.

However, boards which look for the umpteen necessary and sufficient qualities of great leaders are largely wasting their time. In its report on *Developing Leadership for the 21st Century*, Korn/Ferry, a recruitment consultancy, rightly wrote: "Business in much of the developed world still pays too much attention to the search for charismatic leadership, rather than engaging in the more difficult but less chancy task of permitting and developing leadership throughout its organisations." Dana Kaminstein, who works on the Wharton School's leadership programme, says that the majority of what is written about leadership "falls into the trap of romanticising the individual".

The one person blamed more than any other for this is Lee Iacocca, the self-promoting head of Chrysler in the 1980s who published a blockbusting biography called, quite simply, *Iacocca*. In practice, Mr Iacocca's record at Chrysler was, at best, mixed, and nothing like as beneficial to shareholders as that of a soft-spoken successor, Bob Eaton, who adroitly sold the company to Daimler-Benz just before the American car maker hit a rocky patch.

The truth is that there are many people within every corporation who are capable of leading it if they are given the right experience and encouraged to develop certain talents. A number of great companies recognise this and either ask business schools like Wharton or Harvard to run special programmes to help them develop leaders internally, or they do it themselves. Aegon, for example, runs such programmes via its own semi-virtual Aegon University, while GE has a much-admired "experienced leadership programme" which includes opportunities for participants to discuss real live issues with the chairman and board members.

There is a danger that such companies end up preparing people to run other companies. GE is a notoriously rich source of American CEOs. And Nabisco Holdings, a big food company, must be getting something right too. In March 2001 it provided its third head of a major corporation in as many months, with the announcement of Richard Lenny's move to Hershey Foods. He follows colleagues who have gone to head Gillette and Campbell Soup.

It is not easy, however, to design effective leadership programmes. How much time should participants spend in the classroom and how much out there "leading" – be it up a rock face or in a virtual business? The value of real experience is well demonstrated by the way in which some of the top consulting firms have become a rich source of CEOs. It is almost as if the experience that consultants gain from hand-holding clients through hard times constitutes the ideal leadership programme.

This is ironic, since top consulting firms themselves tend not to have a leader in the accepted sense, even though they count among the most successful commercial organisations of recent years. Accenture and McKinsey, for instance, are partnerships which choose one partner to become, essentially, *primus inter pares*. Mr Collins suggests that McKinsey did have the sort of leader that he claims is essential to turn a good company into a great one. Marvin Bower, the legendary nonagenarian and *éminence grise* of "The Firm", is so unassuming that he did not even get rid of the irrelevant Mr McKinsey's name and try to replace it with his own.

Undoubtedly, some of the skills of leadership can only be learnt on the job. Many CEOs report, with hindsight, that it took them about 18 months before they felt they had "mastered" their role at the top. But many of the issues that they face are the same (only larger) than those faced by the leader of any small division within their organisation. Today's "empowered" junior managers are far better prepared to become leaders than were their predecessors.

But boards have to be persuaded to support their gradual (and often expensive) process of development. The reward comes when they have to choose a new CEO, a time that for most of them is not far off. By then they will have a pool of talent to choose from, and their final choice can be determined largely by the circumstances of the corporation at the time. That's far better than rushing off on a search for Elizabeth I in drag.

How to be an e-manager
Ten handy hints

Across the desk of anybody writing about management these days pours a torrent of books about running an e-business. Most start off by saying that everything is different – and then talk as though everything was much the same. It is true that the Internet changes the skills required from managers, but not fundamentally so. Anyone who is a good manager can also become a good e-manager.

However, some qualities have become even more important than they used to be. Here, for any manager too busy wrestling with the Internet economy to plough through the literature, are the top ten things you need says *The Economist's* Frances Cairncross, author of a survey on e-management.

1 **Speed.** The list could, perhaps, stop right here. Being quick is more important than being large – indeed, large companies find it hard to be speedy. "There are very few things that the Internet slows down," reflects MIT Media Lab's Michael Schrage. "Companies that take three or four months to reach a decision find that others have redesigned their websites in that time." Production cycles grow shorter; consumers expect service around the clock; companies do things in parallel that they would once have done sequentially. One way to be speedy is to avoid big-bang decisions. Internet-based technology can help. At Oracle, Gary Roberts, head of global information technologies, points out that Internet applications tend to be smaller than yesterday's proprietary systems, and the software is faster to develop. But speed is also a matter of a company's decision-making processes. Bureaucracy is a killer.

2 **Good people.** Human beings are the most important of all corporate inputs. Companies need fewer but better people: "celebrity teams", as Novell's Eric Schmidt puts it. Employees with new talents, skills and attitudes must be made to feel at home. Completely new jobs have sprung up in the past three years: content manager, information architect, chief e-business officer, chief knowledge officer. Companies need new ways to hire and – trickier – retain these people. They also need new ways to measure their performance.

3 **Openness.** The open nature of the Internet drives its success. The economic rewards that come from belonging to a large network will ensure that the new standards that emerge will remain open. In addition, as the Paris-based OECD pointed out in *The Economic and Social Impact of Electronic Commerce*, a prescient study published in 1999, "Openness has emerged as a strategy." Many e-businesses allow their partners, suppliers or consumers an extraordinary degree of access to their databases and inner workings. To allow another business inside the corporate machine in this way requires trust, and a willingness to expose your weaknesses and mistakes to the world.

4 **Collaboration skills.** The Internet creates many new opportunities for teams and companies to work together. Only as companies learn new ways for their own people to collaborate do they begin fully to realise the opportunities to work with customers, suppliers and partners. Teams may be separated by time zone or by geographic distance, or

they may work for different employers: the spread of outsourcing means that companies manage many more alliances. This calls for a different approach from that required to manage competition.

5 **Discipline.** Can this go with creativity and openness? It has to: "The Internet is all about discipline, protocols and standard processes," insists United Technology's Kent Brittan. When a software program replaces human action, the garbage-in, garbage-out principle applies. Unless companies carefully specify the parameters of a procurement order, for example, it makes no sense to invite tenders in an electronic marketplace. Companies need to insist on a standard look and feel for their websites to avoid confusing customers; and they need to insist on common practices within the company on such issues as purchasing to reap real productivity gains from the Internet.

6 **Good communications.** Given the pace and complexity of change, communicating strategy to staff matters more than ever. Few grasp the Internet's breadth of impact. Communications can no longer be confined within the company, or even within the country. What a company thinks of as external information can turn into the internal sort, and vice versa.

7 **Content-management skills.** All those websites that companies design to reach their staff, their customers or their corporate partners almost always start off by carrying far too much information. Companies are not used to being content providers, and the people who know most about the subject on the site frequently do not, or cannot, manage the site. IBM's Pete Martinez recalls asking the manager of one of his company's intranet sites who its audience was, and what they needed to know. "We took 80% of the information off the site, use rose 3,000%, and the cost of running it fell dramatically." Many corporate managers are simply not used to expressing themselves clearly and concisely.

8 **Customer focus.** New opportunities have opened for companies to deepen their relations with customers. The emphasis has shifted from recruitment to retention, from the commodity to the service and from the mass market to the personalised. Companies are concentrating less on product and process management and more on the customer, treating each as an individual and trying to provide him with precisely the product he wants. This shift, made possible by enriched communications, is altering the whole shape of many companies. On the organisation charts that managers love to draw, the long shapes of product-related "silos" are now criss-crossed with a matrix of lines of

functional responsibility. An executive in charge of retail banking or light trucks, for example, might also be in charge of monitoring fulfilment across the business.

9 **Knowledge management.** The communications revolution has raised the importance of pooling the skills and knowledge of a workforce. The development of sophisticated databases and intranets makes it possible for companies to build a core of knowledge that they can draw upon across the globe. But this is not easy. Managing workers of this kind requires a new sensitivity. Getting intelligent people to share what is in their heads takes more than mere money or clever software – although both can help.

10 **Leadership by example.** Plenty of bosses, especially in Europe and Asia, do not know how to use the Internet, and wear their ignorance as a badge of honour. But chief executives who have never done their own e-mail, or bought something online, or spent an evening or two looking at their competitors' websites, are endangering their businesses. "Top-level management must spend real political capital to create an e-business," insists Forrester's George Colony. This is unlikely to happen if they have no first-hand experience of what the transformation is all about.

Armed with these ten essentials, old-economy managers should see the challenge ahead for what it is: the most revolutionary period they have ever experienced in corporate life. It will be frightening and exhausting, but it will also be enormously exciting. It may even be fun.

8 Regulating the bazaar

IKE AN UNRULY child, the Internet has had its own way so far. But many, including those who cherish it most, believe the time has come for it to grow up and face the real world. If not, Big Brother may have to step in and lay down the law. If that happens American e-tailers might suddenly find they will have to behave like traditional shops and pay sales tax. Marketing firms may have to ask the permission of customers before they sell their private details. Is government intervention really necessary? Or can the fledgling online industry be trusted to regulate itself? How effective could such intervention be when the Internet, a truly global medium, shows no respect for borders? This chapter looks at the issues that will characterise the Internet debate in the coming years.

Regulation: take me to your leader

As *The Economist* reported in "The consensus machine" (June 10th 2000), the Internet has matured to the point where people are increasingly asking: who runs it, and on whose behalf?

The myth that the Internet has thrived only because it is anarchic is now firmly entrenched. Yet myth is what it is. In fact, cyberspace is highly organised and even regulated, and not just for technical standards. What is unique about the Internet is not that it is ungoverned; it is that its regulation has emerged from the bottom up and not the top down. "The Internet's true strength is that, as an institution, it exhibits characteristics of policy formation that appeal to one's sense of liberty," argues Joseph Reagle, a policy analyst at the World Wide Web Consortium (w3c), an Internet standards body.

The process of policy formation on the Internet is not well known to the general public, or even to many avid Internet users. Besides the w3c, there is the Internet Engineering Task Force (IETF), which develops agreed technical standards, such as communications protocols, and its steering group, the IESG, which co-ordinates and approves them. There is also the Internet Corporation for Assigned Names and Numbers (ICANN), which oversees the system of domain names such as .com and .org.

These bodies have certain characteristics in common. They are largely self-created and self-governing. They are open in both membership and arguments, priding themselves on giving all voices a hearing (see Figure 8.1).

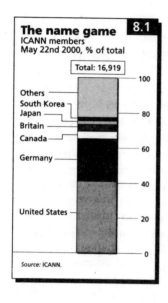

The name game `8.1`
ICANN members
May 22nd 2000, % of total

Total: 16,919

Others
South Korea
Japan
Britain
Canada
Germany

United States

100
80
60
40
20
0

Source: ICANN.

They are largely consensus-based in their decision-taking. And, so far at least, they have worked surprisingly smoothly, even surviving the wholesale commercialisation of the net. Yet the expansion and internationalisation of the Internet are likely now to put new strains on its entire bottom-up system of regulation.

A culture of cautious deliberation prevails in most Internet organisations, particularly in the IETF. Its main mantra, expressed by David Clark of the Massachusetts Institute of Technology, is: "We reject kings, presidents and voting. We believe in rough consensus and running code." The approach has created what Michael Froomkin, of the University of Miami, calls one of the first legitimate international decision-making processes. Any individual can become a member ("no cards, no dues, no secret handshakes", says the task-force's website), just by signing up to a working group's mailing list. Anybody can also show up at the meetings that the task-force holds three times a year. Even network engineers, after all, need occasionally to meet face to face.

This does not mean that all members are, in practice, equal. Not surprisingly, the contributions of some carry a particular weight, not because they have been elected, but because they are so widely respected (although people can lose that status quickly if they rest on their laurels). The late Jon Postel was an example of such an elder. Until his death in October 1998, he had, more or less single-handedly, overseen the numbering system for Internet addresses.

Even so, anybody, however lowly, can propose a standard to the IETF, and thus start a process that is formal enough to ensure that all get a hearing but light enough to avoid bureaucracy. Once a working group has reached a decision, it submits it to the IESG (Internet Engineering Steering Group) for public review and ultimate approval. To become an Internet standard, a new technology must also operate in at least two working products, such as network routers. Decisions in working groups are not taken by formal vote, but by "rough consensus" – more than a simple majority, but not unanimity. The consensus is decided by any method the group chooses. One way is "humming" when a group meets (so nobody can tell who is in favour of a proposal and who against). Those who believe that their arguments have been ignored can appeal to the IESG.

The IETF is not the only example of a well-functioning, meritocratic online "community". Software-development groups known as open-source projects, sometimes comprising thousands of volunteer programmers across the world, are organised similarly. But they rely less on formal working groups and more on "benevolent dictators" to create consensus. The group around Linux, an increasingly popular operating system, for example, is run by Linus Torvalds, a Finnish programmer who wrote the first version of the software. When hackers write new code for Linux, it is scrutinised and discussed, mainly in online discussion groups. Mr Torvalds has the final say about which "patches" will eventually go into the core program.

So far, the Internet decision-making process, like the Internet itself, has been remarkably robust. Yet there are early signs of trouble ahead. A huge row erupted, for example, when IETF members discussed how far their organisation should help law enforcers to conduct wire-taps. Telecoms-equipment makers worried that their products would be required to comply with federal wire-tap laws. But other members were preoccupied by images of Big Brother. In February 2000, an IETF task-force decided not to "consider requirements for wire-tapping". Policy conflicts like these prompted Vint Cerf, one of the IETF's founders, to launch an Internet societal task-force as a forum for deliberating social and economic issues thrown up by the spread of the Internet.

Potential problems loom over the W3C too. So far, it has avoided being gummed up by competing commercial interests. Although it develops standards for the web, and many of its deliberations take place through e-mail, it is far from a traditional online community. Most of the 400-plus members of the organisation, which was founded in October 1994 by Tim Berners-Lee, the inventor of the World Wide Web, are companies that pay $50,000 a year for membership. Mr Berners-Lee first tried to standardise the web within the IETF. But progress in the working group was slow – as he put it in his book, *Weaving the Web*, "partly due to the number of endless philosophical rat holes down which technical conversations would disappear". Because he wanted to move faster, he started his own group.

The W3C is thus a rather different animal from the IETF. Although it also upholds the consensus principle, it is more top-down, with

Mr Berners-Lee acting as a benevolent dictator. Yet over the years, the inner workings of the organisation have become more codified, to the point, Mr Berners-Lee says, that its "process document" is more important than he is. So far, the w3c has developed more than 20 technical specifications. At a conference in mid-2000, it announced details of several important technologies nearing "recommendation status" (w3c-speak for standard), in particular xml (Extensible Markup Language), which enables computers to work out exactly what data on a web article represent and how to process them.

Yet the w3c is no longer uncontroversial, because its decisions have more than technical implications. Critics such as Simson Garfinkel, a technology journalist, argue that the group has become a key maker of public policy – and that it ought to start acting like one, especially by opening its membership and meetings to a broader public.

Online elders admit that policy issues are becoming as important as technical ones. But the w3c is not the place to deal with them, says Mr Berners-Lee. "Technologists have to act as responsible members of society, but they also have to cut themselves out of the loop of ruling the world."

The remaining Internet ruling body, icann, has no choice but to become more than a club of citizen engineers. Its task sounds boringly technical: keeping track of the Internet's names and numbers. The organisation oversees the domain-name system, which links the 12-digit numbers that identify servers connected to the Internet to addresses such as www.economist.com.

But icann's challenges are now more political and economic than technical. It represents all Internet users. Although the net is highly decentralised, its naming system is hierarchical, as it must be if every computer is to be easy to find. Only 13 "root servers" know where one computer has to go to find the address of another. Anybody who controls these has a life-or-death power over the Internet, says David Post of Temple University in Philadelphia.

To complicate things, the economic stakes have become high. Trade-mark owners object to plans to create new "top-level" domains, the designations such as .com. They have invested a lot of money in their names and have often fought or bought off "cybersquatters", people who register web addresses only to sell them later. New top-level domains risk diluting these brands and increasing the costs of policing them. But because the Internet is international, icann also has to deal with geographical interests. The European Union, for instance, would like to create a .eu domain for European websites, because the .com domain is dominated by American businesses and most recognisable English words have been claimed. In June 2000, a British company even started to sell .eu.com names, ahead of ICANN approval. (See Figure 8.2.)

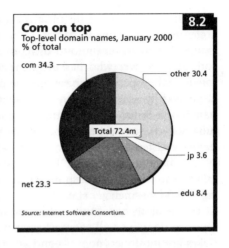

Com on top
Top-level domain names, January 2000
% of total

8.2

com 34.3

other 30.4

Total 72.4m

jp 3.6

net 23.3

edu 8.4

Source: Internet Software Consortium.

Like other Internet bodies, ICANN operates by consensus. It has created a raft of committees, working groups and "supporting organisations". Even national governments have a voice, via a "governmental advisory committee". All these groups are supposed to talk things out. In theory, the 19-member ICANN board only ratifies the consensus, takes care of administration and makes sure that its decisions are implemented, for example, by signing contracts with domain-name registrars. So far, however, ICANN has made more headlines for controversy than for consensus.

It got off to a bad start. In Mr Postel, the organisation lost its benevolent dictator before it was even constituted. The selection of the interim board was perceived by many as shrouded in secrecy and tilted towards corporate interests. And ICANN is in many ways a completely new institutional animal. It is a hybrid between an online community and a real-world governance structure, an untested combination. It is also a new type of international organisation: an industry trying to regulate part of itself, across the globe, with little or no input from national governments.

For critics such as Jonathan Weinberg of Wayne State University, Detroit, ICANN still has to prove itself on all these fronts. It has had difficulties gauging the consensus of such a heterogeneous group. After protests, the board had to take back several decisions, such as a $1 fee on every domain name. And it lacks features that produce accountability in offline institutions, such as an independent review board (one is now planned).

Yet considering its meagre means (only seven full-time employees and an annual budget of $4.3m), ICANN has not done badly. The organisation was successful in wresting the monopoly for domain-name registration from a company called Network Solutions, and also in introducing competition into name distribution. More than 120 registrars are now accredited to sell domain names.

ICANN now has a uniform dispute resolution policy to help resolve controversies over who has the right to a domain name. The World Intellectual Property Organisation, one of four dispute-resolution bodies accredited by ICANN, recently ruled that Internet addresses bearing the names of a British author, Jeanette Winterson, and an American actress, Julia Roberts, should be returned to their rightful owners. Both had their names registered by squatters, who had argued that names of living people are not trademarks. These cases may now set a precedent for others who wish to establish their right to a domain name that has been registered by somebody else.

Yet the moments of truth for ICANN are still to come. The issue of new top-level domains will show whether it can create consensus when the stakes are mostly economic – and what it does if no consensus can be found. If it adds only a token number of new suffixes, many users of the Internet will be disappointed. The consensus in the working group charged with the task is to roll out a few new domains and then evaluate what happens.

More important for ICANN's legitimacy was the election of five board members in November 2000. Originally, the board had opted for an indirect election, with an electoral college to filter out incompetent representatives. But after many at ICANN's March meeting in Cairo had derided this procedure as undemocratic, the board settled for a direct election with candidates selected by a nomination committee, or self-nominated subject to a minimum threshold of support. (See Figure 8.3 on page 148.)

There is still no guarantee that the new board members will be representative of the Internet community. What critics fear most is that the membership – anybody over 16 with a verifiable e-mail and physical address can sign up, at ICANN's website – will be captured by special interests. To some extent this has already happened.

Even if ICANN fails, this does not mean that the Internet's original decision-making process will lapse. No doubt, as the Internet matures, online communities such as the IETF will become more formalised, like offline organisations. Even the anarchic Linux group may have to give itself a constitution if the operating system becomes as pervasive as many in the computer industry expect.

Domain strain

A monopoly can be a good thing – at least when it comes to Internet addresses. There has to be some sort of central governing body to ensure a unified system of domain names, as the strings of characters ending with .com or .net are called. Otherwise, the online world could soon fragment, with some websites inaccessible to some users. This is the *raison d'être* of ICANN.

Yet for the first time, ICANN's monopoly faces a serious challenge. On March 5th 2001, New.net, a start-up based in Pasadena, California, began selling domain names based on suffixes that are not sanctioned by ICANN. For an annual fee of $25, consumers and companies can register Internet addresses with 20 new suffixes (known as top-level domains), including .kids, .sport and .xxx. If ICANN bungles its response, the launch of this service could mark the beginning of the end of a unified cyberspace.

This is not the first attempt to create an alternative to the existing domain-name system. But the previous initiatives, which go by names such as AlterNIC, OpenNIC and Open Root Server Confederation, have failed to catch on with more than a small, politically conscious minority. This is mainly because they have not had the money or credibility to overcome a chicken-and-egg problem: to get Internet service providers (ISPs) to funnel traffic to their servers, they need a large number of users. But to acquire those users, they need ISPs to sign up.

New.net is the first challenger to ICANN with a chance of reaching critical mass. It is backed by Idealab!, a well-financed, though not always successful, dotcom incubator (one of its better-known hatchlings, eToys, filed for bankruptcy in the first week of March 2001). More important, New.net has forged partnerships with leading American ISPs, such as Excite@Home and Earthlink, giving it 16m potential users from the start. And it has found a clever way to extend the official domain-name system. If web users want to have access to a site with a .com or .net address, their requests are handled by the existing infrastructure. If they type in a New.net address, the firm's technology automatically adds the extension "new.net", which routes the request to the firm's own name system.

None of this guarantees New.net's success. But if it takes off, there will be problems down the line. What if, for instance, ICANN wants to add top-level domains such as .kids, .travel or .game – all of which have been proposed to the organisation, but are now also in New.net's portfolio?

In some ways, ICANN has only itself to blame for this mess. It has dragged its feet in providing new domains, thus creating pent-up demand for memorable web addresses. It is mainly ICANN members with

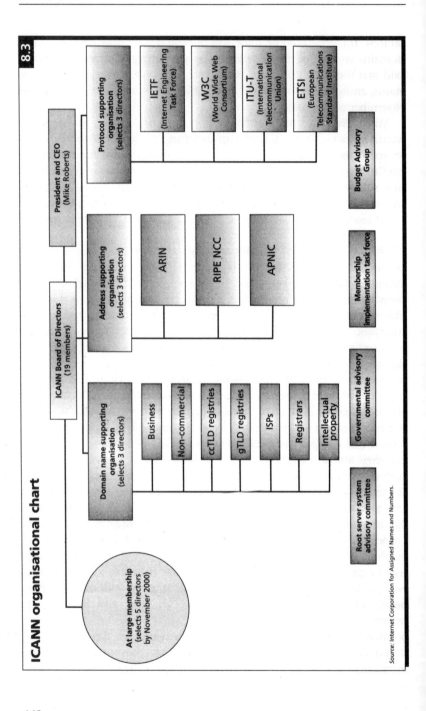

8.3

ICANN organisational chart

President and CEO (Mike Roberts)

ICANN Board of Directors (19 members)

At large membership (selects 5 directors by November 2000)

Protocol supporting organisation (selects 3 directors)
- IETF (Internet Engineering Task Force)
- W3C (World Wide Web Consortium)
- ITU-T (International Telecommunication Union)
- ETSI (European Telecommunications Standard Institute)

Address supporting organisation (selects 3 directors)
- ARIN
- RIPE NCC
- APNIC

Domain name supporting organisation (selects 3 directors)
- Business
- Non-commercial
- ccTLD registries
- gTLD registries
- ISPs
- Registrars
- Intellectual property

Budget Advisory Group

Membership implementation task force

Governmental advisory committee

Root server system advisory committee

Source: Internet Corporation for Assigned Names and Numbers.

famous trademarks that have slowed the process, fearful that new domains would dilute their brands. On March 2nd 2001, ICANN officials said that the introduction of seven new domains (.aero, .biz, .coop, .info, .name, .museum and .pro), which the organisation's board had picked in November 2000, could be delayed for several months.

Might everything turn out all right in the end? The happiest result would be for ICANN to take the challenge from New.net as an opportunity to speed up the introduction of new domains by streamlining its cumbersome administrative procedures, so that a sufficient number of new suffixes can be added regularly and in an orderly fashion. There would then be less reason for competing services such as New.net to exist – and less danger of the Internet becoming infuriatingly balkanised.

Privacy: watching us, watching you, watching them

Privacy is one of the most fought-over battlegrounds of the information economy. At the heart of the debate is a basic dilemma: most people want to retain some control over who knows what about them, and yet information about individuals is key to most successful e-commerce strategies.

There is a famous cartoon published by the *New Yorker* where one dog says to another: "The best thing about the Internet is they don't know you're a dog." Those days of innocence on the Internet are long gone. A more recent cartoon by Tom Toles shows how the Internet has become an increasingly sophisticated means of compiling data about individuals. It shows two dogs talking. The first one repeats that now famous line. The second one disagrees, and says now they not only know you are a dog but they also know that "you are a four-year-old German Shepherd-Schnauzer mix, you like to shop for rawhide chews, you've made 213 visits to the Lassie website, and you had a chat room conversation on August 29th 1999, in which you said that you thought that the dog who played the third Lassie was the hottest".

Detailed information about individuals is the life-blood of most of the burgeoning new service businesses. One of the biggest advantages of e-commerce is said to be better customer service with closer one-to-one ties. Without their growing databases, firms would not be able to tailor their products to individual tastes, handle secure electronic transactions, offer streamlined payment and delivery, or target their advertising and promotion.

But as the race to collect information gathers pace, customers are increasingly wary about where all those personal details are going, how they will be used and who will have access to them. The most obvious result may be a mountain of junk e-mails. But then there are the real dangers. According to Forrester Research, online companies that know customers' shopping habits and history can engage in all kinds of surreptitious discrimination. For example, an inner-city minority teenager may not receive access to the same juicy deals or offers because he is not perceived to have deep enough pockets. Or digital trails that reveal a customer has AIDS may lead to him being snubbed by potential employers or insurance companies. Discrimination on the Internet will be extremely difficult to prove. And there is always the chance that it is based on false or inaccurate data in the first place.

A host of technologies on the Internet helps firms to collect information. Some of the best-known and perhaps most controversial devices are Internet "cookies", tiny software programs placed on consumers' computers when they first visit websites or use shopping carts. They enable companies to track a user's movements on the web and record what Lawrence Lessig, a law professor at Harvard, and one of the best-known commentators on the subject of law and the Internet, calls "mouse droppings". This means that every website visited, every file downloaded, every purchase made at the click of a mouse can be recorded and stored electronically.

The data compiled by cookies are not necessarily linked to user identities. But by combining them with other publicly available data such as credit histories, phone bills, and medical records, companies can accumulate vast databases of knowledge about their customers. For a few cents some medical data sites will even sell you your neighbour's history of urinary tract infections. In America, where the privacy debate is raging, the sale of such personal data held in government and commercial databases, the so-called reference industry, is far more widespread than in Europe, which has stricter laws in place.

A number of high-profile privacy cases have shown the American public how much is at stake in the new information era. When DoubleClick, the largest Internet advertising agency, announced plans to acquire Abacus Direct, a company that provides information to the direct marketing industry, in a $1.7 billion deal in June 1999 it prompted a public outcry and a flurry of legal action. The deal would have given the company access to an extensive database of names, addresses and telephone numbers which it could combine with information it had collected about the shopping habits of online customers. DoubleClick eventually backed down from combining the databases.

In another important case an American security expert found that RealNetworks, a company that produces audio and video software for the Internet, was gathering information about consumer listening habits via its popular program for listening to digital music called RealJukebox. The company had been gathering data from each customer's computer, including a list of all music stored on their hard disk and a serial number that could be used to identify the customer. RealNetworks claims that it never stored the information and that it is now modifying its software so that it no longer transmits the statistics.

Both Intel and Microsoft have run into a storm of criticism when it was revealed that their products – the chips and software at the heart of most personal computers – transmitted unique identification numbers whenever a PC user logged on to the Internet. Both companies hastily offered software to allow users to turn the identifying numbers off, but their critics maintain that any software fix can be breached. In fact, a growing number of electronic devices and software packages contain identifying numbers to help them interact with each other.

Such skirmishes between privacy advocates and those collecting information are occurring with increasing frequency. Taken in context, online companies are last on the list of offenders when it comes to people's privacy concerns. Top of the list by far, according to one poll of American consumers by Jupiter Media Metrix, are the telemarketers. But for online shoppers privacy is a key concern. According to Forrester Research, two-thirds of web users are concerned about their privacy. As a result, they spent $2.8 billion less online in 1999 than they would otherwise have done. Other studies show that privacy is a major concern to Internet users. A March 2000 *Business Week*/Harris poll found that 89% of respondents were uncomfortable with a website profiling their browsing and shopping habits. A survey by America's Federal Trade Commission (FTC) found that 80% of Americans are worried about what happens to information collected about them.

So what is being done to boost consumer confidence in cyberspace? Self-regulation or government intervention is the choice in the current American debate on protecting privacy online. On one side are consumer advocates, who want government oversight. On the other side, online companies led by advertisers and marketers are insisting that they can regulate themselves.

Legislation

There are clear signs that America is heading towards legislation.

Children's interests are already taken care of by the Children's Online Privacy Protection Act (COPPA). The law, which came into effect in April 2000, makes it a federal offence for commercial websites to collect personal information from children under 13 without parental permission. The FTC said that violators could face a $10,000 fine for each offence.

Public pressure is mounting for general legislation. More than 80% of Americans want government regulation of corporate use of personal information, according to an April 2000 study by Odyssey, a market-research firm. This is the darkest fear of most cyber-enthusiasts, who are fiercely proud of the new libertarian paradise. Businesses, too, worry that the heavy hand of government would stifle the development of the Internet and clip the wings of the fledgling e-commerce industry.

In the absence of federal legislation individual states have been leading the way. Many have already passed or are about to pass online privacy laws. This could lead to even greater confusion and the ultimate nightmare of 50 states with 50 different privacy standards. Internet companies are alarmed by the trend. The web's leading person-to-person auction site, eBay, has called for federal legislation to pre-empt individual states' efforts. Independent observers say Congress is unlikely to pass any kind of online privacy law before summer 2001.

The European Union has adopted a much tougher stance. In 1995, it passed one of the most comprehensive and stringent privacy laws in the world, the Data Protection Directive. It aims to give people control over their data, requiring "unambiguous" consent before a company or agency can process them and barring the use of the data for any purpose other than that for which they were originally collected. Individuals must be told how the information will be used. They must also have access to this information and be able to correct or erase it. Each EU country is pledged to appoint a privacy commissioner to act on behalf of citizens whose rights have been violated.

How the directive will work in practice is difficult to say. Many EU countries have yet to bring their own legislation into line. Analysts say it will be too costly and cumbersome to implement. Courts find it almost impossible to pin down a precise enough legal definition of privacy. Privacy lawsuits hardly ever succeed, except in France, and even there they are rare. Policing the rising tide of data collection and trading is probably beyond the capability of any government without a crackdown so massive that it could stop the new information economy in its tracks.

Such heavy-handed legislation is anathema to American firms. They view the EU directive as Draconian and unworkable. They are particularly concerned by the ban on the export of data to countries with less strict regulations because this includes America. The directive could erect a huge barrier to the transatlantic transmission of information. Following an agreement in March 2000, American companies, when dealing with European citizens, must observe the stringent EU privacy rules to obtain "safe harbour" from prosecution. But the Europeans are hinting that they will not enforce the strict terms of the directive against America.

Back home, America's free marketers may be forced to conclude that a more pragmatic approach to the privacy dilemma is required which will inevitably involve legislation. There are already signs that the online industry's opposition to legislation is weakening. Not least because targeted online advertising – the main reason to collect personal data – it seems, is not living up to its promises. Many e-commerce sites that have yet to see a profit are still betting that selling premium-priced ads based on profiling will pay the bills. This may turn out to be a mistake. Analysts say that it is more important on the Internet than it is in other media to know precisely what users do, rather than who they are. It is more effective to try to sell tennis rackets to consumers when they visit a sports site, for example, than when the same consumers are checking stockmarket prices.

Even the cyber-enthusiasts are saying the time has come for a little more law and order. Lawrence Lessig, author of *Code and Other Laws of Cyberspace*, believes that without regulation a combination of market failures and company decisions made narrowly in their own interest will leave everyone worse off: with less privacy, less free speech and less democracy. In other words Big Buck may be more of a threat to e-commerce than Big Brother. Even the FTC, which previously favoured self-regulation, concluded in a May 2000 report that "industry efforts alone have not been sufficient". It has called for wide-ranging powers to protect consumer privacy on the Internet.

Self-regulation

Early efforts by the industry to regulate itself are not encouraging. A survey conducted by the FTC shows that although 88% of websites now display a privacy policy of some sort, their quality leaves much to be desired. Only 20% of sites collecting personal information implement all four widely accepted "fair information practice" principles:

◪ notice about the collection of information;

- ◪ choice of how the information is used;
- ◪ reasonable access to a consumer's own collected data;
- ◪ protection of the data's security.

Studies of members of America's Direct Marketing Association by independent researchers have found that more than half did not abide by even the association's modest guidelines.

Attempts by industry watchdogs such as TRUSTe and the Better Business Bureau (BBB) have not managed to keep companies on the straight and narrow. Both organisations offer privacy seal programmes, which include dispute resolution. TRUSTe's annual charges for its seal range from $299 to $5,000. Websites can display the seal only if they post a privacy statement that meets its standards and submit to a review by a TRUSTe-approved auditing firm. It has about 600 licensees, ranging from Microsoft to small e-tailers. BBB's annual fees are cheaper, ranging from $150 to $3,000. As comparative newcomer to web ethics it has fewer licensees, among them Dell Computer and Equifax, a credit bureau.

Detractors argue that such programmes are not sufficient. In one important case, Toysmart.com, a prominent e-tailer forced into liquidation after it ran out of cash, proposed selling off its customer list, one of its most valuable assets, after it was declared bankrupt. During its short life, Toysmart, once a corporate member of TRUSTe, collected detailed personal information about its online customers, including names, addresses, billing information, shopping preferences and family profiles, including the names and dates of birth of children. The privacy policy posted on its website stated that information collected from customers would never be shared with third parties. The FTC eventually ruled that the sale could go ahead but with a number of restrictions. Nevertheless, the case has provided ample ammunition for those who believe the online industry needs the long arm of the law to guide it.

What kind of privacy legislation, then, can American consumers expect? Probably nothing sweeping. Even the FTC does not want to see self-regulation replaced by legislation, but rather complemented by it. The agency recommends that Congress merely establish some basic privacy rules for consumer-oriented commercial websites, and then give the FTC or another agency more power to enforce these rules.

In the meantime, there is evidence that the fledgling industry is growing up. Companies caught out early in the privacy debacle such as DoubleClick moved quickly to repair the damage. It appointed a privacy advisory board comprising consumer advocates and security experts to

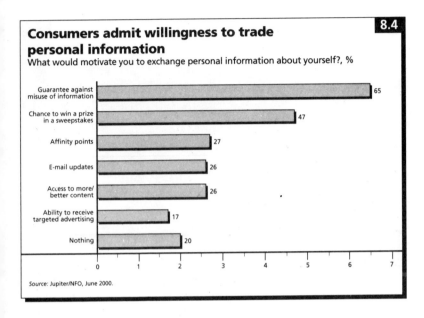

8.4

Consumers admit willingness to trade personal information

What would motivate you to exchange personal information about yourself?, %

Guarantee against misuse of information	65
Chance to win a prize in a sweepstakes	47
Affinity points	27
E-mail updates	26
Access to more/ better content	26
Ability to receive targeted advertising	17
Nothing	20

Source: Jupiter/NFO, June 2000.

review new products and services for potential privacy violations. Among other measures, RealNetworks added a new consumer software privacy statement allowing users to opt out of any information gathering carried out by the company. Other companies will no doubt learn from such mistakes and avoid similar pitfalls.

Some companies have chosen to appoint a privacy officer to tackle the thorny issue. In Washington the first-ever chief privacy officers' convention took place in June 2000. But Jay Stanley of Forrester Research warns that relegating all thinking about privacy to one person could provide companies with a false sense of security: "The Titanic didn't need to have a chief iceberg officer, though it wouldn't have hurt to have had a good lookout." Some companies have resolved the privacy issue by a trade-off. There is growing evidence to suggest that consumers may be willing to trade some of their personal data in exchange for free prizes and cash (see Figure 8.4).

Technology

Technology is also developing to allow users to safeguard their own privacy. For example, browsers, the software for viewing web pages, can be configured to reject cookies (see Figure 8.5). A survey by Arthur Andersen in 2000 revealed that one in eight respondents had configured

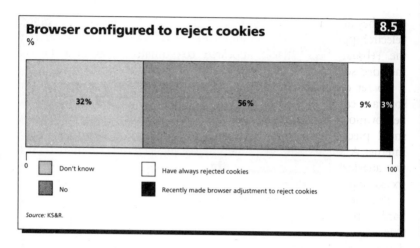

Browser configured to reject cookies 8.5

%

| 32% | 56% | 9% | 3% |

0   100

☐ Don't know   ☐ Have always rejected cookies

■ No   ■ Recently made browser adjustment to reject cookies

Source: KS&R.

their browsers to reject cookies, usually because of privacy concerns.

The Platform for Privacy Preferences Project (P3P) is emerging as a software standard that will help users gain more control over the use of personal information by the websites they visit. Developed by w3c, it will allow users to set privacy preferences in their browsers and will alert them when the websites they click on have privacy policies that differ from their choices. This will save users from the horrible task of reading the privacy policy of every site they visit.

Security: yours securely

Security alongside privacy regularly tops the list of customer concerns in cyberspace. But are things really that bad?

When the Internet's most prominent sites such as Yahoo!, Amazon, buy.com, CNN and eTrade were paralysed by a series of "denial-of service" (DOS) attacks in February 2000 – an avalanche of fake requests for information which overwhelm even the most powerful network computers – some experts wondered if such digital assaults could deal a lasting blow to e-commerce. The attacks demonstrated the vulnerability of even the most sophisticated website technologies, offering scant encouragement to online customers already edgy about security. They also did little to allay the fears of would-be shoppers convinced that cyberspace is a teenage hacker's paradise.

DOS attacks are not new. Computer-security organisations give warnings of threatening programs. The Computer Emergency Response Team of Carnegie Mellon University hears of roughly four DOS attacks a day. They are usually protests directed at smaller websites. A group called "electrohippies" shut the website of the World Trade Organisation. But the February 2000 attacks appeared co-ordinated. And their targets included some of the brightest names in e-commerce.

To set off an electronic avalanche is relatively easy. The necessary software, called *Stacheldraht* (barbed wire) or Tribal Flood Network, can be downloaded from the Internet. The attacker surreptitiously installs a small piece of software on dozens of computers connected to the Internet. A "master" computer then signals these "slaves" to strike. Yahoo! was attacked by 50 computers stuffing its servers with the equivalent of 500,000 typewritten pages a second.

Because the avalanche of data comes from many sources, the attack is hard to resist, and its author is almost certain to remain unidentified. One way to block an assault is to set up a "sniffer" that looks for patterns that could constitute an attack and filters the data stream before it reaches a server. Yahoo! used such software, but it was not powerful enough.

Websites share in the blame. In their rush to establish themselves, security is often an afterthought. Yet most commercial sites need protecting. For instance, when the now defunct eToys filed a trademark-infringement lawsuit against a Zurich-based art group whose website is www.etoy.com, it received DOS threats in return. Just about any computer-based system is vulnerable to external attack. But as companies move more of their core processes and transactions to the Internet and become e-businesses, they become potentially far more vulnerable because the Internet increases the number of entry points exponentially.

Exposure may take a variety of forms. Apart from simple theft, financial documents may be altered and illicit transactions carried out in the company's name. The interception and abuse of credit-card or banking information may compromise a customer. Confidential documents may be made public or passed to competitors. Copyrights and patents may be infringed. Above all, incalculable damage may be done to a firm's brand or reputation.

Without adequate security technology, therefore, e-business rapidly becomes untenable. The trouble is that the Internet was originally designed with interoperability rather than security in mind. Grafting the requirements of business – that transactions should be private, secure, guaranteed and timely – on to the Internet has not been easy.

The first point of defence for most companies is the firewall. In essence, it is a gateway allowing safe external connections to internal

157

applications. These gateways should stop outsiders without the right credentials from getting access to things they should not have access to. There are several other ingredients of Internet security.

- **Encryption.** If information is sent in clear text, anyone can intercept and read it. Encryption, depending on whether it is "soft" or "hard", can make life difficult or next-to-impossible for would-be snoopers. America was originally against any exports of encryption technology. Some governments are demanding a right of access to such keys so that they can catch criminals and terrorists.

- **Authentication of identity.** This, too, can take soft and hard forms. It can amount to a simple password, or it may call for a digital signature. Messages are sent with a hash code that represents a unique signature. When the message is received, the code is checked to see if it matches the code held by the recipient. Information may also be digitally signed as well as encrypted to ensure that it has not been tampered with. Digital signatures may be held and checked by trusted third parties, such as banks or credit-card companies.

- **Virtual private network.** If the above measures are not secure enough, an increasingly popular alternative is the virtual private network (VPN). VPNs offer a controlled pathway through the Internet to which only authorised users have access and along which only authorised data can travel. They "tunnel" through the Internet, wrapping user data in Internet-protocol (IP) packets that hide the underlying routing and switching structure of the Internet from senders and receivers.

- **Public-key infrastructure.** Public-key infrastructure (PKI) is a complete set of products to provide total security. According to the Butler Group, an IT consultancy, such a set should include, among other things, public-key digital certificates (or electronic means of identification), somewhere to store them, means of revoking them, automatic updating of key pairs and certificates before expiry, key storage, back-up and recovery, and secure client-side software. Some companies, such as VeriSign, are offering centrally managed, outsourced PKI services, though the prospect of putting a company's entire security in somebody else's hands may be a psychological bridge too far.

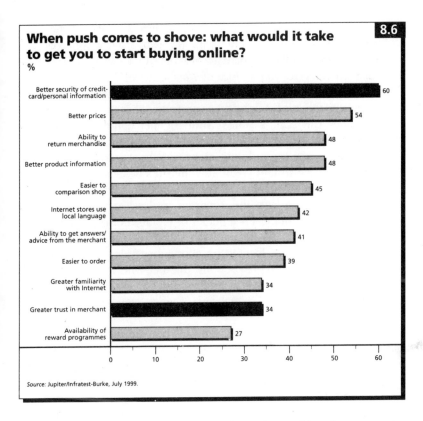

When push comes to shove: what would it take to get you to start buying online?

8.6

%

Better security of credit-card/personal information	60
Better prices	54
Ability to return merchandise	48
Better product information	48
Easier to comparison shop	45
Internet stores use local language	42
Ability to get answers/advice from the merchant	41
Easier to order	39
Greater familiarity with Internet	34
Greater trust in merchant	34
Availability of reward programmes	27

Source: Jupiter/Infratest-Burke, July 1999.

What do Internet users make of all this? Along with privacy, security comes up as a key concern in surveys of online shoppers. In a 1999 poll by Jupiter, 60% of Internet users who do not buy online said that better security for credit-card and personal information would encourage them to try out e-commerce (see Figure 8.6).

In fact, Internet shopping is not as unsafe as many people believe. By and large, the least of the problems with shopping online is the risk that hackers may intercept your messages and steal your credit-card details. To get the same information that customers happily give to any shop assistant, a hacker would have to comb through all the trillions of bytes of Internet transmissions looking for strings of characters that look like credit-card numbers. Even then, they would probably fail: most of the larger online retailers operate their websites from secure servers, which tell the browser to scramble all information before sending it. Breaking such codes is a matter for supercomputers and weeks of effort – hardly

159

worth it for a credit card with a spending limit of $3,000.

Fraud is a more serious worry. In the real world, when you walk into a store you usually get what you pay for on the spot – and the size of the store or its name gives you an idea of whether it will be there next week if something goes wrong. On the Internet, two teenagers in a bedroom can set up a site that looks every bit as professional as those of the biggest retailers. They can scan a store's worth of merchandise out of some catalogue, and make up a grand name, like "The Computer Megaplex". Getting listed by the big indexing sites like Yahoo! is as easy as asking. Endowed with such instant credibility, the site's owners simply wait for the punters to show up: the choice of whether to run a legitimate business or simply to keep the storefront up long enough to collect a stack of credit-card numbers is a matter of morals, not practicality.

The net is waiting for digital cash. Much of the publicity about electronic commerce has focused on efforts to develop a new currency and payment system, tailored for the Internet. The idea is appealing: e-cash could be used anywhere and would not even require a bank account. But clever as such digital cash schemes may be, none has won much support yet.

As technology advances and companies become more security-savvy, hackers will undoubtedly try to outwit their efforts. In the long run, they are unlikely to wreck e-commerce. All the victims of the DOS attacks had reopened their sites in less than three hours. Wall Street remained largely unfazed; indeed, investors bought shares of computer-security firms.

Companies offering security solutions are in for big business. According to Gartner Group, spending on security software is expected to soar from $2.5 billion in 1999 to over $6.7 billion in 2004. Such spending may, however, be in vain. DOS attacks make the headlines but most cyber-crimes are committed by insiders. According to a survey by *Information Security* magazine in October 2000, only 37% of respondents said their company had sustained a DOS attack from an external source. By contrast, 58% said that insiders had abused computer-access controls, and 41% reported that employees or other insiders had electronically destroyed or distributed confidential company information.

Taxation: taxing times

Should e-tailers be forced to hand over a slice of every dollar or should cyber-sales be tax-free?

In America

When American colonists dressed as Red Indians tossed British tea into Boston Harbour in 1773 they were protesting at the unfairness of taxation without representation. But the rebels were also angry because Britain's cash-strapped East India Company enjoyed lucrative tax subsidies that its competitors did not.

Now America's high-street retailers are pitched in a similar battle. Unlike their online rivals, they have to collect sales tax from their customers. If you buy a novel from a Manhattan bookstore, you will pay a combined state and city sales tax of 8.25%. If you purchase the same book over the Internet from Amazon.com, there will be no tax to pay.

This advantage is doing wonders for e-retailers in their battle against traditional high-street stores. If e-commerce grows as big as some predict, this could blow a large hole in tax revenue. In America, sales tax is levied at the state and local rather than the national level, and many state governors are getting nervous about the potential loss of yield from a tax that currently supplies around half of state and local-government revenue.

Forrester Research reckons that in 1999 local and state governments in America lost $525m tax revenue from Internet sales. It predicts that the hole will grow wider as more people do their shopping on the Internet. According to its report, 7% of all purchases will be made online by 2004.

Opponents say that taxing the Internet will stop the nascent e-commerce industry in its tracks and hurt the global economy. Supporters want a level playing field. Some American states decided on pre-emptive strikes, such as slamming taxes on Internet access, which upset the don't-tax-the-net lobby. Now the two sides have been brought together in the Advisory Commission on Electronic Commerce, set up by Congress under the 1998 Internet Tax Freedom Act. The very name of the act gives a strong hint of what the tax collectors are up against: the idea that the Internet is the true land of the free, in a way that offline America no longer is. The act also included a three-year ban on "new Internet taxes" while a permanent arrangement is debated. The inclusion of the word "new", however, may be political wiliness: it leaves open the possibility that the "old" sales tax might simply be extended to currently untaxed e-commerce.

Besides, purchases from an online retailer are not actually tax-free, whatever Americans may have come to believe. Rather, the online retailer may simply have no legal duty to collect it, owing to two Supreme Court rulings on tax disputes involving mail-order companies shipping goods to other states. In 1967, the court said that states could not require an out-of-state company to collect a sales tax on goods coming into the state unless the company had a physical presence or "nexus" within that state. It reaffirmed this decision in 1992, in a case involving Quill, a big catalogue seller. Many lawyers thought this would undermine the argument used in the 1967 case that it was too burdensome for the out-of-state seller to discover what tax the customer should pay.

Legally, most consumers buying goods from outside their state are supposed to pay a "use tax" equal to what the sales tax would have been, but hardly anybody does. America's so-called "tax-free e-commerce" really amounts to mass tax evasion. Online-only retailers such as Amazon, unencumbered with a high-street nexus, have neglected to remind consumers that they may have a legal duty to pay a use tax. Many online retailers have added to their advantage by basing what physical presence they do have (such as warehouses and offices) in the five American states – Alaska, Delaware, Montana, New Hampshire and Oregon – that do not levy a sales tax.

This strategy is not entirely risk-free. Except in states that have explicitly ruled it out, such as California and New York, it is conceivable that the tax authorities will challenge online-only retailers on the ground that using a server or being contacted at a website located within their borders constitutes nexus, obliging them to collect taxes. But under the Internet Tax Freedom Act they have had to wait until 2001 to do so.

All the same, the "tax break", however doubtful, and however unfair to the (mainly less-well-off) people who do not have access to the Internet, has given the online-only retailers a big boost. According to a study by Austan Goolsbee, an economist at the University of Chicago, 1998 Internet sales would have been 25–30% lower if state taxes had been charged on them, if only because (often high) delivery fees have to be added on top. The overseas sales of American-based online retailers probably benefited as well, because they are trading from what is currently an e-commerce tax haven.

Offline retailers who want to sell online are facing serious dilemmas. If they collect tax, they concede a price advantage to their online-only rivals. If they break the law, they risk being taken to court and having to pay back taxes. One short-term way out is to pay the tax on behalf of the consumer, but this is feasible only as long as e-commerce makes up just a small part of the firm's sales.

But according to one report traditional retailers may be overreacting. Jupiter reckons that consumers are far less bothered about sales tax than

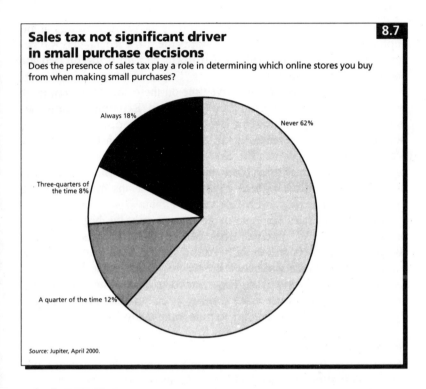

Sales tax not significant driver in small purchase decisions

8.7

Does the presence of sales tax play a role in determining which online stores you buy from when making small purchases?

- Always 18%
- Never 62%
- Three-quarters of the time 8%
- A quarter of the time 12%

Source: Jupiter, April 2000.

some bricks-and-mortar firms like to think. More than half of consumers surveyed said the presence of sales tax never affects their decision on where to shop online (see Figure 8.7).

Another option is to restructure the business so that for tax purposes the online retail operation becomes a separate legal entity from the offline one. This is what Barnes & Noble, a chain of bookshops, has attempted with its bn.com site. There are some legal precedents; for example, Saks Fifth Avenue Folio is a legal non-tax-collecting direct-mail operation run separately from its high-street sibling. But many of America's biggest traditional retailers consider this strategy too risky. According to Walter Hellerstein, a lawyer at the University of Georgia, courts in up to 20 states may not be prepared to accept the legal separateness of what is essentially the same brand online and offline.

Even if agreement on the best tax can be reached, it will still have to be implemented. One way would be for all of America's state and local governments to reach agreement on a solution, but that is highly unlikely because some of them benefit from leaving things as they are. Another would be for Congress to pass a law overriding the previous rulings of the Supreme Court, but Congress has no appetite for a federal-versus-state-government turf war, particularly if it might end up being blamed for "taxing the Internet to death".

Many policymakers feel they have time on their side. At present most state governments are running a budget surplus. E-commerce, worth an estimated $20 billion in 1999, or less than 1% of American retail sales, is not yet hurting tax revenue much: as a report by Ernst & Young, an accountancy firm, put it, "The Sky is not Falling". Yet e-commerce is proceeding in Internet time: blink and it has doubled. If consumers get used to buying online without paying tax, politicians may face strong opposition to changing that happy state of affairs.

Resolving the sales tax issue in America is only the beginning of a broader debate. The Internet does not recognise borders. American consumers can shop online for speciality cheese from France and silk from China, but tariffs and quotas hinder cross-border trade. It will be up to bodies like the World Trade Organisation to discuss the implications. Technology may in future make it easier to collect taxes across borders. But it may also allow tax-evaders to hide more easily.

In Europe

Most rich countries tax consumption quite differently from America. It is usually done at national level and raises far more revenue (see Figure 8.8). Yet some of the problems they face are similar.

Within the European Union, online retailers are supposed to collect value-added tax (VAT), a tax levied on purchases made by individuals but not businesses. Although VAT rates in different EU countries vary widely, the EU has ruled that cross-border retailers should collect the tax at the rate applying in the member state where the purchase is consumed. In theory, this should stop online firms setting up in whichever EU country has the lowest VAT rate on its products and exporting to countries with higher rates. However, enforcing this policy may prove harder than EU officials suppose. As one British customs official explains: "If we visit a company in Britain and find that it is not charging VAT on goods it is shipping to, say, Germany, we will certainly tell them they are supposed to be charging German VAT. But it is not our job to enforce the collection of German taxes or to tell the German government that it is missing out." Nor is it clear who will ensure that firms deliver any tax they collect to the appropriate government. Retailers selling from outside the EU are even harder to keep in line.

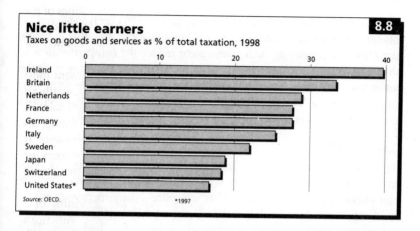

Nice little earners `8.8`

Taxes on goods and services as % of total taxation, 1998

Ireland
Britain
Netherlands
France
Germany
Italy
Sweden
Japan
Switzerland
United States*

Source: OECD.   *1997

With physical goods, the authorities can at least check that items entering the country have had the appropriate duties paid on them. But if online customers find they have to pay extra when their package arrives, they may become irritated enough to pressurise retailers into complying with tax rules. According to Charlie Gilreath, chief executive of Globalfulfillment.com, a firm that helps online businesses with their customers' orders, extra taxes or duties that were not included in the purchase price are among the main reasons that goods ordered online are returned.

The EU has decided that intangibles delivered online should be taxed as services. But collecting tax on services is tricky, and e-commerce can only make it harder. If a supplier sets up in a country that does not require it to collect taxes on the intangible goods it sells, and delivers the product online, the tax authorities in the consumer's country may never know.

Many products that are currently tangible, and thus fairly easy to tax, may become virtual. Already, music can be sent to customers via the Internet rather than in physical form. Books are following suit. The dematerialisation of products could accelerate as Internet bandwidth increases. Clearly, there are limits: nobody has yet devised a way of downloading a Big Mac. However, even with physical goods it may be possible to "unbundle" the price of a good into a tangible component and intangible ones – such as design, advice or customisation – that could be located in a low-tax regime.

Taxing digital goods where they are consumed may prove almost impossible. Collecting a sales tax from the supplier may be easier, and in

America a shift towards such origin-based taxation has been suggested for intangibles. Since the country is a net e-commerce exporter, this is hardly surprising. But imposing such taxes might reduce the competitiveness of American firms if competitors set up in countries that do not impose the origin tax. And even American entrepreneurs may decide to form new companies in a tax-friendlier place. There are plenty of countries competing to attract them.

Conclusion

These are still early days for Internet commerce. An analogy is often drawn with the American Wild West where, despite the best efforts of train robbers, cattle rustlers and other scoundrels, the settlers were able to build a civilised, law-abiding society. Some analysts say that in any new, unregulated industry there are bound to be a few bad guys. Their mistakes will help strengthen the foundations from which e-commerce will prosper and grow. News travels fast in cyberspace. Abuses are quickly found out and punished by consumers. Law and regulation must eventually prevail in the virtual world, as it does in the real one.

9 Brave new world

MANY PEOPLE ARE only just taking on board the idea of PC-based e-commerce, but already technology enthusiasts are touting another new development. Mobile e-commerce is said to be the next big thing. The advent of WAP (Wireless Application Protocol) brings the power of the Internet to the mobile phone. So by dipping into their pocket or handbag, users can have the latest stockmarket prices, news or travel information at their fingertips. According to Analysys, a telecoms research company and consultancy, the annual value of consumer goods and services bought worldwide over mobile networks could reach $13 billion by 2003, or about 7% of all consumer e-commerce. Boston Consulting Group reckons that by that time there will be between 200m and 300m m-commerce users. But if e-commerce is in its infancy then m-commerce has scarcely taken its first breath. Today it is at the same stage of development as the Internet was in 1995. This means service is slow, limited and frustrating. Even the raptures of Amazon's Jeff Bezos have not managed to sway as many fresh converts as fast as mobile-phone firms would like. According to Mr Bezos, m-commerce is "the most fantastic thing the time-starved world has ever seen". But not everyone feels the need to be on the Internet at every available moment. Those who have already glimpsed the future through the tiny screens of their mobile phones are not necessarily impressed. So will m-commerce eventually take off? And if the idea does catch on, how long will it take for companies to make a profit? Here is a brief look at how it all started.

After e comes m

The door to m-commerce was opened partly by luck and partly by design. The phenomenal growth of the Internet and the obsession with mobile phones happened at roughly the same time. But the convergence of the two has been helped along considerably by collaboration between the wireless and computer industries. The product of this happy marriage is the smart phone. Instead of the usual dumb device that only lets you chat, this intelligent device will allow you to check your e-mail, look up the latest news headlines on the web and make calls. In other words, it is a cross between a computer and a mobile phone.

Mobile technology has moved through three main stages. The first generation of mobile phones, based on analogue technology, were large, heavy and difficult to use. Reception was patchy to say the least. The second generation used digital technology, which helped improve reception, and enabled a range of sophisticated services to be offered. Manufacturers also came up with less cumbersome designs for handsets. The third-generation or 3G mobile phones are the intelligent ones that offer the promise of a brave new world accessible from your pocket at lightning speed. You will be able to download video clips, play your favourite games and communicate via a corporate intranet.

The astronomical sums being paid for 3G licences in Europe were clear evidence of the importance telecoms firms attached to being part of the brave new wireless world. In Britain, when the final bids were tabled at the auction for 3G licenses in April 2000, the five successful groups agreed to pay a total of £22.5 billion – three times as much as analysts had predicted. In Germany, the licences sold for a total of 50 billion euros. But the market quickly corrected itself towards the end of the year, when telcos saw their share prices tumble on the stockmarkets. The Swiss government had to postpone its auction after two of the companies bidding decided to merge, eliminating the competition factor in the auction.

Why were the bidders willing to risk so much? According to calculations, the market potential for m-commerce is astonishing. More than 1 billion people are predicted to subscribe to mobile-phone services by 2003. By that time 400m are expected to be using the Internet. More people have mobile phones than have PCS. Furthermore, phone companies know how to charge for their services, something most dotcoms have so far failed to master. It is no wonder that the intoxicating mixture of two of the fastest-growing technologies is making heads spin.

But it is still a huge gamble that might not pay off. There is one corner of the world, though, that offers a sneak preview of what wireless technology has to offer: Japan.

DoCoMo: leader of the pack

With its love of electronic gadgetry, Japan is a testing ground for the global m-commerce project. It is leading the way for two reasons. First, because more people there have mobile phones than have PCS. Second, because of the success of one company, NTT DoCoMo, Japan's biggest mobile-phone operator. Majority-owned by the country's former mono-poly fixed-line operator, Nippon Telegraph & Telephone Corporation, the company began life in 1992. Then in 1999 it launched its smartest product yet, the i-mode, a mobile Internet service.

The tiny handsets, which connect users to the Internet without the need to dial up, come in a variety of flashy colours from "honey platinum" to "lime gold". They have proved an instant hit with Japan's fashion-conscious schoolchildren and are often worn around the neck like a piece of jewellery. One of the most popular and costly designs opens up like a clamshell to reveal a larger display screen than an ordinary mobile phone. Others have full-colour displays and voice recognition.

The menu offers the same kind of selection you would expect to see on AOL, including news and information, games, chat rooms and search facilities. Most Japanese do not own a PC so a journey into cyberspace is truly an other-worldly experience. Unlike European or American users, who are more familiar with the Internet when viewed on a computer screen, the Japanese are quite happy with what they can see from the small display. So far entertainment sites are the biggest attraction, accounting for more than half of all traffic on i-mode. Cartoon downloads and games are popular. But i-mode is also proving to be a great way to keep in touch and make virtual friends, with whom you chat regularly but may never meet. Some phones are equipped with detachable keyboards for writing longer e-mails – furiously punching away at tiny buttons on a phone keypad can become tedious after a while. And it is not just schoolchildren who are using i-mode. The proportion of older users is increasing. Japanese firms are rushing to embrace the service and 30% of i-mode's customers are over 40.

Six months after its launch i-mode had 1m subscribers; 14 months later the figure had jumped to 12m, and by April 2001 DoCoMo had 22m subscribers (see Figure 9.1 on page 170). By the third quarter of 2000 users could access more than 2,000 official i-mode sites and more than 20,000 independent sites. At that time the company achieved a market valuation of about $290 billion, making DoCoMo one of the largest companies in the world. According to analysts, up to one-third of that value was related to the success of i-mode. DoCoMo has been described as a giant sumo wrestler, crushing its rivals everywhere it goes. With no room to grow at home it is now taking on foreign competitors, hoping to win the world title for both cellular and wireless web services.

But DoCoMo is a latecomer to an already overcrowded global market. The battle of the airwaves is well under way. Vast sums of money are at stake as companies jostle for position, hoping to dominate the new market for the next-generation mobile phones and mobile Internet services. For example, in January 1999 Vodafone, a British mobile-phone

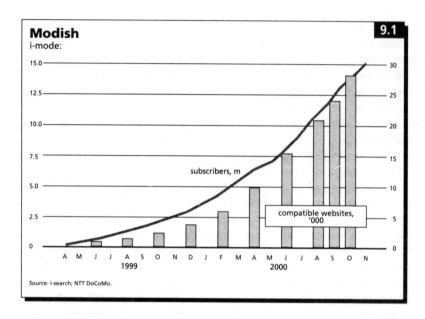

Modish
i-mode:

9.1

subscribers, m

compatible websites, '000

| A | M | J | J | A | S | O | N | D | J | F | M | A | M | J | J | A | S | O | N |
| 1999 | | | | | | | | | | | | | 2000 | | | | | | |

Source: i-search; NTT DoCoMo.

company, bought AirTouch, an American rival, for $58 billion. In 2000 the new company, Vodafone AirTouch, spent $180 billion to acquire Germany's Mannesmann. Deutsche Telekom offered $42 billion for VoiceStream Wireless, a small American mobile carrier.

Amid such turbulence, DoCoMo is quietly going about its business, making small investments throughout Europe and Asia and selecting strategic partners in America. In early 2000, it bought an equity stake in KPN mobile, a Dutch operator. It has also bought stakes in Hutchison Telecom, Hong Kong's largest mobile-phone operator and Hutchison 3G UK Holdings, owner of one of Britain's 3G licences. These moves allow DoCoMo to position itself to become joint owner of 3G mobile licences. It has also linked up with AOL to provide mobile Internet services in Japan, Europe and America and is exploring partnerships with carriers such as BellSouth, Sprint PCS Group, and Cable & Wireless Optus. In November 2000, it unveiled an agreement to pay $9.9 billion for 16% of AT&T Wireless.

How does DoCoMo intend to make money? Minority stakes are unlikely to yield large profits. Instead, the company hopes to cash in on paid services such as news and information services and from local advertising. Back home, DoCoMo has found that banner advertising works for i-mode users. It experiences much higher click-through rates than ads on the fixed-line Internet. To help maximise this revenue stream the company has formed a joint venture with Dentsu, Japan's leading advertising agency.

It is also hoping its huge investments in technology will pay off. DoCoMo has a vast R&D department. With $825m worth of funds and 900 engineers at its disposal, it has managed to create some of the smallest and most sophisticated handsets. So confident is it of its expertise that the company can actually go to equipment makers with the technological specifications in hand. Few others can boast similar capabilities.

Crucial to DoCoMo's rapid growth at home is its use of an advanced packet-switched network, which is more like a computer network than a phone system. As PC is penetration low in Japan, DoCoMo successfully calculated that the i-mode could become the main way on to the web for many users. So it built a more cost-effective packet-switched network alongside its existing digital circuit-switched network and equipped its handsets with a browser that understands HTML, the language of the web. For website owners this means it is quick and easy to adapt their sites for the i-mode because they speak the same computer language. For users it means that i-mode is both simple and fun to use. Rather than having to dial up for a connection the service is "always on" as long as the user is within range of a telephone signal. Users pay ¥300 ($2.80) a month, plus a charge that depends on the amount of data they send or receive – about ¥4 for sending a 500-letter e-mail or ¥20 for downloading a weather report.

The technology has proved a bigger hit so far than WAP, the standard for text-based mobile Internet services developed by the Europeans and Americans after years of wrangling. WAP also uses the technology of the Internet, but unlike i-mode it does not let users roam freely around the web. Instead, users receive a limited set of services that have been selected by the mobile operator. By acting as gatekeeper the operator can control who provides which service and at what cost. It is also much slower because users also have to dial up and wait every time they want to gain access to the Internet.

DoCoMo also earns revenue from its portal site. For example, it earns a 9% commission on transactions such as ordering cinema and airline tickets. However, most websites pay nothing. This is because DoCoMo wants to grow the business by creating new services. Bandai, the firm that gave the world Tamagotchi pets, provides a good example of such co-operation. For a monthly subscription of only ¥100 (about $1), Bandai sends out a new screen saver to i-mode users every day. In July 2000, subscribers downloaded 1.2m new screens. DoCoMo handles the customer billing for such partners.

By constantly seeking innovation DoCoMo aims to keep its customers satisfied. It has cleverly managed customer expectations from the start. It did not try to market i-mode as a mobile Internet service. Instead, it presented i-mode as an inexpensive value-added product, offering information and entertainment services, to enhance the usual voice application. A low pricing strategy has also built demand for the service, which has so far been mainly targeted at consumers.

Despite its runaway success, revenue from i-mode has been modest so far. The company reckons that the service adds about a quarter to the monthly bill of the average user. With 5m customers, that should mean it contributes about $1.5 billion to the firm's total sales. According to Keiji Tachikawa, DoCoMo's president, data and voice traffic will be equally split within five years, but it may not be until 2010 that data are responsible for more than half the firm's revenue.

Consumers will continue to figure highly in DoCoMo's plans for growth. It is working closely with manufacturers such as Matsushita and Sony to enable users to sample and buy music as well as download short video clips of sports highlights. But the company is also planning to move further into the lucrative business market.

The introduction of its new 3G network, originally planned for May 2001 but put back to October 2001, to allow for further tests, will speed up data rates 40 times and allow high-quality streamed video and audio. This will give the biggest boost to i-mode's entertainment and information sites, which together attract 80% of all page hits. There is plenty of pent-up demand: already each of Japan's big five national newspapers boasts 100,000–200,000 mobile subscribers, who pay ¥100–300 per month for the privilege. CNN's Japanese-language i-mode website is also popular, as are specialist weather forecasters and traffic-information sites. Drivers will be able to use the enhanced services to receive colour road maps of the latest traffic jams in Tokyo's permanently congested roads.

The new network will help DoCoMo to boost its business services. It plans to promote i-mode for corporate intranets. Office workers can then read their e-mails or tap into company databases while they are on the move. It will also focus on financial services applications. In March 2000, DoCoMo bought a 5% stake in Japan's first Internet bank, Japan Net Bank, and it has also joined forces with an insurance provider. Financial firms such as Asahi Bank have begun to experiment with i-mode to help with sales. Door-to-door salespeople use it to demonstrate savings products, for instance, or to display up-to-the-minute share prices. The popularity of i-mode with corporate users is likely to grow with the introduction of handsets with added security features. Shoppers will also feel safer. By the end of 2000 they accounted for just 10% of the 150m web-page views that i-mode users rack up every day. DoCoMo reckons that the most popular items sold over the handsets will be books, CDs, and airline and concert tickets. Research by Hakuhodo, an advertising firm, suggests that Japanese consumers want to use their mobile phones to pay their utility bills and to buy all sorts of small items, pointing to a future use for the mobile phone as an "electronic purse". This sounds remarkably like the things analysts say people will want to do with their mobile phones outside Japan in the future.

However, it's still too early to say whether i-mode's success at home will lead to dominance in Europe or America, which lie in second and third place respectively in the m-commerce race. (America has higher PC penetration levels but Europe, benefiting from standardisation on GSM – Global System for Mobile Communications – has a greater penetration of mobile phones. Scandinavia, in particular, is at the cutting edge.) For one thing, affordable fixed-line access to the web is not widely available in Japan so it is not surprising that access via the mobile phone has taken off so fast. Europeans and Americans have cheaper Internet access through their PCS and interactive TVs via which they can use all the consumer and business applications now on the market. Nevertheless, given DoCoMo's technological lead, combined with its determination to stay ahead, Western competitors would be foolish not to take its threat seriously. DoCoMo's role of trailblazer in the brave new world of mobile commerce seems likely to continue for some time yet.

Future waves

DoCoMo may think it has the future in its hands, but others cannot be so sure. M-commerce is still a gamble. If it is to pay off the first people who need convincing are the customers.

From time to time every consumer industry is accused of selling hot air. This time the telecommunications industry may have gone too far. By turning up the hype about the mobile Internet, over-zealous marketers may actually have turned many customers off. M-commerce has proved to be far from being "the Internet in your pocket" as promised.

In the early days, the World Wide Web was dubbed the World Wide Wait because of the length of time it took to load individual pages. Now imagine that with the added frustration of peering at a tiny mobile phone screen. No wonder many people have decided they don't want a second try. In many mobile devices the screen acts like a magnifying glass under which all the problems of the Internet commerce loom even larger. E-tailers initially struggled to make their products seem appealing on a computer screen, especially "high-touch" items like clothes. The challenges of adapting this to the small screen are even greater. Even if the products do look good, most cellular networks don't have enough speed to deliver the images and data in a reasonable amount of time.

Of course, technology is improving all the time. Just think how much easier and faster it is to use the fixed-line Internet today than it was only a few years ago. Most wireless networks do not have the necessary bandwidth or capacity to transmit rich content at high speeds. This is why operators are busy trying to upgrade the networks.

There are two types of next-generation mobile networks and handsets under development. The first, 2.5G or GPRS (General Packet Radio Service), is already being rolled out in many countries. It is a cost-effective way to upgrade Europe's current GSM service. The upgrade will allow service providers to offer a greatly improved m-commerce experience.

But the industry is betting that the demand for m-commerce services will skyrocket. If this happens users will want increasingly sophisticated products, services and devices. Mobile-phone operators will then have to roll out 3G networks and handsets. The extra bandwidth will allow users to view video clips and download music on to their mobile devices. But is that what the customers really, really want? For Japanese youngsters the answer is a definite yes. In Europe and America many people have yet to decide whether they want m-commerce at all. (See Figure 9.2.)

According to a spring 2000 survey by Jupiter Media Metrix, 48% of mobile-phone owners said they would not use or would not pay for m-commerce. The figure jumped to 56% for people without a mobile phone. Those who do use m-commerce are more likely to spend short amounts of time on air to do specific things, unlike many ordinary web users who may spend long periods of time surfing the web with no particular purpose in mind.

According to a November 2000 study (one of the most comprehensive in this area so far) of users in America, Australia, France, Germany, Japan and Sweden by Boston Consulting Group, the most popular m-commerce applications are e-mail, SMS (Short Messaging Service) and accessing news, weather and sports information. Almost half of those surveyed spend less than five minutes on-air in each session, with an average of just 25 minutes a week, compared with 13 hours spent on the fixed-line Internet.

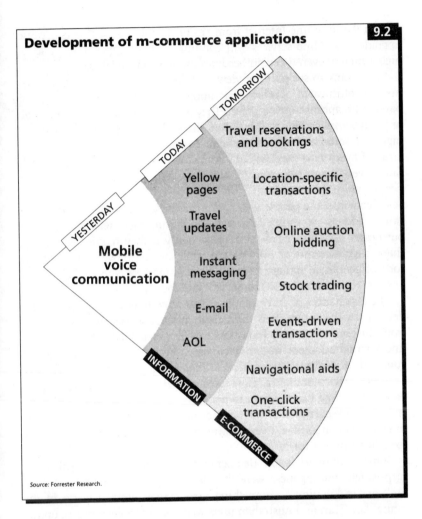

Development of m-commerce applications 9.2

YESTERDAY

TODAY

TOMORROW

Mobile voice communication

Yellow pages

Travel updates

Instant messaging

E-mail

AOL

Travel reservations and bookings

Location-specific transactions

Online auction bidding

Stock trading

Events-driven transactions

Navigational aids

One-click transactions

INFORMATION

E-COMMERCE

Source: Forrester Research.

DoCoMo users spend only 1.5 minutes in an average session to send e-mail, one of i-mode's most popular applications. More experienced users surveyed spent more time on-air, but it was still less than users connecting to the Internet via a fixed line.

Forrester Research has announced similar findings. It says users will want personalised, time-sensitive news and information such as priority e-mails, share-price alerts and travel and online auction updates. For more complex and time-consuming activities, such as in-depth catalogue research and configuring and buying a new PC, users are more likely to rely on the fixed-line Internet from PCS or digital TV sets. This is because upgraded fixed-line services will continue to be cheaper, faster and of higher quality even when 3G becomes more widely available.

This seems to support the view that customers might never want or need sophisticated multimedia applications that require lots of bandwidth and processing power. They may instead want more personal, or "thin", applications that build on the mobile phone's virtue of being highly personal and always available. Forrester says that, although a vast array of fancy new wireless data devices will be manufactured, few will find buyers. Smart phones with additional data services may be all most people will need or want.

Of course, some people will find a use for 3G services, such as online games addicts or sports fans separated from their televisions. Some businesses may also need them, particularly if they require workers to share huge amounts of information while on the move. But will these sorts of people be enough to build a viable market? Nobody has a clear answer. There are still too many "ifs" and "buts".

The experiences of early adopters may show how m-commerce might develop in the future. It is difficult to predict mass-market behaviour from this, but a few early indicators can be gleaned. Like the early fixed-line Internet adopters, m-commerce users are generally rich, young and educated. Asked by Boston Consulting Group to list their top five attractions to m-commerce, most users replied: to save time; to get up-to-date or real-time information; to make communication easier and more effective; to keep in touch with friends and family; and to have security in emergency situations. These answers are similar to those given by early fixed-line Internet users.

Some national and demographic differences emerged. Not surprisingly, the Japanese were the most likely to use the services "for fun" or "to kill time" – something mass-market users may do in the future. American and Australian users were more serious-minded, opting for more business-related applications. Older users were more interested than younger ones in hunting down lower prices and having extra security in the event of an emergency. Other more surprising factors emerged from the survey. For example, most m-commerce use takes place in the home rather than in the office or at school.

So what are likely to be the future "killer apps"? Researchers frequently cite location-based services. Using the mobile phone's ability to signal its exact whereabouts (within about 50 metres), content providers will be able to alert people to useful information. Personal navigation and smart yellow pages that can find the nearest Italian restaurant or golf shop, say, will be popular. Mobile banking is also cited as a potential growth sector, although most financial services companies are still developing their products. In Britain, the banks have been quick to cotton on to the potential. Bank of Scotland has teamed up with BT Cellnet, a mobile-phone company, to launch a mobile-phone banking service. A Woolwich-Vodafone scheme is being tested by 100 of the bank's customers, who have been given WAP mobile phones. Customers may also want to use their phones as a kind of mobile wallet, which allows them to pay for books, CDs and travel services.

If all these predictions are accurate, most people will find that existing networks are enough to provide everything they need from their mobile phones. Mobile-phone operators that have forked out huge sums for 3G licences in Europe may well struggle to recoup their investments. But they would appear to have at least one huge advantage over fixed-line operators when it comes to wringing profits from Internet commerce: unlike traditional telcos, they are under no regulatory obligation to open up their networks. And because they are able to configure their phones to start up with their own portals, they hope to become all-powerful players to rival the likes of Yahoo! and AOL. It is unlikely, though, that online giants such as Amazon will agree to having a preferred position on only one network.

Where does this leave customers? According to Analysys, provided operators can come up with compelling and easy-to-use content, customers will not feel the need to explore the wider mobile web. But not all customers like being hemmed in. Some mobile companies, including Vodafone and Orange, have already been forced to open up their content platforms to third parties.

If DoCoMo's example is anything to go by, the walled-garden approach may be best avoided. Instead of trying to limit users' access to sites, it provided an open platform, which ensured that even the most popular sites got space on i-mode's home page. More than 300 partner sites are accessible through the i-mode portal and the menu on the handset. Other potential partners are queuing up. By adding more services and applications, DoCoMo has continued to attract more customers and encourage the birth of still more sites, creating what it calls a "positive-feedback loop".

Freedom is supposed to be what the Internet is all about. It may be too soon to say whether mobile Internet users will want more or less of it. But the fact that customers have forced some firms to backtrack on their approach provides some indication. Mobile operators that stick to their guns and continue to operate a closed network will come seriously unstuck if they fail to offer the right content at the right price.

There are other reasons to doubt whether there will be enough money in m-commerce to go round. Where profits are to be made they will have to be shared. For example, credit-card companies and banks will want their dues from any money made on payment processing and security. And giants like Sun Microsystems, Oracle and Microsoft will want their share because they will probably be providing back-end services to the operators running the m-commerce systems.

Fresh competitors are springing up to challenge mobile-phone operators' core business of access provision. New mobile virtual network operators (MVNOS) are buying unused capacity at wholesale prices and marketing their own services. Britain's Virgin Mobile is one example. It can rely on the backing of a strong brand, Richard Branson's Virgin Group, which provides travel, entertainment and other services, to secure its place in the market. It signed up about 400,000 British subscribers in less than a year. By inviting customers to use old phones from other carriers, Virgin Mobile has been able to save the cost of providing free or subsidised phones to each subscriber. These savings are passed on to the customer in the form of attractive rates for services such as MP3 music and on-air shopping. The company has linked up with other network operators such as SingTel in Singapore and Cable & Wireless in Australia, where it also plans to roll out its services. Other MVNOS with good customer-management skills, innovative services and strong brands will provide stiff competition.

Mobile-phone operators that try to be all things to all people rather than building solid relationships with strategic partners are likely to come unstuck. According to Forrester Research, the biggest profits for mobile operators are to be made not through direct participation in m-commerce, but through control over the location-based technologies and databases that content providers and merchants will need. Rather than becoming powerful portals, operators might as well be mere commodity providers of transport, just as fixed-line operators are today. Instead of charging for the time spent on-air, they will have to develop new services. In this case, revenue will be closely linked to increased penetration and usage.

Customers will still need some convincing before they come on board in their droves as predicted. Drop-out rates for first- or second-time users will only improve when marketers start to sell the mobile Internet for what it really is at the moment: not an alternative to computer-based Internet access but an addition to it, which can be used for different tasks. M-commerce will probably only take off, though, when it matches the speed, simplicity and low cost of the fixed-line Internet world. For that to happen, privacy and security concerns will need to be addressed.

Downwardly mobile

"I never said I want to be alone, I only said I wanted to be left alone." Hollywood actress Greta Garbo could never have guessed that she would be voicing the fears of future mobile-phone users when she uttered this famous line. But the Internet is intrusive. Like fixed-line users, mobile Internet users are concerned about their privacy. Indeed, the very thing that makes mobile phones so attractive – the fact that they are with you at any time, anywhere – can also be their greatest drawback. Being available 24 hours a day, seven days a week is not everyone's idea of fun. A new buzz phrase for this is "the wireless leash", which can be yanked at any time by friends, colleagues, advertisers and even the boss.

Another new development, also touted as an asset, threatens further to erode privacy. Location technology can conveniently tell you via your mobile phone where the nearest restaurant serving your favourite food is situated, tip you off if a retailer in the area is selling your preferred brand of shirts, or inform you where to find the nearest branch of your favourite coffee shop. This could make your life a whole lot easier. However, your operator will have a pretty good idea of what you are up to and when. This will help the police catch criminals. But for some users it is a heavy price to pay in personal freedom.

Fortunately, technology can solve many of the problems it generates.

- Encryption can help prevent unwelcome ears from listening in.
- Pre-paid mobile users do not have to sign a contract or supply personal details, so they can use their phones anonymously.
- Screening allows users to receive urgent calls immediately and filter out unwelcome or untimely calls, which can be diverted to voicemail.
- Different ringing tones can be used for different calls, so you know whether the boss or the babysitter is trying to reach you.

Security is another serious obstacle in the path of m-commerce. Consumers are worried about sending credit-card numbers and other personal details over the mobile Internet. Over one-third of respondents to Boston Consulting Group's survey said that it is more risky to send information over the mobile network than over the fixed-line Internet. Technology is improving all the time, and more advanced payment systems will develop. DoCoMo has already introduced more secure handsets. Users may also feel more secure if mobile operators handle the billing process themselves. Customers for the i-mode find it much simpler to pay one phone bill at the end of the month rather than receiving different bills for the different services they use. In this case, mobile operators can benefit from their strong brand names and closer relationships with customers.

But perhaps one of the biggest worries of all is health. In Britain, suggestions of a link between mobile phones and brain cancer have sparked a furious debate. Despite thousands of studies around the world, medical evidence on the issue remains ambiguous. Some studies indicate that there is a connection between the two, others rule it out.

In December 2000, the British government launched a £7m research programme into the health effects of mobile-phone use following an earlier study. The study, known as the Stewart Inquiry, recommended a precautionary approach after examining the current scientific evidence on phone safety. It said that although there was no strong evidence that the phones could damage health, there was "preliminary" evidence that subtle biological changes could take place. It said children under the age of 16 should be encouraged to limit the number of calls and to keep them short. Children are thought to be at greater potential risk because their skulls are thinner and offer less protection against radiowave radiation, if a link is finally proved. By the end of 2000, there were 25m mobile phones in use in Britain; one-quarter of these belonged to under-18s.

As part of the precautionary measures, mobile-phone companies are being asked to provide information leaflets for customers detailing the possible risks of using mobile phones. The leaflets will also contain advice about the risks of living or working next to mobile-phone base stations and radio masts. The subject has received a great deal of press attention in Britain because of health fears. At the end of 2000, Mast Action UK (MAUK), an action group, was launched to oppose the positioning of mobile-phone masts close to schools. Britain had about 20,000 base stations in operation in early 2000. At the same time, America had around 82,000 cell sites, each holding one or more base stations.

The World Health Organisation has concluded that for the moment there are no health risks from either mobile phones or their base stations. It says, however, that there are gaps in existing knowledge and further research is required, which could take several years to complete.

An earlier suggestion that hands-free sets could provide a solution if researchers were to establish that radiation from mobiles had a damaging effect on the brain is now being questioned. Two studies commissioned by Britain's Consumers' Association suggest that, far from reducing the amount of radiation reaching the brain, hands-free kits may actually increase it under some circumstances. It has been suggested that the wire connecting the earpiece to the phone acts as an aerial and channels radiation towards the head. Other scientists have dismissed the claim.

Some brain-tumour sufferers have filed lawsuits against some of the world's largest mobile-phone companies and phone manufacturers. They are hoping to achieve similar success to the cancer victims who sued tobacco companies and received huge payouts. These new claimants say that, like the tobacco companies, the phone companies knew about the health risks. But scientists may never establish a firm link. Cellphones emit only tiny amounts of radiation – about one-thousandth of the amount emitted by microwave ovens. Furthermore, people use their phones in so many different ways that epidemiological research is hard to design.

One thing is certain: mobile phones and cars are a dangerous combination. Here, too, technology may eventually play a large part in providing a solution. However, early suggestions that hands-free sets allowing people to talk and drive at the same time may help have proved unfounded. Even when the devices have voice-activated dialling, they still distract drivers' attention from the road.

Conclusion

M-commerce still has a long way to go before it can catch up with e-commerce. Early adopters will put up with the rough ride in the knowledge that things can only get better. Other potential users will continue to play a wait-and-see game. The key word in the future is convergence. Internet users will expect a seamless service whether they access via the PC or the mobile phone. They may book a plane ticket via their PC but will want to have the latest flight details, including the announcement of any possible delays, from their mobile phone. Just as e-commerce watchers turn to Amazon for any clues about the development of e-commerce, m-commerce observers will turn to Japan's DoCoMo to try to predict the future. The mobile Internet may not be perfect yet, but you can be sure that plenty of people are working on it.

Appendix 1   A brief history of the Internet

WHEN HISTORIANS LOOK back on the 20th century, one of the most potent symbols will be the Internet. Touted as one of the greatest catalysts for social and economic change the world has seen, the Internet has even spawned a new measure of how long it takes things to happen: "Internet time", roughly judged to move at four times the normal rate of business progress. Far from being the happy child of hippie parents, this anarchic collection of computer networks was born in a military laboratory and fathered by cold-war paranoia.

Sowing the seeds

The seeds for the growth of the Internet were sown in the early 1960s at the height of the cold war. The US administration was looking for a way to maintain communications in the aftermath of a nuclear attack. An efficient way of networking computers had yet to be found.

Scientists at the Advanced Research Projects Agency (ARPA) of the US Department of Defense teamed up with the Rand Corporation, a military think tank, which was developing such a network.

Paul Baran, a computer scientist at the Rand Corporation and one of the masterminds of the project, conceived a new way of connecting computers. He used the idea of a fishnet, where information could flow along any path rather than from point to point. Splitting data into tiny packets that can take different routes to their destination makes it hard to eavesdrop on messages. And a "packet-switched" network can resist large-scale destruction, even a nuclear attack. If one route is knocked out, packets will simply travel along one that remains intact, allowing communication to continue. The Internet owes its main technical advantage to its military origins.

The idea was shelved by the Department of Defense, but it provided the foundation upon which the Internet would later develop.

Early networking

In 1969 four American universities took the idea and developed the Arpanet. The purpose was to share information and resources between Stanford University, the University of California at Los Angeles (UCLA), the University of California at Santa Barbara and the University of Utah.

The computer-sharing network was a success from the start. E-mail, which was developed in 1972, quickly became the most popular application. However, the main traffic on the network was not long-distance computing. Instead, it was news and personal messages. In effect the Arpanet became a kind of high-speed digital post office.

The network grew steadily, connecting universities and government research centres around America. Then in 1973 it went global, hooking up with University College London and The Royal Radar Establishment in Norway.

Until 1983 the Internet consisted of fewer than 500 "host" computers, almost exclusively in American military labs and academic computer-science departments. But the word was getting out to other academics. By 1987 the Internet had grown to include 28,000 host computers at hundreds of different universities and research labs.

Using it was still difficult and frustrating, but its power was already obvious. No other method to network universities around the world was so universal and so flexible. Internet users invented ways for many people to participate in open discussions, and created software and document libraries on the network and made them accessible to all. This was exciting stuff for computer scientists and some other academics, but it remained a cloistered world.

Setting standards

It became clear that some kind of mechanism to set standards and govern the network was necessary. The InterNetworking Working Group (INWG) was the first body to respond to the challenge. Vinton Cerf, known as the father of the Internet, was elected as the first chairman.

The Arpanet's original standard for communication, developed by Mr Cerf and a colleague called Bob Kahn, was known as Network Control Protocol (NCP). But as time passed and the technique advanced, NCP was superseded by a higher-level, more sophisticated standard known as Transmission Control Protocol/Internet Protocol (TCP/IP). Networks that make use of this protocol became known as internets. Joined together they form the Internet.

Developing networks

Yet during the late 1980s, while the Internet was growing in the academic world, a networking revolution of another sort was taking place outside. Businesses realised that, having traded their mainframes for a multiplicity of PCs, they needed some way to recapture the mainframe's ability to share data and devices such as printers. So they strung wires around their offices and connected the PCs together.

These internal local area networks (LANS) did more than save money; they changed the way people worked. E-mail took off within offices, and soon between them, as companies created wide area networks (WANS) to connect distant workplaces. But there it stopped. Different software and hardware standards used by different companies made creating wider networks a nightmare of incompatibility.

At home, PCS had made computer power affordable, and modems had allowed them to be connected up over telephone lines to commercial online services and bulletin boards (electronic discussion groups and software libraries usually set up by enthusiasts). Both of these grew steadily, but not explosively. Each had disadvantages. The networks offered by CompuServe, the leading online service provider, and others that followed in its wake were national, even global, but they were closed. The providers controlled what was available. Private bulletin-board systems, which had sprung up in their thousands, were unrestricted but usually confined to a small group of users near the host computer.

Around the same time the American government was relaxing its hold on its network. The Arpanet officially ceased to be a research tool and became just another network in 1990. In the meantime, other networks such as the NSFNET, developed by the National Science Foundation and the backbone of today's Internet, had come into being, linking newer, faster, shinier supercomputers, through thicker, faster links. Commercial traffic was allowed on to the NSFNET in 1991.

The World Wide Web
That same year Tim Berners-Lee created the World Wide Web, the software that allows users to exchange information, at CERN, the European particle physics laboratory near Geneva. It was originally designed to help scientists share online information using a single, unified interface.

It soon became clear that the web was useful not only to scientists but also to people in almost any other sphere of human activity. It took off in mid-1993 when Marc Andreesen, then an undergraduate at the University of Illinois, and others wrote a program called Mosaic, which made using the web as easy as pointing and clicking at pictures and underlined words. This led to the explosion of the web and the battle of the browsers, the computer software which allows users to view web pages.

When Mosaic, the first graphical browser, was launched there were about 150 websites holding a few thousand web pages; at the beginning of 1995 there were about 10,000 sites, a number that had grown to 4.5m by mid-1999.

Commercial use of the Internet has skyrocketed, with companies using the Internet to communicate with each other, with their customers, with their partners and with their suppliers. It may come with a "made in the USA" stamp, but the very nature of the Internet, with its ability to link users in any part of the world at any time, has turned e-commerce into a global phenomenon. In Europe, Sweden, Britain and Germany are setting the pace for others to follow. But Asia too is joining in the race, with some countries hoping to transform their entire economies using e-business. Japan is the frontrunner in the mobile e-commerce challenge. And investors are increasingly excited by the prospects offered by emerging China, where the number of Internet users is growing rapidly.

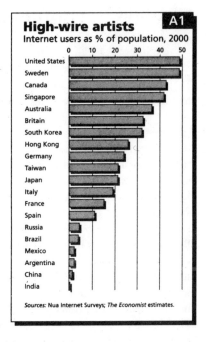

High-wire artists A1

Internet users as % of population, 2000

Sources: Nua Internet Surveys; The Economist estimates.

Appendix 2 Useful websites

Here is a selection of news and information sites on e-commerce.

E-commerce news

www.ecommercetimes.com
E-Commerce Times, news and analysis on e-commerce

www.economist.com
The Economist, articles from the magazine on the Internet and e-commerce

news.bbc.co.uk/hi/English/business/e-commerce
BBC News, top e-commerce stories and feature articles

www.businessweek.com/ebiz/
Business Week, news and special reports on e-commerce

www.ft.com/news/industries/infotechnology
The *Financial Times*, news on the Internet and e-commerce

www.nytimes.com/pages-technology/
The *New York Times*, news on IT, the Internet and e-commerce

www.redherring.com
Red Herring, industry news on IT, the Internet and e-commerce

www.thestandard.com
The Standard, industry news on IT, the Internet and e-commerce

www.wsj.com/pages/techmain.htm
The *Wall Street Journal*, technology news and latest coverage of e-commerce. The site also has a useful chart tracking dotcom closures and lay-offs

www.internet.com
A huge network connecting to different sites covering IT, the Internet and e-commerce

www.news.com
Industry news on IT, the Internet and e-commerce

Organisations

www.commerce.net
A non-profit organisation bringing together leading figures from business, government, technology and academic sectors dedicated to the advancement of e-commerce. Contains news and information

www.eff.org
The Electronic Frontier Foundation, a non-profit organisation dedicated to protecting civil liberties, especially privacy and free speech on the Internet. Founded in 1990, it is based in San Francisco, California

www.ietf.org
The Internet Engineering Task Force, an organisation concerned with the technical infrastructure of the Internet. It describes itself as "an open community" and brings together designers, operators, vendors and researchers from all over the world. The IETF is a member of the Internet Society (ISOC – see below)

www.isoc.org
The Internet Society, a professional body dedicated to shaping public policy, standards and training programmes related to the Internet. It comprises more than 150 organisations (such as the IETF) and 6,000 individual members in over 100 countries. It also contains useful information on the history of the Internet

www.rsac.org
The Internet Content Rating Association, an independent international organisation that helps to protect children from potentially harmful material on the Internet by labelling content. It allows parents to set their Internet browsers to block access to unsuitable material

www.sdmi.org
The Secure Digital Music Initiative, a forum comprising more than 180 companies and organisations dedicated to protecting copyright on digital music. It was launched by the big five music companies – Warner Music, Sony Music, Universal, BMG and EMI – with the aim of trying to replace the Internet's standard for digital downloads with their own. This would allow them to encrypt their products and thus protect their copyright

Research
The following is a selection of consultancies that publish e-commerce research on their websites

www.accenture.com
Accenture (formerly Andersen Consulting)

www.arthurandersen.com
Arthur Andersen

www.bcg.com
Boston Consulting Group

www.ctg.com
Cambridge Technology Partners

www.e-business.pwcglobal.com
PricewaterhouseCoopers
www.mckinseyquarterly.com
McKinsey

Technology specialists

www.analysys.com
Analysys
www.forrester.com
Forrester Research
www.jmn.com
Jupiter Media Metrix

Other resources

www.hbsp.harvard.edu/products/hbr/
The *Harvard Business Review*
cism.bus.utexas.edu/
Center for Research in Electronic Commerce (CREC) at the University of Texas at Austin
www.csulb.edu/web/journals/jecr/
Journal of Electronic Commerce Research (JECR), a quarterly journal published electronically by the California State University, Long Beach
www.pewinternet.org
Pew Internet & American Life Project, a non-profit initiative of the Pew Research Center for People and the Press, an opinion research group based in Washington DC. It publishes the results of academic research on the impact of the Internet on American life
www.whatis.techtarget.com
An online encyclopedia of IT and e-commerce

Appendix 3 Glossary of key e-commerce terms

Amazoned
When a traditional retailer finds part of its business under attack from an online-only competitor. The term was coined following the huge success of Amazon.com, which forced traditional booksellers to formulate their own online strategies.

Banner ad
An advertisement on a web page, usually in the form of an animation designed to attract a user's attention and trigger a click-through to a website. This type of ad was invented by Hotwired in 1994 and is still the most common form of web advertising. Banners are sold on a cost per mille (CPM – or cost per thousand) basis, with advertisers typically paying between $10 and $100 or so for every 1,000 impressions. Banners have not proved as successful as expected. They are seen as bandwidth hungry, adding to the time that it takes to download a web page. According to some estimates, users now click on fewer than one in 50 banners on European websites.

Brochureware
Often used as a derogatory term to describe the first generation of websites, with low or no interactivity. As the name implies, these sites serve as the online equivalent of a company's printed brochure, giving out basic information about products or services and contact details.

Business-to-business (B2B)
The exchange of goods, services, information or money between businesses over the Internet. B2B was proclaimed the next big thing after B2C lost some of its attraction. By implementing B2B solutions, businesses can make huge savings, cutting down stocks and streamlining operations by sharing information across their networks of partners and suppliers. The exchanges that sprang up in the B2B area can be divided into three types: industry-driven (airline industry, oil industry), independent upstarts and private e-marketplaces (General Electric, Wal-Mart).

Business-to-consumer (B2C)

The exchange of goods and services between businesses and consumers over the Internet. B2C marked the beginning of the commercialisation of the Internet, but the sector failed to live up to its promise. Many B2C companies learned to their cost that attracting customers to a website is one thing, but ensuring their visit ends in a purchase is quite different. Fulfilment and delivery problems also abound. Successful B2C players include companies selling low-touch, standardised items like books, CDs and DVDs. Travel services have also proved popular, and many people now buy their plane tickets online.

Bricks-and-mortar

A traditional company with no online presence, as opposed to a pure-play company that exists almost exclusively on the Internet. Heavily criticised for their reluctance to embrace the Internet, most big companies and industry behemoths now have some sort of web presence and are increasingly seen as the dominant online players, with their established brands and loyal customers.

Clicks-and-mortar

Or clicks-and-bricks. A business using a mixture of offline and online sales and distribution channels. A good example is Barnes & Noble, a traditional high-street bookseller that was forced to embrace the Internet following the success of online-only competitor Amazon.com. The company sought to integrate its new channel bn.com with its bookstores. As e-commerce evolved, Amazon.com, along with other pure-plays, moved closer to the clicks-and-mortar model by building infrastructure (bricks) behind the online interface (clicks).

.com

Regarded as one of the most prestigious domain names used to classify web addresses. It was first used to distinguish between American commercial and non-profit organisations by adding the suffix .com to the former and .org to the latter. Businesses hoping to make their mark on the Internet often prefer the .com domain to country-specific ones such as .co.uk. The word dotcom is used to name the pure-play Internet businesses in the B2B or B2C sector.

Cyberspace

A term coined by William Gibson, a science-fiction writer, who used it to describe the geography of the online world in his novel *Neuromancer*. In 1996 he said: "Cyberspace has a nice buzz to it, it's something that an advertising man might have thought up, and when I got it I knew that it was slick and essentially hollow and that I'd have to fill it up with meaning." Today it is used to describe the space on the Internet where people meet, chat, search for information or buy.

Disintermediation

A word borrowed from the banking world that describes how the Internet brings buyers and sellers closer together, allowing them to complete transactions without the use of a middleman. It was initially thought that the Internet would make masses of people in services industries redundant. For example, many airlines now allow passengers to book seats via their websites, reducing the need for travel agents. However, a new type of middleman, an "infomediary", soon emerged with the ability to pool information from airline sites and reservation systems, offering better deals for customers. One example is Priceline.com.

E-tailing

Another term for online shopping. A famous example of an e-tailer is Amazon.com. Founded by Jeff Bezos in 1994 as an online bookstore, the name has become synonymous with e-commerce itself. Amazon now sells everything from wireless phones and DVDs to beauty products and computer software. It also runs its own online auctions. In the brief history of the Internet Amazon is probably one of the most talked-about companies, but like most Internet companies it has yet to turn a profit.

Electronic Data Interchange (EDI)

A standard way of electronically exchanging data between companies that predates the Internet. At its simplest, it is a way to automate purchasing. Retailers often use it because it allows stores to link their suppliers directly to their stock databases. EDI, however, has some serious shortcomings. It can save time and money, but it usually requires an expensive private or dedicated network connection between two established trading partners. It is not interactive, meaning there is no opportunity for discussion or negotiation.

Encryption

A method of scrambling data to ensure that they are unrecognisable to an unauthorised person. It is a technology that makes e-commerce possible because it enables secure financial transactions to be completed over the Internet. Encryption consists of complex mathematical rules known as algorithms, which turn a plain-text message into an unreadable one. All encryption techniques, whatever their level of sophistication, require at least one key to decode the data.

Extranet
A computer network based on Internet technology that typically allows an organisation to communicate with customers, suppliers and other business partners. Seen as an extension of a company's intranet, the network enables a company to share data with external users, hence the name.

Eyeballs
The number of people who look at a specific advertisement, website or other online content. Although somewhat out-of-date now, the term was widely used in the early days of e-commerce as one of the parameters for valuing dotcom businesses.

Intranet
A computer network based on the same technical standards as the Internet but designed for use within a single organisation. Intranets are cheaper and simpler to install than proprietary networks, and companies are increasingly using them to circulate internal information such as phone directories, job openings and training material.

Initial public offering (IPO)
The first sale of publicly traded shares by a previously privately owned company, a process also known as going public. An IPO is often seen as an important stage in a company's development. It generates publicity, crucial for a young company trying to establish its name, and helps in the broader process of establishing its business credentials and raising the necessary cash to further develop the business.

M-commerce
E-commerce conducted via a mobile phone or another wireless device, as opposed to over the fixed-line Internet. Given the teething problems of e-commerce, some powerful arguments will be needed to convince the general public that m-commerce is necessary or worthwhile. Japan has been a testing ground for the technology because of the phenomenal

success of one company, NTT DoCoMo. In Europe, there is great potential for m-commerce because mobile phone penetration is high. Scandinavian countries are at the cutting edge in developing technology for mobile transactions.

Mass customisation

Internet technology can be used to compile detailed information about customer interests and shopping habits. This information can then be used to provide individually tailored products at affordable prices for huge numbers of consumers. Mass customisation is easier for products that can be digitised. It is therefore prevalent in banking, stockbroking and communications. Manufacturers are also beginning to recognise the advantages. The most well-known example is Dell Computer. Its website allows the buyer to design an individual computer and then track it through to delivery.

Online auction

The arrival of the online auction and the success of one company in particular, eBay (one of the few profitable Internet companies), were seen as an end to fixed prices. Since then the Internet has spawned hundreds of businesses based on the auction model because of its ubiquity and cheap access. In the B2C sector, auctions are held for everything from groceries to plane tickets, and in the B2B sector, anything from unwanted stock to whole business units are up for grabs. Priceline.com became one of the media darlings with its reverse auction model, making customers name their price for a plane ticket.

Pure play

Also called a dotcom, a business with an online presence only. Search engines such as Yahoo!, relying on advertising revenue, are one type of pure play. Early e-tailers that existed only in cyberspace and entrusted fulfilment of their orders to third parties are another type. Most of these now have physical assets behind them as well.

Shopping basket

An electronic version of the supermarket trolley. Online customers select the items they wish to purchase together with product details such as price and colour. Once they have finished they head for the "checkout", handing over information about payment and where the goods should be delivered.

Stickiness

Refers to a website's ability to keep a customer within its pages and pin down a sale. In the early days of e-commerce it was thought that most online customers' were fickle. However, experience has shown that online customers are not so different from offline ones; they appreciate the value of brands and of good customer service. Quality content, streaming media, competitions, online chat and online resources are generally seen as good ways of sustaining customer interest.

Wireless Application Protocol (WAP)

A technical standard for text-based mobile Internet services, developed by Europeans and Americans. The first WAP phones were launched in Europe in early 2000, offering access to basic news and other information, but they proved to be a big flop. Users were not able to roam freely around the web and had to dial up every time they wanted to use the service, in a similar way to fixed-line Internet users. Although WAP failed to live up to its expectations in the beginning, the introduction of faster transmission technology could give it a new lease of life.

XML (Extensible Mark-up Language)

A way of describing and sharing data on the Internet. Until the development of this open standard it was not possible to tell the exact nature of the data displayed. XML, like HTML (Hypertext Mark-up Language), uses a system of "tags" to tell a computer how to display the data that it has retrieved. For example, it can tell whether the data refer to a book written by William Shakespeare or a book about William Shakespeare. XML's biggest potential lies in the B2B arena, where its ability to help companies share information will make the automation of many business processes much easier.

Index